THE

ANGLO-SAXON CHURCH:

ITS

HISTORY, REVENUES, AND GENERAL CHARACTER.

BY HENRY SOAMES, M.A.

AUTHOR OF
THE HISTORY OF THE REFORMATION

WIPF & STOCK · Eugene, Oregon

Wipf and Stock Publishers
199 W 8th Ave, Suite 3
Eugene, OR 97401

The Anglo-Saxon Church
Its History, Revenues, and General Character
By Soames, Henry
Softcover ISBN-13: 978-1-6667-3502-4
Hardcover ISBN-13: 978-1-6667-9162-4
eBook ISBN-13: 978-1-6667-9163-1
Publication date 9/15/2021
Previously published by John H. Parker, 1835

This edition is a scanned facsimile of
the original edition published in 1835.

TO

THE REVEREND

HUGH CHAMBRES JONES, M.A.

*ARCHDEACON OF ESSEX, AND TREASURER OF ST PAUL'S
CATHEDRAL, LONDON*

THIS VOLUME IS INSCRIBED,

AS A TESTIMONY OF DEEP RESPECT FOR A HIGHLY EFFICENT AND
ACCEPTABLE DISCHARGE OF IMPORTANT OFFICIAL DUTIES,
FOR QUALITIES OF HEAD AND HEART,
THAT CHRISTIANISE AND EMBELLISH PRIVATE LIFE,
AND FOR A DISINTERESTED VIEW OF ECCLESIASTICAL PATRONAGE
AS A PUBLIC TRUST, BY HIS

OBLIGED AND AFFLCTIONATE FRIEND,

THE AUTHOR.

*Furneux Pelham,
    March 5, 1835.*

CONTENTS.

INTRODUCTION.

	PAGE
Britain converted very early	2
St. Paul possibly her Apostle	3
Joseph of Arimathea	6
Glastonbury	6
Lucius	9
Episcopacy of Ancient Britain	10
St. Alban	11
Arianism introduced	13
Pelagius	13
Pelagianism introduced	15
——— suppressed	16
Settlement of the Saxons	17

CHAPTER I.

A.D.		
	Jutes, Saxons, and Angles, on the Continent	20
	Obstacles to their Conversion	21
	Ethelbert, the *Bretwalda*	23
	——— marries Bertha	24
	——— long, probably, favourable to Christianity	25
	Early Years of Gregory the Great	27
	Elected Pope	29
	Offended by John the Faster	29
	Anecdote of Gregory in the Slave-market	32
596.	Augustine despatched into Britain	34
597.	——— His Arrival in Kent	35

CONTENTS.

A.D.		PAGE
	Augustine, his Establishment at Canterbury	36
598.	——— He sends Laurence and Peter to Rome	37
601.	——— Gregory's Answers to his Queries	39
	Augustine's Conferences with the Britons	42
	Slaughter of the Monks of Bangor	46
604.	Death of Augustine	46
	Foundation of St. Paul's, in London	47
	Apparent Failure of the Roman Mission	48
	Nocturnal Flagellation of Laurentius	49
625.	Marriage of Ethelburga into Northumbria	49
	Dexterity of Paulinus	51
627.	First Conversion of Northumbria	55
630.	Conversion of East Anglia	56
635.	Final Conversion of Northumbria	57
654.	Conversion of Mercia	57
	Final Conversion of Essex	58
	Conversion of Wessex	59
664.	Conversion of Sussex	60
	Roman Triumph at Whitby	61
	Doctrines	63

CHAPTER II.

665.	Consecration of Wilfrid	66
669.	Arrival of Theodore	67
	St. Chad	68
673.	Council of Hertford	68
	St. Etheldred	70
678.	Deprivation of Wilfrid	71
680.	Council of Hatfield	72
	Doctrinal Profession of the Anglo-Saxon Church	72
	Benedict Biscop................................	73
	Patronage given to the Founders of Churches........	74
690.	Death of Theodore	75
	His *Penitential*..............................	76
	Death of Wilfrid	78
693.	Laws of Ina	78
694.	Council of Bapchild	79

CONTENTS.

A.D.		PAGE
696.	Council of Berghamsted	79
	Church-shot imposed by Ina	80
	Tythes usual among Pagans	81
	Monasteries	86
	Pilgrimages to Rome	87
709.	Aldhelm	88
	Bede	89
740.	Egbert	94
	Tripartite Division of Tythes	95
766.	Alcuin	97
746.	Willibrord	100
	Boniface	101
747.	Council of Cloveshoo	102
	Archbishopric of Lichfield	105
787.	First Papal Legates in England	106
	Council of Calcuith	107
	Peter-pence granted by Offa	108
	Image-worship	109
792.	Indignantly condemned in England	110
	The *Caroline Books*	111
	Egbert's *Penitential*	115
	Abstinence from Blood, and from Strangled and Unclean Animals	117
	Uncertainty as to the Use of Fasting for the Dead	118

CHAPTER III.

816.	Council of Celychyth	121
	Incidental Evidence against Transubstantiation	122
	Secular Monasteries	124
	Notice of the Ancient British Church	125
836.	Ethelwulf	127
	St. Swithin	127
854.	Ethelwulf's Decimation	129
855.	—— Journey to Rome	132
858.	—— His Death	133
	Alfred's Visits to Rome	134
	—— His neglected Education	137

CONTENTS.

A.D.		PAGE
871.	Alfred's Accession	139
878.	—— His Retirement	141
	—— His Victory over the Danes	143
	—— His Literary Works	144
901.	—— His Death	145
	—— His Infirmities	146
	—— His Economy of Time	147
	—— His Economy of Money	149
	—— His Provision for Ecclesiastical Dues	151
	—— His truncated Decalogue	152
	—— His Theology	153
	Erigena	155
904.	Alleged Interference of Pope Formosus	158
928.	Council of Grateley, under Athelstan	161
	Doctrines	162

CHAPTER IV.

	The Monastic System	164
	Birth of Dunstan	167
	His Education	170
	His Phrenzy	171
	He is tonsured, and retires to Glastonbury	173
	Introduced at Court	173
	Driven from it	174
	Argues against Monachism	176
	Adopts the Benedictine Habit	177
	Introduces it at Glastonbury	178
943.	Council of London	179
	Archbishop Odo	181
	His Canons	182
	Ethelwold	183
	Foundation of Abingdon	183
	Dunstan driven into Exile	185
	—— restored	186
957.	—— advanced to the Episcopate	188
959.	—— made Archbishop of Canterbury	189
961.	Council of Andover	191

CONTENTS. ix

A.D.		PAGE
	Defined Civil Penalties for recovering Tythes	192
	Church-shot reserved for the Ancient Minsters	194
	Hardships undergone by the Married Canons	196
	Oswald	197
	Relics and Pilgrimages	199
968.	Council of Winchester	201
	The speaking Crucifix	202
975.	The Canons reinstated	203
978.	Council of Calne	204
	Fall of the Floor there	205
	Edward the Martyr	205
	Ethelred the Unready	206
979.	His Coronation	207
988.	Death of Dunstan	207
	His Resistance to Papal Interference	209
	Alleged Removal of his Remains from Canterbury	210
1008.	Council of Eanham	212
	Church Dues defined, but not enforced by Penalties	212
1014.	Council of Haba	216
	Church Dues enforced by Penalties	217
	Elfric	218
	—— His Education	219
	—— Commissioned to regulate Cerne Abbey	221
	—— His Homilies	222
	—— His Grammar	223
	—— His Epistle to Wulfsine	223
	—— His Epistle to Wolstan	224
	—— His Scriptural Translations, and other Works	225
	—— Obscurity of his History	226
	—— Probable Sketch of it	227
	—— Probable Cause of its Obscurity	229
	Canute's Ecclesiastical Laws	236
1043.	Edward the Confessor	237
	—————— His Ecclesiastical Laws	238
1052.	Stigand	240
1062.	Foundation of Waltham Abbey	241
	Doctrines	242
	Additional Note on Elfric	247

CHAPTER V.

Salvation offered universally	249
Practice the only Test of Sound Religion	251
Humility represented as indispensable	252
The Human Soul God's Image	253
The Bondage of the Will	253
Divine Grace indispensable	254
The Creed and Lord's Prayer to be explained	254
Apocryphal Legends	255
Strict Observance of Sunday	257
Festivals	260
Fasts	262
Abstinence from Blood, and various Meats	263
Election, Examination, and Engagements of Bishops	265
Their Legislative Rights	267
Their Jurisdiction in the County Courts	268
Their Sees	268
Their Duties and Restrictions	270
Examination for Orders	272
Regulations for the Clergy	274
Endeavours to keep them unmarried	275
Ministerial Gradations	276
Anglo-Saxon Monks	278
Regulations provided for them	280
The *Trinoda Necessitas*	281
Guild-ships	282
Coronation Oath	283
Anglo-Saxon Laws relating to Baptism	284
Marriages	285
Wakes	287
Burial in Churches	288
Dedication of Churches	288
Anglo-Saxon Buildings	289
Organs	290
Ordeals	290
The Truce of Religion	294
Water and Oil used as Charms	295

CONTENTS.

	PAGE
Commutations of Penance	296
St. Chad's Horse-wain	299
St. Cuthbert	299
St. Etheldred	300
St. Frideswide	301
St. Edmund the King	302
St. Oswald	303
St. Guthlac	304
Anglo-Saxon versions of Scripture	305
Conclusion	310
King Edgar's Proclamation	313

PREFACE.

In preparing the *Bampton Lectures* of 1830, it became obvious that the subject could not be thoroughly understood, without various historical details and miscellaneous particulars, inadmissible in a limited course of sermons. Materials for supplying these deficiencies were naturally accumulated while the undertaking was in progress. Many more have been collected since. Late events appeared to give encouragement for completing, arranging, and publishing this mass of information. England is overspread, more or less completely, with endowed places of religious worship, uniform in doctrine and discipline, of very ancient foundation, and immemorially protected by the State. It has, also, no small number of religious endowments, far from uniform as to doctrine or discipline, and of no ancient foundation, but fully protected by the State. The propriety of such protection, in the latter case, has been conceded by all parties. It seems to have occurred to no man that these modern foundations are become public property, because they are no longer private inheritances. Hence we have heard nothing of their just liability to seizure for any purpose whatever, either religious, or local, or fiscal; nor have individual holders been tempted by a prospect of appropriating to their own emolument such parts of them as may fortunately be in their hands. Hitherto this line of argument has been reserved for our ancient religious foundations. These are often treated not only as mere creatures of some legislative act, but also as justly convertible by like authority, to any purpose, either public or private, or to both conjointly, as expediency or accident may suggest. The enactment, however, which this view assumes, has not found admittance into collections of the national records; certainly an extraordinary fate for such a statute. Nor is it less unaccountable that no trace of it appears in those monkish chronicles which comprise our ancient history, and which are ordinarily copious, nay, even rhetorical, when they have to mention some advantage gained by religion. A legislature also that provided churches would hardly overlook the size of parishes. This, however, an uninquiring mind might assign to accident, or caprice. Many rural parishes, indeed, are so small as to raise the wonder of a townsman, and to render plans, drawn from cases widely different, neither very practicable nor important.

Anglo-Saxon Ecclesiastical History throws light upon these difficulties. It introduces to notice an active and able Asiatic, our first acknowledged metropolitan, who formed the plan of inducing Englishmen to build and endow churches on their estates, by tempting them, as Justinian had his own countrymen, with the patronage of their several foundations.[1] It shews this policy to have been approved by Athelstan, one of the wisest, most powerful, and most energetic of Anglo-Saxon princes; who strengthened it by granting the rank of thane to such proprietors as would not see their tenants unprovided with a place of worship.[2] It records an exhortation of the archbishops, given solemnly at a *witena-gemot* early in the eleventh century, to the building of churches " in every place."[3] They would hardly have acted thus at such a time, without sanction from the legislature. Thus we find the national authorities urging and alluring opulent individuals to build and endow churches upon their lands, during the whole

---

[1] See Page 74.   [2] Page 162.   [3] Page 215.

period of nearly four hundred years—from Theodore to the Conquest. It is known, that many of these foundations are of a subsequent date, and, probably, existing parochial subdivisions were not consummated under six hundred years. Our ancient and uniform religious endowments arose then, like the multiform religious foundations of later times, from the spontaneous liberality of successive individuals. Formerly also, as now, there was every variety in the magnitudes of property. Because, however an estate was small, its lord commonly would not rest contented without a church upon it. Nor often did he forbear to shew whose accommodation was first consulted, by placing the new erection close to his own home, although both the chief population, and the house provided for its minister, might be at some distance. Parishes, therefore, owe their actual dimensions to no negligence or caprice, but to the accidental inequalities of private property.

This private origin of English parochial religious foundations is obviously the clue to existing rights of patronage. Hence the verse familiar to canonists, in days when church-building was common, or had lately been so,

Patronum faciunt dos, ædificatio, fundus.[1]

---

[1] J. DE ATON, *Const. Legit. totius Regionis Angl.* f. 105.

The church's *dowry* of glebe had notoriously been settled upon it by some land-owner, who likewise raised the fabric, and provided more effectually for the maintenance of its minister, by resigning in his favour one-tenth of all that his own possessions around should hereafter produce. Such public spirit justly demanded a suitable acknowledgment. None could be more so, than a freehold right of selecting, under proper control, that functionary who was to realise the liberal donor's pious intentions. This was nothing beyond an equitable return to an individual, who had not only provided his neighbours with a place of religious worship at his own expense, but had also rendered this liberality available to them, and to those who should come after them, by building a parsonage, by surrendering inalienably a part of his own property as glebe, and by burdening irredeemably the remainder. Undoubtedly the justice thus done to founders has withdrawn a very large number of benefices from professional emulation. But the laity have really no great practical reason to complain of this. They thus, however, draw important pecuniary benefits from the Church, and they are thus additionally bound to respect ecclesiastical rights. A man may have little value for religion, or may dislike that of his fathers; but surely he cannot be justified in encroaching upon the patrimonies of his kinsmen or neighbours. Now, this character attaches to a great proportion of English parochial preferments. A landowner has presented a younger son to a living in the gift of his family, or another person has invested one child's portion in an advowson, or presentation; advancing like sums to settle his remaining children in secular callings, or situations. Charity forbids a belief that the lay brother can desire, or could even endure, to have the clergyman's portion confiscated to swell his own rent-roll, or pay his own taxes.

Our larger ancient churches have, indeed, been founded by the crown, and so have many of the smaller. But no reasonable or safe principle will allow the denial to such foundations of all that inviolability which rightfully belongs to those that originated in the public-spirited sacrifices of individuals. If even ages of possession are no secure title to a royal grant, many a child of affluence must bid farewell to hereditary splendour, and enter a profession, or sue for a pension.

Undoubtedly the great bulk of our ancient religious revenue arises from tythes, and these may be hastily regarded as wholly derivable from legislative liberality. But were this undeniable, a new appropriation, advantageous, even temporarily, to any other than the landlord, is obviously very difficult while he remains. It would, however, be a monstrous folly to present individuals of the richest class with a large augmentation to their fortunes, which they have neither inherited nor purchased, and to which, therefore, they have no more just or equitable claim than they have to some adjoining estate. If, instead of such idle prodigality, a fiscal appropriation were advocated, it would be trifling with the hopes of undiscerning occupiers. The tax-gatherer would disappoint them bitterly. For commissioners, clerks, and surveyors, patronised by the ruling party, some fortunes might unquestionably be provided, and many comfortable situations. The pressure of taxation, too, might be somewhat modified, or even lessened. But this advantage, hardly perceptible to individuals, would be fatally counterbalanced by a national disregard of all that ought to render property secure.

A sufficient knowledge of our ancient history gives, however, great reason to doubt the legislative origin of tythes. They seem to have been paid by the Anglo-Saxons before the legislature interfered to enforce them. There are, in fact, traces of them in every age and country.¹ Hence this appropriation has not unreasonably been considered as dictated by that patriarchal creed, which men have nowhere been able wholly to forget. When an early Anglo-Saxon proprietor, therefore, founded a church, he solemnly dedicated the tythes of his land for its maintenance, without any legal compulsion, or any hesitation or reserve. His foundation was an evidence of his piety; and such a man could feel no disposition to deny a religious claim which even heathens admitted. A similar spirit, however, would inevitably be wanting to some among the representatives or posterity of any man. Individuals would arise eager to forget that they acquired the estate under certain deductions. It was to restrain this dishonourable rapacity, that the Saxon legislature at length interfered, and that repeatedly. At first, it was hoped that solemn injunctions, or ecclesiastical censures, might sufficiently remind selfish men of their duty to religion, and of the terms on which they had become possessed of land. Hence Athelstan's legislature pronounced tythes demandable both upon crops and stock, requiring them to be strictly rendered.² Edmund the Elder again

---

[1] Page 81.　　　[2] Page 161.

gave legislative weight to this injunction.[1] Mere admonition, however, will not long strive successfully against the necessities, artifices, and avarice of mankind. Edgar's legislature was, accordingly, driven to compel, by civil penalties, the due discharge of that claim to which every landowner had found his possessions liable.[2] A precedent for this act of justice was, indeed, afforded by Alfred's treaty with Godrun. The great king was contented to naturalise a colony of his Danish invaders in the eastern counties; but he would not allow these unwelcome settlers to escape from liabilities immemorially fixed upon their several estates. Well, however, did he know the lawless rapacity with which he had to deal. He, therefore, provided pecuniary fines for keeping the new proprietors to the only terms on which he was willing to place them in possession, or, indeed, considered himself able.[3] From his reign more than nine hundred years have now elapsed; from Edgar's, not much less. So long, then, has English landed property been inherited, or otherwise acquired, under a system of protecting by civil penalties those rights to tythe with which proprietors, greatly anterior to Alfred, had burthened their

---

[1] Page 180.   [2] Pages 191, 192.   [3] Page 151.

estates. How importantly this immemorial deduction has affected every sale of land, the very numerous tythe-free properties, now in England, afford evidence alike ample and irresistible.

Among such as feel unwillingly the force of this, there are some who would still fain appropriate more than they have purchased or inherited, by making tythes release them, in a great degree, from assessment to the poor. Ordinarily they pour contempt upon antiquity; now they gladly seek its aid. They maintain that tythes were originally granted with a reserve of either one-fourth, or one-third, for charitable purposes. Anglo-Saxon history will shew that views like theirs are of very ancient standing. Evidently there were thanes anxious to regard the religious rent-charge, under which they had acquired their several estates, as an exemption from all further provision for indigence. The papal legates at Calcuith expressly denied this principle:[1] so did Archbishop Odo, a hundred and fifty years later.[2] It could, undoubtedly, find some shelter under venerable names. The missionary, Augustine, claims a fourth part of the tythes for the poor;[3] Egbert, archbishop of York, a third.[4]

---

[1] Page 107.   [2] Page 183.   [3] Page 40.   [4] Page 95.

This latter claim could also plead subsequently the great authority of Elfric.[1] But even he lived while the parochial subdivision of England was in progress. Hence came recommendations for the quadripartite or tripartite division of tythes: they arose from the minster-system, and were intended for it. To supersede this, however, in a very great degree, by the universal diffusion of a parochial clergy, was a leading object of national and individual piety during several ages. A reason, then, may readily be found for the silence of both statute and canon law, upon the quadripartite or tripartite division of tythes. The principle has reached posterity under the mere sanction of three celebrated individuals, all guided by foreign canonists, and all chiefly conversant with a clerical body settled round a large church, both to serve it, and to itinerate in the neighbouring country. Scanty as are these authorities, a wary advocate would, probably, dispense with one of them. It appears from Egbert, that the " year's tenth *sceat* was paid

---

[1] " The holy Fathers have also decreed, that tythes be paid into God's Church, and that the priest go to them, and divide them into three parts; one for the reparation of the church, a second to the poor, a third to God's servants who attend the church."—JOHNSON's *Transl. sub ann.* 957. SPELM. i. 578. WILK. i. 253.

at Easter."[1] If, therefore, his authority be good for a third of the tythes to relieve the poor, perhaps it may be equally good for every tenth groat from the dividends, from the gains of all placemen, trading and professional men, not holding a church benefice, and from all annuities. Nor do Anglo-Saxon monuments refuse to the Church other authority, and that of a more formal character, even for such a claim as this. The laws of Edward the Confessor impose expressly tythes upon trade.[2] Those, however, who would claim for the poor one-fourth, or one-third of the tythes, need feel but little disappointment from unexpected deficiencies in early canons and enactments. The famous statute of Elizabeth has pretty thoroughly brought their favourite principle into active operation. One-fourth of the tythes, or even more, is commonly insufficient to defray assessments for the poor on that property, the glebe, and the parsonage. Private charity makes inroads upon the remainder to an extent of which persons, unacquainted with clerical expenditure, are very little aware.

---

[1] Page 97. Wilkins (i. 123) renders the Saxon *cum decimum obolum annuum solvimus*. The *sceat*, however, which answers to his *obolum*, was equivalent to ten *sticas*. Eight of these made a penny, worth a modern three-pence.—HICKES, *Diss. Epist.* 111.

[2] Page 238.

Another fourth of the tythes, or even a larger portion, during an incumbency, is often absorbed by the house, buildings, and chancel, together with dilapidations.

Besides tythes, however, the ancient religious foundations in our parishes are endowed with rent-charges to repair the church, and to supply the exigencies of public worship. It certainly does not appear that these are anterior to the Saxon conversion; they plead no higher authority, then, than that of ancient legislation: this plea they can powerfully urge. *Church-shot* was imposed by Ina;[1] and, in all probability, if his legislature did not follow here a known and approved precedent, its own example quickly acted upon every kingdom of the Heptarchy. Alfred, accordingly, stipulated with Godrun, that, in addition to tythes, *light-shot* and *plough-alms* should be regularly paid by the new Danish proprietors.[2] As years rolled on, these claims naturally encountered many cases of denial or evasion. Hence, the legislature under Athelstan,[3] Edgar,[4] and Ethelred,[5] lent them new force, by providing civil penalties for their recovery. The latest of these enactments has an antiquity of more

---

[1] Page 80. [2] Page 151. [3] Page 161.
[4] Page 192. [5] Pages 212, 216.

than eight hundred years: so long, then, at the least, has landed property been inherited, purchased, or otherwise acquired, under a liability to rent-charges, independently of tythes, statutably settled upon our ancient parochial places of worship. Any such rent-charge, settled upon a modern place of worship, though comparatively a mere matter of yesterday, would undoubtedly be claimed as only a debt of justice. Vainly would an occupant plead religious repugnance to such an application of his money: perhaps he might be reminded of Jewish scruples, upon the lawfulness of paying tribute to Cæsar.[1] A sympathy so acute between purse and conscience would certainly have little chance of meeting with respect.

It is true that parochial collectors have long ceased from application for *church-shot*, *light-shot*, and *plough-alms*. Those who delight in throwing unworthy imputations upon the Church, may be at a loss to account for this forbearance. Such as would reason calmly upon known facts, will, probably, view the modern church-rate, raised for the very purposes answered by these ancient payments, as merely their successor and representative. That rate is no offspring, then, of some blind prescription,

---

[1] St. Matt. xxii. 17.

but as regularly derived from legislative acts, yet extant, as any other public burden. Its name and form, indeed, are changed; but here the payer has no reason to complain: he probably foresaw this, and easily consented. In country parishes, church rates are trifling, unless under the rare occurrence of extensive works required. For such an emergency, there are some who would again make the tythes alone responsible. Perhaps, as men are fond of an ancient lineage, these reasoners may be glad to learn that their class is as old as Canute at the least: that prince, however, declares, that church-repair rightfully concerns the whole community:[1] nor is any other principle reasonable. The rebuilding, or even the repair of a spacious pile, might absorb the tythes of several years, leaving no remuneration for the duty, if the living were a rectory; if a vicarage, wholly stripping an unfortunate impropriator of his resources.

If an innovating party were, however, driven into an admission of violence to founders, and hardships to possessors, an apology would, probably, be sought in the Reformation; but, surely, no precedent is afforded here as to polity. Episcopacy was rooted in this country

---

[1] Page 236.

on the Saxon conversion: hence every ancient religious foundation was established with an eye to place it under the superintendence of a bishop. When, therefore, episcopal incumbents were superseded under the Commonwealth by Presbyterians, undoubtedly violence was done to those pious intentions which gave us our ancient churches. But of any such injustice the Reformation is guiltless; it left religious endowments, of remote establishment, under the very kind of governance that had been originally provided for them.

It likewise left untouched the exterior condition of all parochial incumbents, and of the dignitaries in some cathedrals. None of these were disturbed in their rights, revenues, or privileges, if only willing to recognise the principles regularly sanctioned by their own body, constitutionally consulted. It is true that all restraint was withdrawn upon their discretion as to marriage; but ancient ecclesiastical history shews no departure here from the intentions of those to whom we owe our churches. It exhibits clergymen ordinarily married, whether employed about a cathedral or in a rural parish. Clerical marriages, in fact, although eventually pronounced uncanonical and rendered penal, were never illegal: nor was free license for them any thing else than a return to that principle which had originally prevailed.

It is the same with the substitution of canons for monks in a few cathedrals. Anglo-Saxon ecclesiastical history stamps the Benedictines as intruders, and their expulsion as an act of justice to founders.[1] The Reformation, therefore, affords no precedent bearing either upon polity or station, for interference with the clergy, termed secular by Romanists. Of that ancient body, the present ecclesiastical estate of England is the lineal successor and the lawful representative.

Nor did the Reformation make any change in our Church's orthodoxy. It was one of Theodore's earliest cares to settle a national establishment upon the principle of assent to the first four general councils:[2] exactly the same base was laid by the Reformers. At Calcuith this base was somewhat widened; assent being there given to the first six general councils.[3] But Elfric subsequently shews that this extension was not viewed as interfering with Theodore's original principle:[4] it was not, in

---

[1] Pages 196, 202, 203.   [2] Page 72.   [3] Page 107.
[4] " These four synods are to be regarded as the four books of Christ in his Church. Many synods have been holden since; but yet these are of the greatest authority."— JOHNSON's *Transl.* SPELM. i. 581. WILK. i. 254.

fact, material; it was little more than a fuller admission of those doctrines which have been pronounced orthodox by the consent of ages.[1] If the Reformers, therefore, had afforded entrance to any such opinions as pass under the name of Unitarian, obvious injustice would have been done to that liberality which has provided our ancient religious endowments. To this innovation, however, Cranmer and his friends were no more inclined than Theodore himself: they jealously guarded the great landmarks of belief which antiquity has established, and which the founders of our churches were equally scrupulous in respecting.

In one capital article of faith, undoubtedly, the Reformation effected a signal change: it banished from our churches a belief in the corporal presence; but how this had gained possession of them had never been thoroughly examined. It was, however, notoriously a doctrine solemnly affirmed by no earlier leading ecclesiastical assembly than the fourth Lateran council; a body sadly late[2] for adding to the creed, and about which scholars out of Italy

---

[1] The fifth general council is the second of Constantinople, assembled in 553: it condemned the errors of Origen. The sixth general council is the third of Constantinople, assembled in 680: it condemned the Monothelites.

[2] 1215.

were, besides, divided in opinion. Eventually, the Council of Trent stamped a new authority upon transubstantiation.[1] But there was no reason why England should assent: her voice was not heard in the deliberations. Her authorities, however, were then investigating the question at home, and they came to a different conclusion. An independent body was fully justified in acting thus in any case, for which, direction would be vainly sought from ancient councils. In this case, the authorities of England were *more* than justified. In expelling transubstantiation from our churches, they prevented a leading doctrine from being taught in them, which their founders had expressly repudiated. The disclaimer of ancient England is, perhaps, even stronger here than that of modern. Had transubstantiation, then, when first regularly examined by the national authorities, been imposed upon incumbents, a like violence would have been done to the piety which provided our ancient religious endowments—that was done when Episcopalians were ejected—and that would be done if Unitarians were admitted.

---

[1] In 1551. The *Forty-two Articles* were agreed-upon in 1552.

In common with her continental neighbours England had adopted other doctrines, and religious usages, found embarrassing on the revival of learning. Scholars vainly sought authority for them in Scripture, or in the earlier monuments of theology, or in conciliar decisions of acknowledged weight: hence arose a general anxiety for the solemn and sufficient investigation of these difficulties. On the continent, this call was answered in some degree at Trent; in England, by an appeal to the national authorities. Again, the two parties disagreed: English divines rejected principles and practices unsupported by Scripture, or primitive antiquity, or universal recognition. Evidently here, too, an independent body was fully justified: nor was violence done to those intentions which had endowed the secular clergy. Image-worship had been indignantly rejected in ancient England.[1] Of other principles abandoned by the Reformers, no one, excepting transubstantiation, had attracted any particular notice. Anglo-Saxon monuments offer dubious traces of them, but no more: undoubtedly they were not received as articles of faith. Appeals against them have, accord-

---

[1] Page 110.

ingly, been often made, and far from rashly, to our ancient Church. They were, in fact, lingering remains of exploded Paganism, which had defied extirpation, and which a spirit of insidious compromise had gradually invested with something of a Christian character. But even when a firm footing had been gained by these excrescences, they had no operation upon discipline, and rarely bore upon any vital question of doctrine; they merely came before a reflecting mind as unexamined admissions of one age, which were fairly open to revision from another. If that other should decide upon pruning them away, evidently the religious fabric, both spiritual and visible, would retain its full integrity and purity. With such questions as our Lord's divinity, transubstantiation, and episcopacy, the case is widely different.

Attention to subjects of so much interest may be invited, it is hoped, neither unusefully nor unacceptably. The religion of our fathers and its venerable endowments are now become, more than usually, topics of discourse; yet few appear to enter upon these discussions under the advantage of previous inquiry. For this, perhaps, a reason may be found in the books containing such of the required information as has been already published. These are generally neither of modern date, nor likely to meet the eye of general readers, nor to engage their notice. The present undertaking, therefore, may afford facilities for extending an acquaintance with many facts, now demanding urgently correct opinions: it offers also some particulars not hitherto before the public; and it may complete modern collections upon our earlier affairs, by a fulness of detail where points occur of little prominence in civil history. Care has been taken to keep the work within moderate dimensions. No fact, it is believed, of any moment has either been omitted, or hastily passed over; but various persons and incidents, mentioned in older books, do not appear in this, because they are neither interesting nor important to posterity. From this desire of excluding every thing unnecessary, the intention of closing the volume by a copious Appendix was abandoned. Several Saxon pieces were prepared for the press; but, although useful, they were very far from indispensable, and their insertion would have augmented considerably both bulk and expense. No document has, accordingly, been printed, except the record of Edgar's two legislative assemblies: these have been hitherto overlooked, although well deserving notice. It was needful, therefore, to print the authority on which they appear in the present work. One of the places mentioned has not been identified; nor has it been found possible to give a literal translation of some sentences in the record.

INTRODUCTION.

CONVERSION OF ANCIENT BRITAIN — ATTRIBUTED VARIOUSLY TO APOSTLES — JOSEPH OF ARIMATHEA'S ALLEGED SETTLEMENT AT GLASTONBURY — LUCIUS — CHRISTIAN BRITAIN EPISCOPAL FROM THE FIRST — ST. ALBAN, THE BRITISH PROTOMARTYR — INTRODUCTION OF ARIANISM — PELAGIANISM — ARRIVAL OF THE SAXONS.

WITHIN little more than a century from our Saviour's passion, Justin Martyr[1] asserted, that every country known to the Romans contained professors of the Christian faith. Britain, he does not, indeed, expressly mention; but it has allowably been inferred, from his testimony, that her population had then become acquainted with the Gospel.[2] Irenæus adds probability

---

[1] A. D. 140 is the age assigned by Cave (*Hist. Lit.* Lond. 1688, p. 36) to Justin Martyr. He appears from Tatian (*Contra Græcos*, ad calcem Just. Mart. Paris, 1636, p. 157,) to have been put to death by the machinations of Crescens, a philosopher, whose enmity he had incurred by an exposure of his hypocrisy. This martyrdom happened in the year 166. "The author of the Alexandrian Chronicle sets the death of S. Justin down in this year, and we have not any certainer proof."—DU PIN's *Eccl. Writers.* Engl. Transl. Lond. 1696. I. 51

[2] Οὐδὲ ἓν γὰρ ὅλως ἐστὶ τὸ γένος ἀνθρώπων, εἴτε βαρβάρων, εἴτε Ἑλλήνων, εἴτε ἁπλῶς ᾡτινῶν ὀνόματι προσαγορευομένων, ἢ ἁμαξοβίων, ἢ ἀοίκων καλουμένων, ἢ ἐν σκηναῖς κτηνοτρόφων οἰκούντων, ἐν οἷς μὴ διὰ τοῦ ὀνόματος τοῦ σταυρωθέντος Ἰησοῦ εὐχαὶ καὶ εὐχαριστίαι τῷ Πατρὶ καὶ ποιητῇ τῶν ὅλων γίνωνται.—S. JUST. MART. *cum Tryphone Judæo Dialogus.* Ed. Thirlby. Lond 1722, p. 388 Ed Paris, 1636, p 345.

B

INTRODUCTION.

to this inference.[3] He speaks in one place of our holy religion as propagated to earth's utmost bounds by the apostles and their disciples. In another, he names the Celts among nations thus enlightened.[1] A Celtic race was then seated in the British isles, and may reasonably be included, especially when Justin's language is recollected, within the enumeration of Irenæus. All doubt, however, upon the early conversion of our island, is removed by the testimony of Tertullian. He speaks of British districts *inaccessible to Roman arms but subdued by Christ*.[2] Had not the faith of Jesus obtained considerable notice in more polished quarters of the island, it would hardly have won a way into its remoter regions. Tertullian's authority, therefore, establishes abundantly, that when the second century closed,[3] Christianity was far from a novelty among the tribes of Britain. Great probability is thus given to that statement of Eusebius,

---

[3] Assigned by Cave, (*Hist. Lit.* 40.) to the year 167. He appears to have been born A. D 97, and to have lived beyond the age of 90.

[1] Ἡ μὲν γὰρ ἐκκλησία, καίπερ καθ' ὅλης τῆς οἰκουμένης ἕως περάτων τῆς γῆς διεσπαρμένη, παρὰ δὲ τῶν ἀποστόλων καὶ τῶν ἐκείνων μαθητῶν παραλαβοῦσα τὴν εἰς ἕνα Θεὸν πατέρα παντοκράτορα τὸν πεποιηκότα τὸν οὐρανὸν καὶ τὴν γῆν, καὶ τὰς θαλάσσας, καὶ πάντα τὰ ἐν αὐτοῖς, πίστιν. (D. Iren. adv. Hæres. l. 1. c. 2. Lut. Par. 1675, p. 50.) Καὶ οὔτε αἱ ἐν Γερμανίαις ἱδρυμέναι ἐκκλησίαι ἄλλως πεπιστεύκασιν, ἢ ἄλλως παραδιδόασιν, οὔτε ἐν ταῖς Ἰβηρίαις, οὔτε ἐν Κελτοῖς.—*Ibid.* c. 3. p. 52.

[2] " Britannorum inaccessa Romanis loca, Christo vero subdita." *Tertull. adv. Judæos.* Lut Par. 1664, p. 189.

[3] Tertullian's birth is considered by Cave to have taken place before the middle of the second century. " The treatise *adversus Judæos* is supposed by Pamelius to have been written in the year 198, by Allix, after Baronius, in 208."—Bp. KAYE *on the Writings of Tertullian.* Camb. 1826, p. 50

which attributes British acquaintance with the Gospel to *some of the apostles*.[1] Hence also the mind is prepared for assenting to the obscure intimation of Gildas, the earliest of our national historical writers, which would lead us to conclude that the light of Christianity had shone upon his countrymen before their signal defeat under Boadicea.[2]

The high antiquity of Britain's conversion being thus established, her authors have naturally been desirous of connecting it with some of the more illustrious names in religious history. Among the apostles, accordingly, James the son of Zebedee and brother of John, Simon Zelotes, Simon Peter, and St. Paul, have been variously named as the evangelists of our island. The first three cases are not, however, supported by sufficient authority to render them worthy of more than a passing notice.[3] Of St. Paul's personal services to Britain, there are presumptions of some weight. Clemens Romanus affirms that great apostle to have preached as far as *the utmost bounds of the west*.[4] St. Jerome says, that he imitated the Sun of

---

[1] Ἑτέρους ὑπὲρ τὸν Ὠκεανὸν παρελθεῖν ἐπὶ τὰς καλουμένας Βρετανικὰς νήσους.—Euseb. *Demonst. Evang.* l. 3. c. 7. Par. 1628, p. 112.

[2] "Interea glaciali frigore rigent insulæ quæ velut longiore terrarum secessu. Soli visibili non est proxima, verus ille non de firmamento solum temporali, sed de summa etiam cœlorum arce tempora cuncta excedente, universo orbi præfulgidum sui lumen ostendens Christus suos radios, id est sua præcepta indulget, tempore ut scimus summo Tiberii Cæsaris, quo absque ullo impedimento ejus propagabatur religio."—Gildas *de Excidio Britanniæ, inter Monumenta S. Patrum* Bas. 1569, p. 833.

[3] The evidence upon which these cases rest, and remarks upon it, may be seen in Abp. Usher's *Brit. Eccl. Antiqu.* p. 3.

[4] Διὰ ζῆλον ὁ Παῦλος ὑπομονῆς βραβεῖον ἀπέσχεν, ἑπτάκις δεσμὰ φορέσας, ῥαβδευθεὶς, λιθασθεὶς, κῆρυξ γενόμενος ἔν τε τῇ ἀνατολῇ, καὶ ἐν τῇ

Righteousness in going from one ocean to the other,[1] and that his evangelical labours extended to *the western parts*.[2] By such expressions Britain was commonly understood.[3] Theodoret accordingly asserts, that St. Paul *brought salvation to the isles in the ocean*.[4] Elsewhere he mentions the Britons among converts of the apostles.[5] In another place he says, that St. Paul, after his release from imprisonment, went to Spain, and thence carried the light of the Gospel to *other nations*.[6] In the sixth century, Venantius Fortunatus,[7] and in the seventh, Sophronius, patriarch

---

δύσει, τὸ γενναῖον τῆς πίστεως αὐτῷ κλέος ἔλαβεν, δικαιοσύνην διδάξας ὅλον τὸν κόσμον, καὶ ἐπὶ τὸ τέρμα τῆς δύσεως ἐλθών.—S. CLEMENS *ad Cor.* inter *SS. Patres. Apost.* Coteler. Lut. Par. 1672, p. 94.

[1] Qui (Paulus) vocatus a Domino, effusus est super faciem universæ terræ, ut prædicaret evangelium de Hierosolymis usque ad Illyricum, et ædificaret non super alterius fundamentum, ubi jam fuerat prædicatum, sed usque ad Hispanias tenderet, et a Mari Rubro, imo ab Oceano usque ad Oceanum curreret; imitans Dominum suum et solem justitiæ."—HIERON. *in Amos.* l. 2. c. 5. Par. 1602, tom. v. col. 249.

[2] " Ut Evangelium Christi in Occidentis quoque partibus prædicaret."—HIERON. *Catal. Script. Eccl.* Opp. tom i. col. 349.

[3] " Fuisti in ultima Occidentis insula."—CATULL. *in Cæsar.* Carm. xxix. Stillingfleet (*Antiqu. Brit. Ch.* p. 38,) produces many other authorities to shew that Britain was esteemed the *extreme west.*

[4] Καὶ εἰς τὰς Σπανίας ἀφίκετο, καὶ ταῖς ἐν τῷ πελάγει διακειμέναις νήσοις τὴν ὠφέλειαν προσήνεγκε.—B. THEOD. *Interpr. in Psalm.* 116. Opp. Lut. Par. 1642, tom. i. p. 871.

[5] Καὶ Βρεττανοὺς —— καὶ ἀπαξαπλῶς πᾶν ἔθνος καὶ γένος ἀνθρώπων δέξασθαι τῷ σταυρωθέντος τὰς νόμους ἀνέπεισαν.—THEODORET. *Sermo.* 9. *de Legib.* Opp. tom. iv. p. 610.

[6] Ὡς ἀθῴως ἀφείθη, καὶ τάς Σπανίας κατέλαβε, καὶ εἰς ἕτερα ἔθνη δραμὼν, τὴν τῆς διδασκαλίας λαμπάδα προσήνεγκε.—THEOD. *in Epist.* 2. *ad. Timoth.* Opp. tom. III. p. 506.

[7] Apud Usser. *Brit. Eccl. Antiqu.* p 4.

of Jerusalem,[1] speak expressly of St. Paul's mission to Britain. Upon the whole, therefore, a native of our island may fairly consider the great Apostle of the Gentiles as not improbably the founder of his national Church.[2]

The Greek Menology asserts, that Aristobulus, whom St. Paul salutes in his Epistle to the Romans,[3] was ordained by him bishop of the Britons, and established a church among them.[4] Two individuals also, Pudens and Claudia, greeted in the Second Epistle to Timothy,[5] have been identified with a married couple mentioned by Martial, of whom the lady was a Briton.[6] It is of course inferred, that Claudia must have been zealous to spread that holy faith among her pagan countrymen, which she and her husband had happily embraced. Of all scriptural

---

[1] Magdeburg. Centur. et alii. *Ibid.*

[2] Bp. Burgess, while he filled the see of St. David's, laid before the clergy of that diocess, in a very learned and able charge, the evidence for St. Paul's mission to Britain, and he thus states his own conviction upon the question: "We may finally conclude that the testimony respecting St. Paul's preaching in *the utmost bounds of the west*, that is, in *Britain*, is indisputable."—*Tracts on the Origin and Independence of the Ancient British Church.* Lond. 1815, p. 52.

[3] Rom. xvi. 10.

[4] See the passage in Usher. *Brit. Eccl. Antiqu.* p. 5.

[5] 2 Tim. iv. 21.

[6] "Claudia, Rufe, meo nubit peregrina Pudenti."—MART. lib. iv. epigr. 13. *ad. Ruf.* The particular country of this *foreign* lady appears from the following passage in another epigram·

"Claudia cœruleis cum sit Rufina Britannis
Edita, quam Latiæ pectora plebis habet!"
Id. lib. xi. epigr. 53.

personages, however, Joseph of Arimathea has been most extensively regarded as the British apostle. Being despatched, we are told, from Gaul by St. Philip, he was allowed to fix himself with his twelve companions at Glastonbury, then ordinarily called the isle of Avalon.[1] Against this relation, though long undisputedly current, a fatal objection, however, arises from the silence of Saxon authorities. Glastonbury was a place renowned for sanctity among many generations preceding the Norman conquest; indeed, probably from times of the most remote antiquity.[2]

---

[1] " Sanctus autem Philippus, ut testatur Freculphus, lib. ii. cap 4, regionem Francorum adiens, gratia prædicandi, plures ad fidem convertit et baptizavit. Volens igitur verbum Christi dilatari, duodecim ex suis discipulis elegit, et ad evangelizandum verbum vitæ misit in Britanniam : quibus, ut ferunt, charissimum amicum suum, Joseph ab Arimathia, qui et Dominum sepelivit, præfecit. Venientes igitur in Britanniam, anno ab incarnatione Domini sexagesimo tertio, ab assumptione beatæ Mariæ decimoquinto, fidem Christi fiducialiter prædicabant. Rex autem barbarus quandam insulam sylvis, rubis, atque paludibus circumdatam, ab incolis Ynswitrin nuncupatam, in lateribus suæ regionis ad habitandum concessit."—MALMESB. *De Antiqu Glaston. Eccl.*, ap. USSER. *Brit. Eccl Antiqu.* p. 7.

[2] " In ea" (Glestonia, sc.) " siquidem ipsius loci primi catholicæ legis neophytæ antiquam dō dictante repererunt ecclesiam, nulla hominum arte constructam, immo humanæ saluti celitus patratam." (Brit. Mus. MSS. Cotton. Cleopatra. b. 13. f 61.) This extract is made from an octavo volume of high antiquity, and of uncommon interest; the life of Dunstan, which supplies the citation above, having been written by a contemporary, and the particular MS. having been consulted by William of Malmesbury, Josselin (who compiled, under Abp. Parker's direction, the *Antiquitates Britannicæ*), and Abp Usher. These curious facts appear from the following entries in contemporary hands, f. 58 .

" Hunc librum, cuius auctor, ut apparebit lectori, claruit tempore ipsius Dunstani, de quo agit, reperi inter veteres libros manu-

Encompassed by watery marshes and sluggish streams, its British name was *Ynys vitryn*, the *Glassy Isle*. Among pagans, islands had commonly borne a sacred character, and Christian teachers were naturally willing to make use of spots and erections which exploded heathenism had not only rendered suitable, but also by religious rites had invested with popular veneration. The isle of Avalon was probably such a spot.[1] It is likely that Druidism had left there, on its extinction, a residence desirable for the now triumphant Christian teachers, and had rendered their labours more generally acceptable by the sanctity with which it had long distinguished the abode thus provided to their hands. On the Saxon invasion, Avalon's water-locked recesses might have served as a shelter for a congregation of native Christians, and a wattled church of their erection being, probably, found there at a subsequent period, might have been eventually used by the invaders on their own conversion.[2] Had this ancient

---

scriptos monasterii Augustinensis Cant. anno Dñi 1565. mens. August.—JOĀ. JOSSELINUS.

" Ibi hunc ipsum librum a Gulielmo Malmesburiensi repertum esse ; ex libro ejusdem de Antiquitate Glastoniensis monasterii apparebit —JA. USSERUS."

[1] From the following passage in the MS. cited above, f. 63, it might seem that Glastonbury was famed for sanctity so early as the fifth century Otherwise it is not likely that St. Patrick would have fixed himself there, and that he should be thought to have died there.

" Porro Hibernensium peregrini per dictum locum Glestoniæ, sicut et cæteræ fidelium turbæ magno colebant affectu, et maxime ob beati Patricii senioris honorem ; qui faustus ibidem in Dño quievisse narratur."

[2] " Ecclesia de qua loquimur (Glest. sc.), quæ per antiquitatem sui celeriter ab Anglis ealꝺe cince, id est, *vetusta Ecclesia*, nuncupatur, primo virgea."—SPELM. *Conc.* 1. p 17.

place of worship been thought to possess pretensions of a character yet more illustrious, it is by no means likely that Saxon veneration for the spot would have overlooked them. We may, therefore, not unreasonably conclude that Joseph of Arimathea's connexion with Glastonbury depends upon no tradition anterior to those Norman times,[1] from which it has descended to posterity.

As much less uncertainty, however, attaches to the date of Britain's conversion than to the names of her evangelists, the case of Lucius can hardly claim the importance often assigned to it. This king of Britain, we are informed, was impressed so much in favour of Christianity, that he sent Eluan and Medwin to Eleutherius, the Roman bishop, for farther instruction.[2] His ambassadors are said to have been courteously entertained in Rome, instructed in the faith of Jesus, baptized, and finally ordained. On returning home, Lucius is represented to have received baptism by their persuasions, and to have founded a church

---

[1] "It seems to be a little suspicious, at first view, that so considerable a part of the antiquities of this church should be wholly past by, by the most ancient and inquisitive writers of our affairs; so that neither the true Gildas, nor Asserius, nor Marianus Scotus, nor any of the ancient annals, should take the least notice of this tradition" (respecting Joseph of Arimathea).—STILLINGFLEET'S *Antiqu. of the Brit. Churches*, p. 6.

[2] Bede (*Eccl. Hist.*, l. 4, ed. Wheloc. p. 28.), assigns this application of Lucius to some time within a short distance of the year 156. The alleged conversion, however, of this prince, is rather uncertain as to date. Abp. Usher (*Brit. Eccl. Antiqu.* p. 20) has collected, from various writers, no fewer than twenty-three different dates, ranging from 137 to 199, to which that event has been referred.

in Britain, which flourished until the persecution of Diocletian.¹ These transactions have been referred to various dates; but hardly any authorities will allow us to consider them as anterior to the latter half of the second century. Lucius, then, must have been contemporary with Justin Martyr and Irenæus, and, at farthest, not more than a single generation removed from Tertullian. Now, in the time of the former writers, we have every reason to believe that Christianity had already taken root in Britain. Such is known to have been the fact in Tertullian's days. Lucius, therefore, might seem to have sought from a very distant quarter information which lay within his reach at home. It should, however, be observed, that no notice is taken of any demand for religious instruction in a letter of reply attributed to Eleutherius. From this he seems to have done no more than apply for authentic particulars of Roman jurisprudence.² Although it may, then, be probable that some petty prince, styled in Latin Lucius, was among the earlier of British converts to Christianity,

---

¹ Bed., i. 4, p. 28.

² See a translation of it in Collier's *Eccl. Hist.*, i. 14. It is a very suspicious document, upon several accounts, especially as to antiquity, not being "met with till a thousand years after Eleutherius's death, and where it was first found is altogether uncertain. The author of the *Customs of London* printed it in the twelfth year of Henry VIII.; afterwards Lambert inserted it among the laws of Edward the Confessor: but here it is printed in an italic letter, as a mark of its being spurious. Hoveden's manuscripts, of about four hundred years standing, take no notice of it; and, which is remarkable, his contemporary, Geoffrey of Monmouth, who did not use to suppress or overlook any British antiquities, says nothing about it."—COLLIER.

yet he can hardly have been contemporary with its introduction to the island. If any, therefore, would fain derive his conversion from papal intervention, and claim authority for the Roman see over every church which its prelates have planted, they must fail of establishing such a claim over Britain from this alleged transaction.

The care, universally marking primitive Christianity, to provide a bishop for every church,[1] necessarily connects the stream of British prelacy with apostolic times. National confusions, by destroying evidence, have, indeed, prevented modern Britain from ascertaining the earliest links in the chain of her episcopal succession. But it is satisfactory to know that her prelates presented themselves upon the first occasion likely to furnish an authentic record of their appearance. Constantine, desirous of terminating the Donatistic schism, convened a council at Arles.[2] The signatures of three British bishops are appended to the canons there enacted.[3]

Subsequently, when the younger Constantine and his brother Constans endeavoured to secure religious

---

[1] 'Ο χωρὶς τῦ ἐπισκόπυ, καὶ τῶν πρεσβυτέρων, καὶ τῶν διακόνων τί πράσσων, ὁ τοιῦτος μεμίανται τῇ συνειδήσει, καὶ ἔστιν ἀπίστυ χείρων.—IGNAT. ad Trall. inter Mon. S. PP. p. 10.

[2] In 314, Labb. et Coss. i. 1422.

[3] " Eborius episcopus, de civitate Eboracensi, provincia Britannia.

" Restitutus episcopus, de civitate Londinensi, provincia supracripta.

" Adelfius episcopus, de civitate Colonia Londinensium, exinde sacerdos presbyter. Arminius diaconus."—*Ibid.* 1430.

By *Civitas Colonia Londinensium,* it is hardly doubtful that Colchester is to be understood.

unity by summoning the principal ecclesiastics to Sardica, this council also was attended by British bishops.[1] Several of that body likewise obeyed the mandate of Constantius, in attending the council of Ariminium, holden a few years later in the fourth century.[2] Nor has it been considered otherwise than highly probable, that episcopal delegates from Albion were among that most illustrious assembly, the first council of Nice.[3]

Before Britain thus appeared among ecclesiastical authorities, her constancy was severely tried in the fire of persecution. In common with other parts of the Roman empire, she suffered under that insane and atrocious policy by which Diocletian glutted the vengeance of baffled Paganism. It was during this gloomy reign of terror that St. Alban obtained the crown of martyrdom. When the persecution began, he was a Pagan, but his humanity would not allow him to refuse an asylum under his roof to a proscribed Christian priest. While hospitably sheltered there, the pious clergyman's religious fervour so effectually won Alban's

---

[1] The Council of Sardica was holden in 347. For the attendance of British bishops there, see Usher (*Brit. Eccl. Antiq.*), p 105.

[2] " Ita missis per Illyricum, Italiam, Aphricam, Hispanias, Galliasque, magistris officialibus, acciti ac in unum coacti quadringenti et aliquanto amplius occidentales episcopi, Ariminium convenere: quibus omnibus annonas et cellaria dare Imperator præceperat: sed id nostris, id est, Aquitanis, Gallis, ac Britannis, indecens visum, repudiatis fiscalibus, propriis sumptibus vivere maluerunt. Tres tantum ex Britannia, inopia proprii, publico usi sunt, cum oblatam a cæteris collationem respuissent: sanctius putantes fiscum gravare, quam singulos."—SULPICII SEVERI *Hist. Sacr.* l. ii. inter *Mon. S. PP.* p. 539.

[3] Usser. *Brit. Eccl. Antiq.* p. 105.

veneration, that he readily received instruction in the faith of Jesus. At length the priest's retreat was discovered; but Alban, now a zealous Christian, had become bent upon saving him at every hazard. He dressed himself, accordingly, in his clothes, and thus disguised, he was dragged before the Roman governor. The deception being discovered, he was bidden to choose between sacrificing to the gods, and the punishment intended for his fugitive friend. In answer, he declared himself immovably resolved against offering an insult to his holy faith. He was then tried by scourging, and this proving insufficient to daunt his courage, he suffered decapitation. He resided at Verulam, or Werlamcester, as the Saxons eventually called it. The place of his martyrdom was the hill overlooking the spot then occupied by that ancient city. Here, in after-times, arose the noble abbey of St. Alban's, a worthy commemoration of Britain's earliest blood-stained testimony against Gentile errors. After Alban's example, many other members of the ancient British church surrendered their lives rather than deny their Saviour.[1] Thus, in Britain, as elsewhere, Diocletian's persecution, though serving to render Paganism odious and contemptible, by an exhibition of vindictive rage and impotent intolerance; enabled Christianity, after displaying numerous examples of heroic self-denial, to emerge from a stormy time of trial, more vigorous and illustrious than ever.

Old churches, accordingly, were soon repaired, new ones built, and Christians, who had timidly con-

---

[1] Hom. in Pass. S. Alban. ap. *Wheloc. in Bed.* p. 36.

cealed themselves during the persecution, again came forward, bringing from their hiding-places an ardent zeal to spread the faith of Jesus.[1] Constantine's accession followed shortly after; when Britain became the seat of a flourishing and extensive church. During the progress of its complete establishment, Arianism distracted the Christian world. This heresy appears, however, to have been slow in reaching the British shores.[2] At length, seemingly when the fourth century was verging towards a close,[3] Arius, already popular in other divisions of the Christian world, found followers in the church of Albion.[4]

An entrance being thus afforded to a spirit of rash vain-glorious disputation, as usual, another enemy to religious peace quickly took advantage of the breach. Pelagius, probably called Morgan

---

[1] " Nam qui superfuerant, sylvis ac desertis, abditisque speluncis se occultavere, expectantes a justo rectore omnium Deo carnificibus severa quandoque judicia, sibi vero animarum tutamina. Igitur bilustro supradicti turbinis, necdum ad integrum expleto, emarescentibusque necis autorem nepharie edictis, lætis luminibus omnes Christi tyrones, quasi post hyemalem ac prolixam noctem temperiem, lucemque serenam auræ cælestis excipiunt, renovant ecclesias ad solum usque destructas, basilicas sanctorum martyrum fundant, construunt, perficiunt."—GILD. de Excid. Brit. p, 834.

[2] Stillingfleet. Antiqu. Brit. Ch. p 175.

[3] Usser. Brit. Eccl. Antiqu. p. 106.

[4] " Mansit namque hæc Christi capitis membrorum consonantia suavis, donec Arriana perfidia atrox ceu anguis transmarina nobis evomens venena, fratres in unum habitantes exitiabiliter faceret sejungi, ac si quasi via facta, trans oceanum, omnes omnino bestiæ feræ mortiferum cujuslibet hæreseos virus horrido ore vibrantes, lætalia dentium vulnera patriæ novi semper aliquid audire volenti, et nihil certe stabiliter obtinenti, infigebant."— GILD. de Excid. Brit. p. 834.

among his countrymen, by birth a Briton,[1] following a prevailing fashion of his day, resolved upon a residence in Rome. Being remarkable there for piety and mortification, with considerable abilities, although his learning was far behind them, he quickly gained a high degree of credit. His principal companion and warmest admirer was Celestius, an Irishman of great subtlety and readiness of wit. Unfortunately for both these insular ascetics, they became acquainted with Rufinus, who, after having resided in the East for thirty years, had returned into his native Italy deeply tinctured with Origen's peculiar opinions. From this eminent, though injudicious acquaintance, Pelagius and Celestius learned to doubt the doctrine of original sin. They soon proceeded to reason against the necessity of divine grace for fulfilling the will of God. These principles, at first, were cautiously proposed, in conversation chiefly, and rather as questions deserving a fuller examination than they had hitherto received, than as positions entitled to implicit confidence.[2] By mooting them, however, often and shrewdly, Pelagius rapidly acquired a new hold upon popular attention. Doctrines, indeed, to say nothing of their novelty,

---

[1] "Pelagius *Brito*."—BED. *Eccl. Hist* i. 10. p. 51.

"Patrio nomine *Morgan* dictum fuisse aiunt. *Morgan* autem Britannis *Marigenam*, sive *Pelago ortum* denotat: unde et Latinum *Pelagii* deductum est vocabulum."—USSER. *Brit. Eccl. Antiqu.* p. 112.

[2] *Ibid* 110. The Pelagian heresy seems to have arisen about the year 400. (*Ibid.* 114.) For the doctrines of Pelagius, this work of Abp Usher may be consulted, pp. 117, 122, 123, 129, 170

so flattering to human pride, could hardly fail of extensively attracting admirers. To arrest their progress, St. Austin laboriously employed his powerful pen. The controversy naturally drew from him strong assertions of grace and predestination: these have occasioned, in modern times, many exulting appeals to his authority. Such passages, however, are probably largely indebted for their force to the strong recoil of ardent passions, and a vigorous intellect wound up in the heat of argument.

After their ill-famed celebrity was gained, neither Pelagius nor Celestius appears to have revisited the British Isles. Their opinions, however, were introduced; chiefly by means of Agricola, son of Severianus, a Gallic bishop. Auxiliaries of native origin, it might seem, seconding Agricola's endeavours, Pelagianism soon became extensively popular in Britain. The leading ecclesiastics remained firm to their ancient principles; but their opposition to the tide of innovation proving insufficient, they requested assistance from the neighbouring church of Gaul. The summons was answered in the persons of Germanus bishop of Auxerre, and Lupus bishop of Troyes. These able prelates, by their eloquence in the pulpit, by their influence in private society, and by the arguments which they used in a council convoked at Verulam, succeeded in imposing silence upon the Pelagian party. They then returned to the continent. On their departure, British Pelagianism revived, and the native clergy, again despairing of its extinction by their own unaided powers, implored Germanus to pay their island a second visit.

The pious Bishop of Auxerre, listening readily to this application, took with him Severus bishop of Treves, a disciple of his former coadjutor, and set sail for Britain. Upon this occasion, as upon the former one, the preaching, arguments, and persuasions of the foreign prelates were followed by the complete abasement of Pelagianism. The visitors, however, now were not to be satisfied until they had made effectual provision for perpetuating their triumph. They persuaded, accordingly, their insular friends to act upon an edict of Valentinian, and drive into exile the teachers whose innovating doctrines had caused so much dissension.[1]

Soon afterwards the British Church was grievously despoiled of her ancient splendour. The country, abandoned by its Roman masters, became a prey to domestic faction, and to predatory movements of barbarian tribes occupying its northern regions. Intolerable miseries, arising from this latter cause, impelled the harassed and pusillanimous authorities of southern Britain to seek assistance from some restless and intrepid soldiers of fortune, then wandering, as it seems, in quest of plunder.[2] This impolitic and disgraceful call was promptly answered. The foreign warriors immediately became highly serviceable, and having recommended more extensive invitations to their countrymen, such a force was formed as quickly drove the Picts and Scots back to their mountain-fastnesses. But the victors now

---

[1] Usser. *Brit. Eccl Antiqu.* 176. Stillingfleet's *Antiqu. Br. Ch.* 194.

[2] Turner's *Hist Angl Saxons* Lond. 1828 ı, 254

cast a longing eye upon the fair fields delivered by their valour. A prize, so noble and unprotected, naturally proved a temptation too great for the cupidity of mere pirates.[1] The bold auxiliaries accordingly became invaders, nor did they cease to struggle for the mastery, until the miserable remains of British power were driven from every seat of its long-established glory, into quarters of the island, remote, inaccessible, and comparatively worthless.

---

[1] " Statuunt inter se dividere victores alienigenæ insulam bonis omnibus fecundissimam: indignum judicantes eam ignavorum dominio detineri, que ad defensionem suam idoneis posset prebere sufficientem alimoniam, et optimis viris."—ABBO. FLORIACENSIS. *Passio Sancti Eadmundi.* Bibl. Bodl. MSS. Digby. 109, p. 4.

ANGLO-SAXON ECCLESIASTICAL HISTORY.

CHAPTER I.

FROM AUGUSTINE TO THEODORE.
597—669

THE ANGLO-SAXONS — OBSTACLES TO THEIR CONVERSION — ETHELBERT AND BERTHA — GROWING DISPOSITION TOWARDS CHRISTIANITY — GREGORY THE GREAT — AUGUSTINE — SUCCESS OF HIS MISSION — CLAIMS MIRACULOUS POWERS — PROPOSES QUESTIONS TO GREGORY — INEFFECTUALLY ENDEAVOURS TO UNDERMINE THE INDEPENDENCE OF THE ANCIENT BRITISH CHURCH — TEMPORARY CONVERSION OF ESSEX — LAURENTIUS — TEMPORARY CONVERSION OF NORTHUMBRIA — CONVERSION OF EAST ANGLIA — FINAL CONVERSION OF NORTHUMBRIA — CONVERSION OF MERCIA — FINAL CONVERSION OF ESSEX — FURSEY — CONVERSION OF WESSEX — CONVERSION OF SUSSEX — TRIUMPH OF THE ROMAN PARTY IN NORTHUMBRIA — DOCTRINES.

ANGLO-SAXON Ecclesiastical History admits of an advantageous distribution into four several portions. The first exhibits a nation passing from Paganism to Christianity, and a foreign church struggling for ascendancy over one of native growth. The second embraces a period in which ancient England made her most conspicuous intellectual progress, and in which were laid securely the foundations of an ecclesiastical establishment. The third is rendered interesting by the splendid services of Alfred, but it paints an age of national distress, and of literary declension. The fourth is also deeply marked by civil difficulties, and prevailing ignorance. Dunstan has, however, given it a peculiar character, by planting the Benedictine system among Englishmen. Immediately began a serious interference with vested rights, the natural parent of obstinate dissension.

The Anglo-Saxon people sprang from three piratical tribes, of Gothic origin. Two of these were seated in the neck of the Cimbric Chersonese, now known as Jutland, and in three islands off its western coast.[1] The Jutes, probably, lived within that peninsula. The emigration of their tribe does not, however, seem to have been extensive, its British settlements being confined to Kent, the Isle of Wight, and the southern part of Hampshire.[2] The Angles, whose continental home lay in the modern districts of Sleswick and Holstein,[3] emigrated entirely,[4] and spreading over the north-eastern, midland, and northern coun-

---

[1] North Strandt, Busen, and Heiligland, or Heligoland. The last of these, now reduced by repeated incursions of the ocean to a mere rock, was anciently of much greater extent than it is at present.—*History of the Anglo-Saxons*, by SHARON TURNER, F.A.S. Lond. 1828, i. 114.

[2] Bedæ *Historia Ecclesiastica Gentis Anglorum.* Ed. Wheloc. Cant. 1643, p. 58. Dr. INGRAM's *Saxon Chronicle*, Lond. 1823, p. 14.

[3] " Porro Anglia vetus sita est inter Saxones et Giotas, habens oppidum capitale, quod sermone Saxonico Slesuuic nuncupatur, secundum vero Danos, Haithaby.—*Chronicum Ethelwerdi.* ed. Savile · inter *Scriptores post Bedam.* Lond. 1596, f. 474.

[4] " Anglia, which has ever since remained waste." (*Sax. Chr.* 15.) Perhaps, however, this language is not to be understood quite literally, for Bede qualifies it by *perhibetur.*

ties of South Britain, eventually gave name to the whole country. The Saxons, nearest neighbours of these, as coming from that region, between the Eyder and the Elbe, called Old Saxony by our ante-Norman ancestors,[1] found new abodes in Essex, Middlesex, and in those counties, west of Kent, which lie between the Thames and the Channel. That the Angles, no less than the Saxons, were descended from the Teutonic branch of the Gothic family, not the Scandinavian, is attested sufficiently by the Anglo-Saxon tongue. This could hardly fail of exhibiting a closer affinity with the modern Icelandic, had the tribe most conspicuous in planting it on British ground, owned perfect identity of origin with nations yet inhabiting the north-western extremities of continental Europe. Anglo-Saxon, however, is a language assimilating rather with German than Icelandic.[2]

All these invading tribes were Pagans. Nor were the earlier years of their settlement in Britain favourable to their adoption of the Christian creed. It is true, that the people whose fair possessions lured them from their Scandinavian abodes, had risen into opulence under an abandonment of Gentile errors. This people was aroused, however, into a long course

---

[1] Bed. 58.

[2] " That the Angles were a Teutonic race is not only probable, but almost certain, from the fact that the dialect of these invaders so soon coalesced into one common tongue, and assumed a character so decidedly Teutonic, that, with the exception of a few Normanisms, introduced in later times, there is scarcely a vestige deserving notice of the old Scandinavian, or of Danish structure, to be found in the Anglo-Saxon."—Preface to RASK's *Anglo-Saxon Grammar*, translated by THORPE. Copenhagen, 1830, p. xii.

of sanguinary conflict with its treacherous invaders, when it found itself menaced by them with nothing short of slavery or extermination. Hence, during considerably more than a century from Hengist's arrival, South Britain was unceasingly distracted by the various miseries of intestine war.[1] Such a season obviously denies a field to missionary zeal. It is, therefore, probable that the native clergy made no attempt, while their nation yet struggled for existence, to humanise its unrelenting enemies by communicating to them a knowledge of the Gospel. The

---

[1] Hengist did not establish himself in the kingdom of Kent until after the battle of Aylesford, fought in 455, in which battle his brother Horsa was slain. Thus, as these two brothers first lent their dangerous aid in 449, six agitated years, at least, elapsed between the period of their arrival in Britain, and that of their nation's earliest rational prospect of a secure establishment within the island. (*Sax. Chr.* 15. *Ethelwerd. Script. post Bed* 474). The Britons did not abandon Kent until after the battle of Crayford, two years later. Nor subsequently did they cease to contend vigorously with the unwelcome colonists Of these intruders, however, a new body succeeded in planting itself in Sussex, under Ella, soon after 477, the year in which it landed there. In 495, Cerdic landed (probably in Hampshire), and he was enabled eventually to lay the foundations of the kingdom of Wessex; but it was not until after an arduous struggle of twenty-four years. Nor was it then, until after the lapse of about seventy years, that his descendants pushed their conquests to the Somersetshire Avon and the Severn. While this protracted warfare was raging in the south; the east, the north, and the middle of England were successively overrun by Saxons and Angles; principally by the latter Nor was it before the year 586 that this latter people founded the great midland kingdom of Mercia. Even then, however, the British spirit was not subdued: a few sanguinary contests, occurring at intervals afterwards, plainly shewing that the new comers were necessitated to continue upon the alert against the hostility of the people whom they had dispossessed

Pagan warriors were besides likely to draw new prejudices against Christianity from the very success which usually waited upon their arms. Britain's trust in the Cross had not secured her fortunes from constant declension: while a reliance upon Woden had been encouraged unceasingly by victory. A people unpractised in sound argumentation, and unacquainted with true religion, would hence hardly fail of concluding that its own deities were more kind, and probably more powerful also, than those of its opponents. Vainly would Christianity solicit the favourable notice of such minds thus prepossessed. It is plain that a considerable change must be wrought in the whole frame of a society like this, before it could be gained over to calm reflection upon the religion of a people prostrate under its assaults.

No sooner, however, had Providence effected such a change, than England, happily, could take full advantage of it. Her principal monarch then was Ethelbert, king of Kent; a prince whose authority reached the Humber,[1] and who, under the designation of *Bretwalda*,[2] enjoyed an admitted precedence over all the Anglo-Saxon potentates. This powerful sovereign appears to have ascended his father's throne,

---

[1] *Bed.* ed. Wheloc. l. 1. c. 25, p. 75. Ethelbert, probably, had extorted a tributary acknowledgement, or some other mark of subserviency, from all the petty princes established to the south of the Humber. Malmesbury (*Script. post Bed.* Lond. 1596, 6, 4), speaks of him as having subdued all the Anglo-Saxon nations, except the Northumbrians. But Bede's words hardly seem to bear a construction so wide

[2] The Saxon Chronicle (p. 88) says that Ethelbert was the third Anglo-Saxon prince thus distinguished. Ella, king of Sussex,

about the year 560,[1] and probably ten years afterwards,[2] he married Bertha, daughter of Cherebert, king of the Franks. This princess, coming of a Christian family, was not allowed to pass over into Kent until ample stipulations had been made for the free profession of her holy faith. She came, accord-

---

was the first, and Egbert, king of Wessex, the last Bretwalda. Of this designation it seems impossible to define the exact import. Mr. Turner has shewn that it could not have arisen from an absolute conquest over the contemporary sovereigns. That it implied, however, a considerable degree of influence over the whole, or the greater part of England, must necessarily follow from the language of Bede. See *Hist. of Angl. Sax.* i. 331.

[1] Bede's text is made to say that Ethelbert died in the year 613, after a reign of fifty-six years. (l. ii. c. 5, p. 119). This account throws his accession back to the year 557. This is the year, accordingly, assigned to that event by the Saxon Chronicle (p. 25). But the ancient chronicler here makes Ethelbert to have reigned no more than 53 years. According to this portion of his narrative, therefore, the Kentish *Bretwalda* must have died in 610. Afterwards, however (p. 30), the Saxon Chronicle makes Ethelbert to have died in 616, and to have reigned 56 years. With these dates Henry of Huntingdon agrees. (*Script. post Bed.* f. 187). Malmesbury contents himself with remarking the discrepancy between the ancient authorities, and desiring his readers to form their own opinion as to the facts. (*Ibid.* f. 4). Had he known King Alfred's translation of Bede, he would have been at no loss to decide upon the subject himself. That illustrious remnant of our great monarch's literary labours makes Ethelbert to have died *about the year* 616. Now, as Alfred follows his author's printed text in assigning a reign of fifty-six years to the celebrated King of Kent, there can be little doubt, that by Malmesbury's time, some error had crept into the MSS. of Bede, and that, according to the venerable writer's original statements, Ethelbert really died about the year 616, after a reign of fifty-six years.

[2] Inett considers Ethelbert to have married " about the year 570." This is not unlikely, as he came young to the throne, and required a few years to attain that importance which rendered him an eligible match for the Frankish princess.

ingly, attended by Luidhard, a Frankish bishop, and for her accommodation, a British church, erected in honour of St. Martin, on the eastern side of Canterbury, but long desecrated, was again rendered suitable for Christian worship. Thus, when the sixth century had, perhaps, thirty years to run, a Christian congregation was formed in the principal seat of Anglo-Saxon power. Nor, as its leading member was the most illustrious female in the island, can we reasonably suppose that it long failed of making converts. Intelligence accordingly arrived at Rome, that among the English nation *an anxious desire* prevailed for admission within the Church of Christ.[1] How far any such anxiety had affected Ethelbert personally, there are no direct means of ascertaining. But Gregory the Great, from whose epistles we learn the bias of his people, intimates to Bertha, that *she ought early to have inclined him favourably*[2] towards her own religion. As

---

[1] " Pervenit ad nos Anglorum gentem ad fidem Christianam, Deo miserante, *desideranter velle converti.*" (GREGORII PP. I. *Epist.* 58, l. v. *Labb et Coss.* tom. v. col. 1244). " Indicamus ad nos pervenisse Anglorum gentem, Deo annuente, velle fieri Christianam."—(*Ejusd. Epist.* 59. *Ibid*).

The former of these epistles is addressed to Theodoric, and Theodebert, kings of the Franks; the latter, to Brunichild, queen of that nation. The object of both epistles is to recommend Augustine, on his passage through Gaul, to the favourable consideration of these royal personages. Mrs. Elstob has printed English translations of these epistles in the appendix to the homily on St. Gregory's day.

[2] " Et quidem *jamdudum* gloriosi filii nostri, conjugis vestri, animos prudentiæ vestræ bono, sicut revera Christianæ, debuistis inflectere, ut pio regni et animæ suæ salute fidem quam colitis sequeretur." (GREG. PP. I. *Epist.* 59, lib. 9). A translation of this Epistle is in Mrs. Elstob's Appendix, p. 18.

this intimation occurs amidst a mass of compliment, it is, probably, a mere allusion to a fact, sufficiently known, but unfit for public mention. Of Ethelbert's politic temper, his influence beyond his patrimonial territories is an undeniable evidence. Such a man's habitual prudence would restrain him from a hasty avowal of an important change in his religious opinions. Nor, after his formal conversion, would he fail of wishing that a secret, laying him open to a charge of dissimulation, should not be needlessly divulged. Had not Ethelbert, however, long looked upon Christianity with an approving eye, it is most unlikely that, when publicly called upon to embrace it, he should so readily have obeyed the summons.[1]

---

[1] Bede says (l. ii. c. 5, p. 120), that Ethelbert died twenty-one years after he had received the Christian faith. The venerable author's royal translator, Alfred, goes farther; adding that the Kentish *Bretwalda* died at this interval, after his *baptism*. His death, however, took place, it seems, in 616. He might, therefore, have become a Christian in 595. The Saxon Chronicle, however, assigns the arrival of Augustine to 596, and Bede (l. i c. 23, p. 73), says that it took place in the fourteenth year of the Emperor Maurice, and that that emperor acceded in 582. Bede's chronology, therefore, coincides with that of the Saxon Chronicle, and is, most probably, its authority. Hence, it seems, we must understand, not that Ethelbert died at the distance of twenty-one years complete from his conversion, but in the twenty-first year after that event. He must, accordingly, have been baptised almost immediately after the arrival of Augustine. John of Tinmouth, accordingly (*Historia Aurea*, Pars. 3, Bibl. Lameth. MS. 12. f. 7), says, *Æthelbertus rex Cantiæ anno vicesimo-primo post fidei susceptionem, migravit ad Dominum.* A splendid MS. containing Lives of Saints, in the Bodleian Library (MSS. Bodley, 285, f. 116), likewise says, *Itaque post suscepte fidei sacramentū, cum per viginti et unum annos juxta examinationis lancem secundum equitatem divini juris*

From one of the more eminent of Roman bishops this happy summons flowed. Gregory, honourably distinguished among popes as the Great, sprang from an illustrious family, and inherited a papal fortune, his great-grandfather Felix having filled the opulent see of Rome. His early instruction was not altogether unworthy of hereditary affluence, and he proved an apt scholar. Gregory, notwithstanding, lived and died ignorant of Greek, then a living language, necessary for understanding the best authors, and spoken vernacularly at his sovereign's court.[1] This deficiency might seem immaterial to one intended for a mere civilian, and his education was, probably, conducted with no other view, since he was appointed, at an early age, governor of Rome, his native city. He now was tried by one of those alloys which Providence mercifully uses for chastising the insolence of prosperity, and rebuking the envy of depression. His habitual state of health was miserable. Hence he soon anxiously sought an escape from public life, and an uninterrupted course of religious meditation: the only proper occupation, as it seemed, for a mind encased in a frame like his. He founded, accordingly, six monasteries in Sicily, and one in his native city. To this he himself retired. Rome resounded with the praise of such mortification and magnanimity. Hence he was not long left in the obscurity

---

temporalis regni sceptra rite gubernaret, die vicesimo-septimo (no month mentioned), *mundialibus rebus exemptus est*

[1] *Quamvis Græcæ linguæ nescius,* he says of himself to Anastasius, an Isaurian presbyter. GREG. PP. I. *Epist.* 29, lib. vi. *Labb. et Coss.* v. 1274.

of his retreat. Pelagius II. ordained him deacon in 582, and sent him as apocrisiary to the imperial court.[1]

He remained at Constantinople, highly esteemed, until the death of Tiberius, in 586. It being usual that a new papal resident should wait upon a new emperor, Gregory then returned to Rome, bearing with him, in proof of satisfaction given by his mission, some of those wretched relics from which the Romish hierarchy has gathered so great a load of well-earned infamy, and the Romish laity such deep debasement. But although fully smitten by the prevailing spirit of superstition, he possessed a self-devoted spirit, worthy of the apostolic age. A raging pestilence filled Rome with mourning and consternation. Gregory braved the horrors of this avenging scourge, seeking to disarm the wrath of Heaven, and to mitigate the popular distress, by solemn religious exercises. Under his guidance, all the citizens formed themselves into seven choirs, which perambulated their half-deserted streets, mournfully chanting penitential litanies. This noble disregard of every thing but duty, led grateful Rome to name him unanimously the successor of Pelagius, who had lately perished in the plague. Such elections, however, had no more than a conditional validity. Unless the

---

[1] Such officers were called *Apocrisiaries*, because they returned the ἀποκρίσεις *answers*, that is, of their principals, to inquiries or proposals made at the several courts to which they were delegated. Ecclesiastical apocrisiaries were ordinarily received at the court of Constantinople only from the patriarchal sees. Deacons were generally chosen for this office by the Roman pontiffs. Du Cange *in voc.*

emperor confirmed them, they were void.[1] Gregory wrote to Constantinople, earnestly beseeching the denial of this confirmation. He determined also upon flight, and finding guards appointed to frustrate his intention, he was conveyed away, like St. Paul, in a basket, and sought the concealment of a wood. All these incidents naturally cast additional lustre upon his elevation. His messenger to the imperial court was intercepted, and in place of his own letter, another was transmitted, earnestly supplicating the emperor to confirm the choice of Rome. This request found a ready acquiescence; and Gregory's retreat being easily discovered, he was joyously conducted to the pontifical chair.

Of this he became a very active occupant. His equanimity, however, was not proof against lofty pretensions in a rival see. John the Faster, bishop of Constantinople, a prelate almost adored in that capital, from his extreme rigour in ascetic mortifications, assumed, under imperial sanction, the title of *Œcumenical bishop.* Inconceivably offended, Gregory styled himself *Servant of the servants of God,*[2] an ostentation of humility yet retained by the princely

---

[1] " Nil enim tum a clero in eligendo pontifice actum erat, nisi ejus electionem imperator approbasset."—PLATINA *in Pelag.* ii. ed. 1529, p. 65.

[2] " Superstitiosum *Universalis* vocabulum, quod Johannes, Constantinopolitanus antistes Episcopus insolenter sibi tunc temporis usurpabat, more antecessorum suorum Pontificum, sub districtissimæ interminationis sententia refutavit, *et primus omnium se in principio epistolarum suarum* SERVUM SERVORUM DEI *scribi satis humiliter definivit.*"—*Vita S. Greg. M.* Auctore Paulo Diacono. *Acta SS. Ord. Benedict.* Lut. Par. 1668, i. 386.

pontiffs, though so long unruffled by Oriental arrogance. He reminded, also, the Emperor Maurice of St. Peter's high prerogatives, *and yet,* he added, *that pillar of our faith is never called Universal Apostle.* The Faster's assumption he paints, accordingly, as an insult to the priesthood, and a scandal to the Church.[1] Nor was he able to conquer a resentful feeling towards Maurice for lacerating so severely his pride of station. Hence, when that emperor fell under the murderous hand of Phocas, the usurper, infamous as he was, not only met with a ready recognition from the Romans, but also with fulsome compliments from their bishop.[2]

---

[1] Greg. PP. I. *Epist.* iv. 32, ap. *Labb. et Coss.* v. 1181. In this epistle Gregory charges his rival, the Faster, with downright hypocrisy. He says " Ossa jejuniis atteruntur, et mente turgemus. Corpus despectis vestibus tegitur, et elatione cordis purpuram superamus. Doctores humilium, duces superbiæ, ovina facie lupinos dentes abscondimus." It is not possible to acquit such language of gross intemperance, when applied to a person of strict morality, and of ascetic habits. Nor did Gregory here, in all probability, render justice to the Faster. That prelate was not likely to be an absolute hypocrite, and these words paint him as nothing else. That he was, however, much of a self-deceiver, there can be little question, and his case deserves the serious notice of every one who may become acquainted with it. Had John really made these acquisitions in humility which were in accordance with his outward acts of mortification, he would not have given such violent offence to Gregory. He may serve, therefore, to remind us, that even under a striking appearance of extreme humility, men are very liable to overlook a most dangerous degree of pride within.

[2] " Aliquando vero cum misericors Deus mœrentium corda sua decrevit collatione refavere, unum ad regiminis culmen provehit, per cujus misericordiæ viscera in cunctorum mentibus exultationis suæ gratiam infundit. De qua exultationis abundantia roborari nos citius credimus, qui benignitatem vestræ pietatis

As a counterpoise to the encroaching spirit of his Eastern rivals, Gregory naturally thought of extending the influence of his own authority in an opposite direction. Britain presented an inviting field. Her ancient Church, which in better days would probably have spurned any Roman attempt at interference, had been miserably curtailed by the Saxon conquest, in importance and extent. An auspicious opening was now offered, by means of Ethelbert and his Christian spouse, for raising on its ruins a new ecclesiastical establishment. Gregory was well aware of these advantages, and judiciously determined upon improving them. His determination is referred by the earliest of our church historians to an impulse from on high.[1] Nor is this view unreasonable. Providence undoubtedly often acts upon the minds of men, and orders their affairs, to further its own benevolent designs.

Political motives for Gregory's generous enterprise were not likely to be assigned, at any time, by those who deeply venerated the see of Rome. A garrulous and wonder-loving age could not refer it even to heavenly motions, without making them depend upon a striking incident. In Bede accordingly,

---

ad imperiale fastigium pervenisse gaudemus. *Lætentur cæli, et exultet terra*, et de vestris benignis actibus universæ reipublicæ populus nunc usque vehementer afflictus hilarescat." (GREG. PP. I. ad Phoc. Imp. Epist. 38, lib. xi. *Labb. et Coss.* v. 1530). " Considerare cum gaudiis et magnis actionibus gratiarum libet, quantas omnipotenti Domino laudes debemus, quod remoto jugo tristitiæ ad libertatis tempora sub imperiali benignitatis vestræ pietate pervenimus."—Id. ad eund.—*Ib.* 1533.

[1] *Bed.* 1. 23, p. 73.

after Gregory's history is finished and his epitaph recorded, appears the following tale.[1] While yet a private clergyman, this famous pontiff was one day passing through the slave-market of his native city. There his eye was forcibly arrested by some light-haired, fair-complexioned youths, who stood exposed for sale. " Whence come these lads?" he asked. " From Britain:" was the answer. " Are the people Christians there?" he then inquired. " No: Pagans:" he was told. " Alas!" he said, " how grievous is it, that faces fair as these should own subjection to the swarthy devil!" His next question was: " What do you call the tribe from which these young people spring?" " Angles:" said the dealer. " Ah! that is well:" the future Pope rejoined. " Angels they are in countenance, and coheirs of angels they ought to be. Where in Britain do their kindred live?" " In Deira:"[2] was the reply. " Well again," Gregory said; " it is our

---

[1] *Bed.* ii. 1. p. 108. The venerable historian says that he received the story *traditione majorum.* It is detailed also in the *Homily on the Birth-day of S. Gregory,* published in the original Saxon, accompanied by an English translation, by Mrs. Elstob, in 1709, and by Paulus Diaconus.— *Vita* S. GREG. *Acta SS. Ord. Ben.* i. 391.

[2] *Dei ira* means in Latin, *God's anger.* The Saxon district, known as *Deira* in Latin, was that portion of Northumbria which lay between the Humber and the Tees, and which was occasionally independent of Bernicia, the northern portion. The Saxons called it *Deora mægthe,* or *Deora rice,* words meaning, there can be little doubt, the *province,* or *kingdom of wild beasts (deer).* It is likely that the form and pronunciation of this name, which a slave-dealer would probably give correctly enough, were not exactly suitable to the punning use of it placed in Gregory's mouth.

duty to deliver them from *God's ire.* Pray, who is king of the land so significantly named?" " Ella," replied the merchant. " Ah!" the pious inquirer added; " *Allelujah* must be sung in that man's country." Fired by this occurrence, Gregory resolved upon undertaking personally a mission into Anglia. Nor did the pope discourage his intention; but the Roman people would not allow their highly valued fellow-citizen to enter upon a labour so remote and perilous. Thus Gregory is exhibited as bringing to the pontificate those benevolent intentions towards Pagan Anglia, which were eventually realised under his direction. It is at least certain, that after his elevation he directed a priest named Candidus, manager of the papal patrimony in Gaul,[1] to buy some English lads of seventeen or eighteen, for education as missionaries among their countrymen.[2] This fact, probably, has brought Gregory himself upon the scene, to contrast his dark Italian hue with the bright complexion of a northern clime, and to point a dialogue with verbal play.

The prospect, however, of evangelising Britain by means of young people to be educated expressly

---

[1] " Churches in cities whose inhabitants were but of moderate substance, had no estates left to them out of their own district; but those in imperial cities, such as Rome, Ravenna, and Milan, where senators and persons of the first rank inhabited, were endowed with estates in divers parts of the world. St. Gregory mentions the patrimony of the Church of Ravenna, in Sicily, and another of the Church of Milan, in that kingdom. The Roman Church had patrimonies in France, Africk, Sicily, in the Cottian Alps, and in many other countries."—F. PAUL's *Treatise of Ecclesiastical Benefices.* Lond. 1736, p. 30.

[2] GREG. PP. I. Epist. v. 10. *Lab. et Coss* v 1217.

for the purpose, being distant and uncertain, Gregory's honourable zeal impelled him to think of a more expeditious course. He accordingly selected Augustine, prior of the monastery of St. Martin, in Rome, as leader of a devoted band, willing to attempt at once the conversion which he so anxiously desired. Augustine, having engaged several monks as partners in his toils, left the ancient capital of Europe, and made, it seems, his first considerable halt among the monastic recluses of Lerins. To these devotees the difficulties of his undertaking were necessarily better known than they could have been at Rome. At Lerins, accordingly, becoming utterly discouraged, he determined upon applying for Gregory's leave to withdraw from an enterprise apparently so hazardous and hopeless. But the pontiff would hear nothing of this despondence. He rebuked the missionary's pusillanimity, refused to cancel his obligations, and commanded him to lose no time in reaching Britain, fully relying upon God's protection and support. Augustine now rallied his spirits, proceeded northwards, and providing himself with interpreters in Gaul,[1] set sail for the chalky cliffs of Kent. He

---

[1] Malmesburiensis nostri illam de communi utriusque gentis sermone observationem libet adjicere: *naturalis lingua Francorum communicat cum Anglis, eo quod de Germania gentes ambæ germinaverunt:* illa nimirum lingua, *quam Franci transrhenani terunt;* et qua Carolum magnum Francorum regem usum fuisse, ex Vita ipsius paulo ante confirmaverat.—Quo minus mirum videri nobis debeat, quod a Beda proditum invenimus, Augustinum et socios, conversionis Anglorum opus aggressos, *accepisse, præcipiente Papa Gregorio, de gente Francorum interpretes.*"—USSER. *Brit. Eccl. Antiq.* 222.

landed in the isle of Thanet, and thence despatched a messenger to Ethelbert, informing him of his arrival, and declaring that he had journeyed thus far from home in hope of shewing him the way to heaven.[1]

By the Kentish prince, however well the message might have pleased him, it was cautiously received. He gave no permission to his Roman guests for a farther advance into the country, until he had gone himself to make observations. Augustine's arrangements for this royal visit did honour to his knowledge of human nature. Forming a procession of his monks, one of whom bore a silver cross, another a picture of the Saviour, while the remainder chanted litanies, he came forward into the *Bretwalda's* presence. Ethelbert might really have felt some fears of magic. At all events, there were those around him who would hardly fail of expressing such apprehensions, and an appearance of over-haste in approving the Roman mission seemed, probably, very far from politic. Augustine's first reception, accordingly, was in the open air; magic arts being thus considered less likely to take effect. The prior explained his object as no other than an anxious wish for guiding the king, and all around him, to those everlasting joys above, which it was the privilege of his ministry to promise, on conversion. "Fair words and promises are these," Ethelbert replied; "but being also new and uncertain, I cannot relinquish for them principles long and universally professed among my countrymen. Your

---

[1] Augustine appears to have received his commission from Gregory in 596, and to have landed in Kent in 597.— WHARTON *de Vera Success. Archiep. Cantuar Angl. Sacr.* i. p. 89.

distant pilgrimage, however, and your charitable purpose of communicating to us what seems of surpassing excellence to yourselves, justly claim our hospitality. I shall, therefore, provide you with a residence, and the means of living. Nor do I restrain you from endeavours to spread your opinions among my people." The residence provided was at Canterbury, and the missionaries entered that city to take possession of it, with all those imposing solemnities of the cross, the picture, and the chanted litany, which had dignified their introduction to the *Bretwalda*. Of their speedy success there are abundant assurances. Ethelbert, probably long a concealed Christian, seems to have openly professed himself a convert soon after their arrival. Nor, obviously, could such an example fail of operating extensively upon the people.

When sufficiently established, and attended by a considerable congregation in the ancient church of St. Martin, Augustine felt his time to be come for venturing upon a more extensive field. His instructions, however, and those principles of ecclesiastical polity which had ever guided Christians, forbade him to make dispositions for the general diffusion of his holy faith until he had formally assumed the episcopal character. He seems, accordingly, to have crossed over into Gaul, and to have advised with Etherius, archbishop of Arles,[1] upon a public appearance as metropolitan of the English nation. On his return

---

[1] "Neque Londinensis, neque Cantuariensis Archiepiscopus, sed universali nomine *Anglorum Episcopus* creabatur, ut liberum sibi sit, in quacunque vellet regni regione sedem suam collocare." (Parker. *Antiqu. Britan.* Lond. 1729 p 18) " Consecratus

into Kent, he sent to Rome, Laurence a priest, and Peter a monk, with news of his success. Among their intelligence, these messengers were, it seems, to give accounts of miracles wrought by him, as Augustine alleged, in confirmation and furtherance of his mission. There are no days, however loud in claims to illumination, not even when such claims are far from unfounded, incapable of affording multitudes eager to believe any thing supernatural. Nor are persons ever wanting equally eager to claim the power of indulging credulous people with food suitable to their appetite for wonders. At the close of the sixth century, when the leaden age had long pretty thoroughly set in, even in the chief seats of intellectual cultivation, an ignorant, a more than semi-barbarous country, like Jutish Kent, must necessarily have pre-

---

erat ab Eucherio, archiepiscopo Arelat. A. 602, et sedit annos 16, ait liber *Taxar. Ep. Wint. MS.* Wren. et *MS. Trin* Ab Ætherio, A. 597. Beda Lib 1. cap. 27. 16 Kal. Dec. 597 *Chron. W. Thorn* p 1760. Cui in hoc maxima fides est adhibenda " (*Godwin de Præsul.* Cant 1743, p. 37, note) Wharton (de Vera Success. Archiep. Cantuar. *Angl. Sacr.* p 89) has inferred from two epistles of Pope Gregory, that Augustine was consecrated to the episcopate before he originally passed over into Kent The first of these epistles (*Labb et Coss* v. 1289) acknowledges the kindness shewn by Brunichild, queen of the Franks, " erga fratrem et *coepiscopum* nostrum Augustinum " The second of these epistles (*Ib.* col. 1307) thus speaks of Augustine, to Eulogius, bishop of Alexandria . " Qui, data a me licentia, *a Germaniarum episcopis episcopus factus,* cum eorum quoque solatiis, ad prædictam gentem (*Anglorum,* sc.) in finem mundi perductus est." Guided by these authorities, Wharton reasonably concludes that W Thorn was rightly informed when he placed Augustine's consecration in 597, the very year of his arrival in Kent If, therefore, he went subsequently over to Etherius, it must have been to advise with him, not to receive consecration from him, as Bede relates

sented a most inviting field to any one possessed of the public eye, and disposed to gratify it by an assumption of miraculous endowments. Augustine appears to have been sufficiently forward in thus gratifying his adopted countrymen. He might, indeed, occasionally have really suspected some degree of truth in his pretensions. For among parties desirous of his wonder-working intervention, some must have laboured under nervous ailments. In such cases, a strong excitement and firm conviction would naturally render any juggling process productive of temporary benefit. In cases positively hopeless, he lulled his conscience, probably, under a little *pious fraud* (as language poisonously runs), by the false and execrable maxim, that "the end justifies the means." Gregory's disposition for scrutiny was equally dormant. He seems to have heard of Augustine's miracles with all that implicit credulity which in his day was generally prevalent. His, indeed, apparently, was a mind enamoured of the marvellous. At all events, his politic habits readily made him patronise a wonderful tale, whenever it seemed likely to raise the dignity of his see, or advance a favourite notion. He merely, therefore, contented himself, in noticing the supernatural attestations claimed for Augustine's mission, with gravely admonishing him against the danger of being puffed up under a consciousness of such extraordinary privileges.[1] Gregory provided, besides, the seeds of future debasement to the church so happily founded, by consigning to her new prelate various

---

[1] GREG. PP. I. Epist. ix. 58. *Labb. et Coss.* v. 1470.

relicks, the false, frivolous, and disgusting incentives to a grovelling superstition. He likewise transmitted vestments proper for celebrating the divine offices; and with still more commendable care for the rising community of Christians, he added several valuable books. Gregory the Great can, therefore, not only claim the honour of having embraced a favourable opportunity for delivering England from Paganism, but also of having laid the foundations of her literature, by presenting her with the first contributions towards the formation of a library.[1]

Augustine likewise received answers to certain questions proposed by him to the pontiff. In the first of these, he requested an opinion as to episcopal dealings with inferior clergymen, especially with reference to oblations laid by faithful Christians on the altar.

---

[1] The following appear to have been the books sent by Gregory. 1. A Bible, in two volumes. 2. A Psalter. 3. A book of the Gospels. 4. Another Psalter. 5 Another book of the Gospels. 6. Apocryphal Lives of the Apostles. 7. Lives of Martyrs. 8. Expositions of certain Epistles and Gospels. The Canterbury Book in the library of Trinity Hall, Cambridge, which supplies this interesting information, closes the brief catalogue with these expressive words — HÆ SUNT PRIMITIÆ LIBRORUM TOTIUS ECCLESIÆ ANGLICANÆ.

Wanley considered the Gregorian Bible to have been extant in the reign of James I.; being led to think so, from an apologetic petition of the Romanists to that prince. He considered neither of the Psalters to be extant, but thought a very ancient Psalter among the Cottonian MSS. to be copied from one of them. Both books of the Gospels, though imperfect, he considered to be extant, one in the Bodleian library, the other in the library of Corpus Christi College, Cambridge. The other books he considered to be lost. Their substance, however, probably remains in the Saxon homilies. See ELSTOB's *Homily on the Birth-day of S. Gregory,* p. 39.

As a general guide, Gregory recommends a habit of consulting Scripture; and, in pecuniary matters, a compliance with Roman usage. This assigned one-fourth of clerical resources to the bishop, for the maintenance of his family and the exercise of hospitality; an equal share to the clergy; a third such to the poor; and the remaining portion to maintain the fabric of the church.[1] Augustine, however, was ad-

---

[1] From this recommendation, given by an Italian prelate at the outset of a mission which had just obtained a favourable reception among the Kentish Jutes, various interested parties are anxious to infer that church-rates and poor-rates legally fall upon tithe-property alone. Such reasoners cannot be expected to inquire whether Gregory's recommendation has ever been adopted by any national council or parliament; or even whether the tithe-property is equal to the demands which their inference would make it answer

Upon the usages of Rome, Father Paul supplies the following information. "It was, therefore, ordered in the Western Church, about the year 470, that a division should be made into four parts: the first was to go to the bishop; the second to the rest of the clergy; the third to the fabric of the church, *in which, beside that properly so called, was also comprehended the habitation of the bishop, of the other clergy, of the sick, and of the widows;* and the fourth part went to the poor."—*Treatise of Ecclesiastical Benefices,* p. 18.

Now, even supposing Gregory's recommendation to have been subsequently embodied in the canon, or statute law of England (which it never was), and that it was originally intended for a body of parochial clergy, scattered on separate benefices all over the country (which it certainly was not), yet English incumbents would have no reason to shrink from it. Assessments for the poor, actually or virtually made upon their tithes, houses, and glebes, together with their own private charities, rarely absorb less than a fourth of their tythes; often more. The repairing and rebuilding of chancels and glebe-houses, dilapidations paid on vacancies, and other like charges, will generally be found, in the course of an

monished upon the propriety of expending his own fourth as much as possible in common with his clergy, keeping steadily to those monastic obligations which he had contracted whilst at home. But any of the inferior ministers, whom inability for continence had induced to marry, were to be indulged in consuming their portions at residences of their own.

Augustine, secondly, remarking upon varying religious usages prevailing in different churches, demands which of them appeared most eligible for his individual adoption? Gregory leaves these matters to his own discretion, expressing a conviction that he would naturalise in England such usages, whether Roman, Gallic, or any other, as might seem best adapted to the feelings and edification of his converts.

The third question, relating to robberies in churches, is answered by directions for punishing such offences by fines, or by personal chastisement, as the cases should severally require. To the fourth question, whether two brothers might marry two sisters? an affirmative reply is returned. The fifth, relating to marriages between different degrees of kindred, is met by various directions suited to particular cases. The sixth, as to episcopal consecration by a single prelate, whom distance might prevent from obtaining others of his order to assist him, elicits a sanction for such a consecration, under Augustine's peculiar circumstances. The seventh, as to the nature of his

---

incumbency, to have absorbed little or nothing less than another fourth of the tithes received. As to episcopal claims upon parochial tithes, they were voluntarily relinquished, for the purpose of planting the country with a body of rural clergy.

intercourse with the bishops of Gaul and Britain, induces Gregory to say, that, in case of his correspondent's passage over sea, he ought not to take any thing upon himself among the native prelacy, but that in Britain all of his order were committed to him: the ignorant for instruction, the weak for persuasive confirmation, the perverse for authority. The remaining questions relate to the baptism of women during pregnancy, their admission into the church after child-birth, and to certain scruples arising from the sexual functions.[1]

Augustine received about the same time, from Gregory, the insidious compliment of a pall.[2] He was charged also to establish twelve suffragan bishops, and to select an archbishop for the see of York. Over this prelate, who was likewise to have under his jurisdiction twelve suffragan sees, he had a personal grant of precedence. After his death, the two archbishops were to rank according to priority of consecration.[3] Augustine's views were now directed to the consolidation and extension of his authority. Hence he repaired to the confines of Wales, and sought an interview with the native prelacy of Britain. The place rendered memorable by this meeting seems to have been under the shade of some noble tree, afterwards known as *Augustine's Oak*,[4] situated, probably,

---

[1] BED. i. 27, p. 96.

[2] For various particulars respecting the *Pall*, extracted from a work of high antiquity, and from De Marca, see the Author's *Bampton Lectures for* 1830, p. 178.

[3] BED. i. 29, p. 99.

[4] " The matter is not so clear but that the place called *Au-*

within the modern county of Worcester. The influence of Ethelbert was used in bringing the parties together, and Augustine declared his principal object to be no other than to secure British co-operation in the great work of converting the Saxons. But then he qualified his application for native aid by insisting upon a complete uniformity in religious usages. The Britons adhered to a very ancient mode in fixing the festival of Easter,[1] and varied in many other particulars from Roman practice. In doctrine, the two churches appear to have been identical. This would not, however, content Augustine. The native Christians were equally intractable; clinging with fond affection to those peculiarities of their national church which bespoke its high antiquity, and which seem, in fact, to connect it immediately with Asia, the cradle of our holy faith. Finding ordinary argument evidently hopeless, Augustine proposed a recourse to miracle. The pretensions, he said, favoured by this attestation, were, undeniably, those that ought to prevail. This was admitted, but with difficulty; suspicion probably arising, that in seeking assent to an abstract proposition, nothing else was intended than to cover some stratagem suited for misleading the multitude. At all events, no time was lost in using the admission. A man was introduced, by birth an Angle, exhibiting marks of blindness. The Britons were invited to pray for his release from that calamity. No considerable assemblage can want the vain and indis-

---

gustine's Oak may as well be a *town* as a tree, so called from some eminent *oak* in, at, or near it."—FULLER's *Church Hist.* 60.

[1] See the Author's *History of the Reformation*, 1. 437.

creet. British ecclesiastics, accordingly, accepted the treacherous invitation. Of course, their prayers proved ineffectual. Augustine then stepped forward, bent his knees, and offered an earnest supplication. This ended, the man was found in full possession of his visual faculties. As usual among people uncivilised, or nearly so, the whole arrangements and execution appear to have been admirable. Hence Augustine's principles were approved by acclamation. The leading Britons, however, professing incompetence to receive them without the general consent of their countrymen,[1] requested a second conference, in which they might appear more numerously supported.

To this repaired seven bishops, and various native divines of distinguished learning. In their way, they consulted a hermit, highly esteemed for prudence and holiness. "If Augustine," said the recluse, "be a man of God, take his advice." They then urged the difficulty of ascertaining whether he might be such a man or no. "This is not so difficult," they were told. "Our Lord enjoined, *Take my yoke upon you, and learn of me, for I am meek and lowly in heart.*[2] Now, manage to be at the place of meeting after the foreigner, and if he shall rise at your approach, then you may think him to have learnt of Christ. If he should receive you sitting, and shew any haughtiness, then maintain your ancient usages." As the ears of Augustine yet tingled with applause extorted by admiration of a miracle, no test could be more unfortunate. When he saw the Britons, accordingly, though

---

[1] Bed. ii. 2, p. 111 [2] St. Matt. xi. 29

so numerous and respectable, he did not deign to lift himself from his chair. "I ask only three things of you," he said; "one, that you should keep Easter as we do; another, that you should baptise according to the Roman ritual; a third, that you should join us in preaching to the Angles. With your other peculiarities we shall patiently bear." But the Britons were disgusted alike by his discourtesy and by his pretensions to ecclesiastical jurisdiction over them.[1] They replied, therefore, "We shall agree to no one of your propositions. Much less can we admit as our archbishop him who will not even rise to salute us." Augustine now seeing himself completely foiled, became enraged, and hastily said: "If you will not have peace with brethren, you shall have war with enemies. If you will not shew your neighbours the way of life, their swords shall avenge the wrong in putting you to death." In these words has been sometimes discerned rather a deliberate threat than a random prophecy. After no long interval, about twelve hundred British monks, from the great monastery of

---

[1] It is not clear from Bede whether Augustine's claims to archiepiscopal jurisdiction were brought forward at the first, or at the second conference, or even whether they were formally brought forward at either The venerable historian says nothing of them among the conditions proposed, but he mentions the refusal of them in the final answer given after the second conference. *At illi nihil horum se facturos, neque illum pro archiepiscopo habituros esse respondebant* (11. 2, p. 112). The British clergy could hardly be ignorant of Augustine's pretensions, and they must have known, therefore, without any formal communication, that if they agreed to his propositions, they would be next required to acquiesce under his superiority.

Bangor, in modern Flintshire,[1] were savagely slaughtered on the field of battle, by Ethelfrid, an Anglian chief. "Who are all these unarmed men?" the warrior asked. "Monks," was the reply, "brought hither, after a three days' fast, to pray for success upon their country's arms." Ethelfrid rejoined, "These are active enemies, then, no less than the others; for they come to fight against us with their prayers. Put them to the sword." Of this cruelty, sometimes attributed to his intrigues, Augustine was probably altogether guiltless.[2] But his unbecoming pride, and unwarrantable claims to jurisdiction, naturally engendered a violent antipathy in the British Christians, who refused communion with the Roman party no less than with the Pagan Saxons.[3]

Augustine was called away soon after the failure of his ambitious hopes. Death did not, however, surprise him before he had been duly careful to provide for the continuance of that Church which his useful and honourable labours had founded. Ricula, sister to his friend and patron Ethelbert, was married to

---

[1] This Banchor was distant but ten or twelve miles from Chester, as Ranulphus Cestrensis, and Bradshaw, in his *Life of St. Werburg*, say. Leland, in his *Itinerary*, describes the place as *standing in a valley, and having the compass of a walled town, and two gates remaining half a mile distant from each other.*"— STILLINGFLEET'S *Antiquities of the British Churches*, 205.

[2] Bede appears to have said of him (p. 114), after relating the slaughter of the Bangor monks, *quamvis ipso jam multo ante tempore ad cælestia regna sublato*. But there is nothing answerable to these words in King Alfred's Anglo-Saxon translation. Hence they have been considered as an interpolation.

[3] HUNTINGDON. *Script. post Bedam*, 189.

Sebert, king of the East Saxons. This petty prince he found the means of converting, and of persuading to receive a bishop. The prelate consecrated for this mission was Mellitus, one of the company sent by Gregory to his aid, after he had become tolerably established. The see to which Mellitus went was London, then the capital of Sebert. Ethelbert ordered a church to be built there in honour of St. Paul, and thus provided a site for two noble cathedrals; one, spacious above all contemporary fanes, and magnificent above most; the other, second only to St. Peter's as a monument of Grecian architecture, and, besides, the glory of Protestant Christianity. Justus, another of the second missionary band sent over by Gregory, was consecrated by Augustine to a see founded at Rochester,[1] within the territory under Ethelbert's immediate authority. He consecrated also Laurentius as his own successor.[2] But here his arrangements terminated; a plain proof that he was nothing more than the pioneer in evangelising the Anglo-Saxons. Augustine, however, justly claims the veneration of Englishmen. An opening through which their ancestors received the greatest of imaginable services, was rendered available by his address and self-devotion. A grateful posterity may well excuse in such a man something of human vanity and indiscretion.

After Augustine's death, Laurentius imitated his

---

[1] In 604. WHARTON de Vera Successione Archiep. Cantuar. *Angl. Sacr.* i. 90. Wharton thinks Augustine to have died in the same year. His death has, however, been referred to various years down to 616.

[2] BED. ii. 3, p. 116.

example in seeking to undermine native partiality for ancient usages. He wrote letters, in conjunction with Mellitus and Justus, to the principal Scottish ecclesiastics, complimenting them at the expense of their brethren in other British regions,[1] and exhorting them to a conformity with Rome. A similar letter was addressed to the inferior clergy of South Britain; their superiors, probably, being considered proof against any such attempt. A complete failure, however, again waited upon Roman ambition; Gregory's mission seemed, indeed, now on the very eve of a final miscarriage. Ethelbert, having lost Bertha, married, in his declining age, a second wife. After his death, his son and successor Eadbald insisted upon espousing this female, aggravating that indecency by an open relapse into Paganism. His kinsmen, also the sons of Sebert, now deceased, had looked with longing eye upon the whiteness of some bread used in administering the holy communion, and desired a taste of it. "You must first be baptised," was the answer. "The bread of life is reserved for such as have sought the laver of life." This refusal was requited by the expulsion of Mellitus, who retired into Kent. He there found both Justus and Laurentius agreed with him in regarding the Roman cause as hopeless. All three, accordingly, determined upon withdrawing from the isle. This resolve was quickly executed by Justus and Mellitus.[2] Laurentius was to follow them without unnecessary delay. When,

---

[1] "Sed cognoscentes Britones, Scotos meliores putavimus."—*Ib.* ii. 4, p. 118.
[2] *Ib.* ii 5, p 122

however, his preparations for departure were completed, he desired a couch to be spread in the church, that he might spend his last night upon a spot endeared to him by so many grateful labours. No doubt Eadbald's spirits rose as the sun declined, under an agreeable conviction that reproof and importunity from Laurentius were likely to trouble him no more. How unwelcome then to his eyes must have been the archbishop's agitated countenance early in the morning! " I come," said the prelate, uncovering his shoulders, " to shew you what I have undergone during the night. St. Peter stood at my side while I slept, reproached me sharply for presuming to flee from my charge, and scourged me most severely; as these marks will testify!" Eadbald heard the missionary's tale, and gazed upon his livid shoulders with deep uneasiness. He might even dread a renewal of former arguments enforced by some nocturnal flagellation. He consented, accordingly, to dismiss his father's widow, to receive baptism, and to recall Mellitus and Justus from the continent.[1] The latter he fixed again at Rochester, but he was unable to re-establish the former in London.

A sister of his named Ethelburga, or Tate, was asked in marriage by Edwin, a powerful prince who ruled Northumbria. Eadbald, however, would only hear of the suit under condition that his sister, like her mother, Bertha, should be protected in the free exercise of her religion. Edwin not only stipulated

---

[1] BED. II. 6. p. 124.

this, but also professed a willingness to embrace Christianity himself, if he should find its pretensions able to stand the test of a sufficient inquiry. Paulinus, accordingly, one of the second missionary band sent over by Gregory,[1] having been consecrated to the episcopate by Justus, now archbishop of Canterbury,[2] accompanied Ethelburga into the north. His patience was there sorely tried by the strength of Edwin's pagan prejudices. But his Italian address being keenly on the watch for favourable incidents, proved eventually an over-match for the semi-barbarian's obstinacy. Quichelm, king of the West Saxons, desiring to seize his country, sent a colourable message to Edwin by one provided with a poisoned weapon. The assassin speciously explained his pretended business until every eye around was fixed upon his countenance: then he rushed furiously upon his intended victim. Edwin would, undoubtedly, have perished, had not Lilla, a faithful thane, suddenly sprung forward and received himself the deadly blow. On the same evening, being that of Easter-day, Edwin's queen was delivered of a daughter, afterwards named Eanfleda, and his own acknowledgments were warmly offered to the imaginary gods of Scandinavia, both for the happy termination of Ethelburga's painful anxiety and his own wonder-

---

[1] BED. i. 29. p. 98.

[2] Laurentius appears to have died in 619, and he was succeeded by. Mellitus, who never regained his original see of London. On the death of Mellitus in 624, Justus was translated from Rochester to supply his place. —WHARTON de Verâ Success. *Angl. Sacr.* i. 91, 92.

ful escape. " I must give hearty thanks to Christ, my Lord," said Paulinus, " for the queen's easy and safe delivery. Nor can I forbear from thinking that this mercy is partly owing to my earnest prayers in her behalf." Edwin then asked, " And will you pray for my success in an expedition that I shall undertake against the cowardly traitor, Quichelm?" The answer was: " Yes: but I fear that Jesus will not hear me unless you resolve upon becoming his disciple." Edwin pledged himself to this qualification at an early opportunity, and as an earnest of that engagement he desired Paulinus to baptise his infant daughter, with twelve of his household. He then marched against Quichelm, and succeeded in killing or capturing all who had been any way concerned in the late attempt upon his life. When returned, however, victorious to his home, the force of early prepossessions rallied, and he declared himself unable to renounce heathenism until his more eminent subjects had approved.[1]

Paulinus was acquainted with a scene that often powerfully struck the mental eye of Edwin. It seems to have been a secret; for Bede supposes the bishop to have learned it by revelation from above. His real informant most likely was the queen. Edwin having succeeded to the Northumbrian throne when hardly out of his cradle, was quickly set aside, and then stealthily conveyed away. Ethelfrid, who had usurped his crown, sent emissaries after him into every corner of the island where he took temporary

---

[1] Bed. ii. 9. p. 132.

shelter. At length he found protection at the court of Redwald, king of East Anglia. This prince, being assiduously plied by Ethelfrid with promises and menaces, began to waver. A friend of Edwin was informed of this, and advised instant flight. The royal youth had just retired to rest, but he hastily left his chamber and withdrew beyond the dwelling, distracted by anxious apprehension. He had already wandered over most of England in quest of safety, and he was now utterly at a loss to see any farther hope. As night wore away he probably sank into an agitated slumber. A majestic personage now roused attention, whose countenance and dress were wholly new. Edwin strained his eyes in agony. "Wherefore," said his unknown visitor, "sit you mourning here while other mortals quietly repose?" He was answered, "It can be no concern of yours whether I spend the night abroad or on my couch." The figure said: "Do not think me unaware of your distress. I know it all. What will you give me, then, to set your heart at ease and make Redwald spurn every overture of your enemy?" Edwin eagerly promised any thing that ever might be in his power. "Again: what would you give," the stranger added, " if I should enable you, not only to trample on your foes, but also to outstrip the power of every neighbouring king?" Edwin pledged himself, if possible, more largely than before. He was then asked: "Should he who cheers you thus with unexpected hopes be found quite equal to crown them with success, would you take hereafter his advice if he should recommend a course of life different from any ever followed in your family, yet far more excellent?" This also met with a hearty affirmative reply. "When this signal shall be repeated, *remember, then, your pledge.*" As these words were spoken the figure pressed his right hand solemnly on Edwin's head, and immediately disappeared. After a short interval the young Northumbrian saw that kind friend approach whose warning had aroused him from his bed. Now he was, however, told that Redwald, influenced by the queen, had not only given up every thought of betraying him to Ethelfrid, but was even ready to furnish him with troops for driving that usurper from his throne.[1] He did aid him thus, and Edwin regained his patrimonial sovereignty.

After his triumphant return from taking vengeance upon Quichelm, Paulinus desired an interview. In this he slowly raised his right hand and pressed it earnestly upon the royal head. Edwin started and trembled violently. "You know this signal?" the Italian said; "you know it to have been originally given by one whose words have most exactly been fulfilled. *Remember, then, your pledge.*" Edwin fell at the missionary's feet and earnestly inquired his meaning. "By God's mercy," Paulinus added, "when even hope had fled your life was saved. By the same mercy you have wonderfully prevailed over all your enemies and regained your paternal throne.

---

[1] "*A. D.* 617. This year was Ethelfrith, king of the Northumbrians, slain by Redwald, king of the East Angles; and Edwin, the son of Ella, having succeeded to the kingdom, subdued all Britain, except the men of Kent alone."—*Saxon Chronic.* Dr. Ingram's *Transl.* p. 32.

A third, and a greater instance of his mercy, yet awaits acceptance. *Redeem your pledge:* and the God, who has led you through so many dangers to gain and to secure an earthly throne, will remain your friend until you reach the glories of his own eternal kingdom." Before such an appeal Edwin was powerless. He professed himself anxious to redeem his pledge, as Paulinus claimed; and he desired only to delay baptism until he could receive it in company with his leading men.[1]

These duly met in a solemn assembly, and Paulinus having pleaded in favour of Christianity, Coifi, a Druidic pontiff apparently,[2] thus addressed the royal president:—" It seems to me, O king, that our paternal gods are worthless, for no one has worshipped them more devoutly than myself; yet my lot has been far less prosperous than that of many others not half so pious." A chief then said: " The life of man, O king, reminds me of a winter feast around your blazing fire, while the storm howls or the snow drives abroad. A distressed sparrow darts within the doorway: for a moment it enjoys the cheering warmth and shelter from the blast; then, shooting through the other entrance, it is lost again.

---

[1] BED. ii. 12. p. 141.

[2] " Coifi, the pontiff, by whose persuasions Edwin embraced Christianity, is no other than the title of the chief of the Druids."—(PALGRAVE'S *Rise and Progress of the English Commonwealth.* Lond. 1832, i. 155.) An etymological reason, rendering this opinion highly probable, is subjoined in a note; and it is fairly inferred, that the ancient Druidical superstition having escaped extinction while Britain was generally Christian, had found protection, together with, at least, a partial adoption, among the pagan Saxons.

Such is man. He comes we know not whence, hastily snatches a scanty share of worldly pleasure, and then goes we know not whither. If this new doctrine, therefore, will give us any clearer insight into things that so much concern us, my feeling is to follow it." Before such arguments, resembling so strikingly those of Indian warriors in America, Northumbrian paganism fell. Coifi was foremost in making war upon the superstition which had so severely baulked his worldly hopes. His priestly character obliged him to ride upon a mare, and forbade him to bear a weapon. The people, therefore, thought him mad when he appeared upon Edwin's charger with lance in hand. He rode, however, to a famous temple, pierced the idol through, and ordered the building to be burnt.[1] Soon afterwards Paulinus kept a most impressive Easter by holding a public baptism at York, in which Edwin, his principal men, and a great multitude of inferior people, were solemnly admitted into the Christian church.[2]

Paulinus was now established in York as his episcopal see; and this being known at Rome procured for him the customary compliment of a pall.[3] His mission, however, eventually failed. His patron, Edwin, being attacked by Cadwalla, a British prince, and Penda, king of the Mercians, fell in battle.[4] Frightful destruction followed, and Northumbria

---

[1] BED. II. 13. p. 143.   [2] *Ib.* ii. 14. p. 145.

[3] *Ib.* ii. 17. p. 150. York, it may be remembered, was intended for an archiepiscopal see.

[4] *Ib.* II. 20. p. 157.

completely relapsed into paganism. Paulinus, with Queen Ethelburga, sought safety on ship-board, and sailed into Kent.[1] The see of Rochester becoming vacant shortly afterwards, Paulinus was chosen to fill it, and he remained bishop there until his death.[2]

Edwin's faithful friend, Redwald, had made a temporary profession of Christianity, moved by arguments and persuasions which assailed him during a visit into Kent. On returning, however, into East Anglia, his wife, and others whom he valued, easily prevailed upon him to relapse into idolatry; but his brief adherence to the truth was far from fruitless: it naturally undermined the prejudices of others. Carpwald, accordingly, his son and successor, embraced the Gospel on Edwin's recommendation. Shortly afterwards this prince was assassinated, and his brother, Sigebert, was driven an exile into Gaul. There he was baptised; and having regained the East Anglian throne, he received Felix, a Burgundian bishop, for whom he founded an episcopal see at Dunwich, in Suffolk.[3]

Edwin's conversion proved similarly advantageous for his own dominions. It paved the way for a ready and permanent reception of our holy religion, though not by Roman instrumentality. When Edwin prevailed over his rival Ethelfrid, the sons of that prince took refuge in Scotland, where they became Chris-

---

[1] In 633. GODWIN *de Præsul.* 651, note.

[2] BED. ii. 20. p. 159. Paulinus died in 644. GODWIN *de Præsul.* 651.

[3] *Ib.* ii. 15. p. 148. This see of Dunwich was founded in 630. GODWIN *de Præsul.* 423.

tians. Oswald, one of them, having established himself in great power on the Northumbrian throne, soon determined upon Christianising his people. Happily his exile had shewn him how to accomplish this without Roman intervention; probably odious to him from its connexion with Edwin. He sent accordingly for missionaries to his friends in Scotland; and Aidan, a bishop of uncommon merit, answered the summons. In finding a see for this exemplary prelate, no regard was paid to papal arrangements. Aidan fixed himself at Lindisfarne, or Holy Island,[1] as did also his successors, Finan and Colman, like him, Scots, unconnected with Rome, repudiating her usages and despising her assumptions. It was under these prelates of British origin,—it was under a religious system of native growth, that the north of England was evangelised.

More completely still was the whole centre of South Britain indebted for this inestimable benefit to the native clergy. There no Roman preacher first took possession of a field which labourers, more happily circumstanced, afterwards cultivated with lasting success. Peada, king of the Mercians, offering marriage to a Northumbrian princess, was accepted on condition of embracing Christianity. He received, as the bishop of his people, Diuma, a Scot by birth, who was consecrated by Finan, the prelate of Northumbria.[2] Diuma's three immediate successors were also

---

[1] BED. III. 3. p. 167. Aidan was consecrated to the see of Lindisfarne in 635. GODWIN *de Præsul.* 718, note.

[2] *Ib.* III. 21. p. 219. Diuma appears to have been consecrated bishop of Mercia in 656. Diuma's three immediate suc-

members of the national church; and under these four prelates all our midland counties were converted.

Equal zeal was displayed by the national church, and with equal success, in the kingdom of Essex. That region had been sunk in unheeded heathenism since the failure of Mellitus. One of its princes, however, named Sigebert, had become a frequent guest at the Northumbrian court, and he was there converted. At his desire Chad, a member of the national church, repaired into Essex. He received, eventually, episcopal consecration from Finan, prelate of Northumbria; and it was chiefly by his exertions that the modern diocese of London was reclaimed from Gentile superstition.[1]

Nor was East Anglian Christianity without extensive obligations to the ancient church of Britain. The prelates of East Anglia seem indeed constantly to have been in communion with Rome; but the people's conversion was greatly owing to the labours of Fursey, an Irish monk.[2] Only two counties, therefore, north of the Thames—those of Norfolk and Suffolk—were ever under Roman superintendence during their transition from paganism to Christianity, and these two were largely indebted to domestic zeal

---

cessors were named respectively Cellach, Ihumhere, and Jaruman. WHARTON in Thom. Chesterfield. *Angl. Sacr.* i. 424.

[1] BED. iii. 22. p. 221. Chad appears to have been consecrated by Finan in 654.—GODWIN *de Præsul.* 172.

[2] *Ib.* iii. 19. p. 209. This missionary appears to have possessed a dreamy temperament and a poetical imagination. Hence he purchased for himself a memorable name among believers in purgatory.—See *Bampton Lectures*, p. 353.

for their conversion. Every other county, from London to Edinburgh,[1] has the full gratification of pointing to the ancient church of Britain as its nursing mother in Christ's holy faith.

In this patriotic gratification the southern counties cannot so largely share. The West Saxons were chiefly converted by means of Birinus, a Roman monk,[2] whom Pope Honorius sent over into England.[3] His labours, however, owed probably a large portion of their success to Oswald, king of Northumbria, who had arrived at the West Saxon court as suitor to the king's daughter. At such a time it was found an easy matter to convert both the young princess and her father, Kynegils. To the latter Oswald stood sponsor; nor did he leave the south until he had accomplished arrangements for providing Birinus with an episcopal see at Dorchester, in Oxfordshire.[4] Thus the West Saxon church was importantly indebted for its establishment to a powerful professor of the ancient national religion. Its second bishop also was Agilbert, a Frenchman, who had long studied in Ireland,[5] and who had undertaken the duties of a missionary among the West Saxons at the desire of Oswy, king of Northumberland.[6] The principles and habits of this prelate must have been, therefore,

---

[1] The southern counties of Scotland were included in the ancient kingdom of Northumbria.—INETT, i. 60.

[2] RUDBORNE. Hist. Maj. Winton. *Angl. Sacr.* i. 190.

[3] The arrival of Birinus is referred to 634; the baptism of Kynegils, to the following year.—*Ib.* note.

[4] BED. III. 7. p. 176.   [5] *Ib.* 177.

[6] RUDBORNE. *Angl. Sacr.* i. 192.

sufficiently conformable to those of the ancient national church. His successor was Wine, an Anglo-Saxon by birth, and a monk of Winchester. In usages he probably followed Rome; but he does not appear to have conceded her any jurisdiction, for he sought consecration in Gaul, not from the archbishop of Canterbury.[1]

The Gospel, having thus won its way over other parts of England, at length obtained an establishment in Sussex. The people were prepared for its admission by a small community of native monks settled within their territory. These recluses, however, made no great impression upon the surrounding country; but Ædilwalch, king of Sussex, returned from the Mercian court a Christian. He had been baptised there at the recommendation of Wulfhere, king of Mercia, who stood sponsor to him,[2] and who was a member of Britain's national church. Ædilwalch's people were indeed chiefly converted by means of the famous Wilfrid, then a wanderer, and always a zealous partisan of Rome.[3] In Sussex, therefore, the cases of Essex and Northumbria were reversed. In these latter countries a Roman introduction prepared the way for British success: among

---

[1] BED. iii. 7. p. 177.

[2] Wulfhere gave to Ædilwalch a substantial proof of his sponsorial affection in the Isle of Wight, which he conquered and made over to him.—*Sax. Chr.* 47.

[3] *Ib.* iv. 13, p. 293. Wilfrid obtained from Ædilwalch the peninsula of Selsey, where he fixed an episcopal see about the year 680 (LE NEVE, 55). After his return to the north, the South Saxon diocess was governed for a time by the neighbouring bishops of Winchester.

the South Saxons Britain made an opening through which Rome prevailed.

Her complete and final prevalence over the national church flowed from female influence and the dexterity of her agents. Eanfleda, who had been driven from her native Northumbria in infancy with Paulinus, returned thither, after an education among her maternal relatives in Kent, as the wife of Oswy, then king of the country, and *Bretwalda*.[1] Inheriting all the religious constancy of her mother, Ethelburga, and of her grandmother, Bertha, she would not abandon Kentish usages for those of Northumbria. Her son also was intrusted to the tuition of Wilfrid, an able Englishman of the Roman party, whose attainments had been matured in southern Europe. Oswy, however, continued firm to the religious profession of his youth. Easter was accordingly celebrated at his court on different days; one party enjoying its festivities, while another placed in strong contrast with them the austerities of Lent. At length Oswy consented to purchase domestic peace by hearing a solemn argument in the monastery which he had recently founded at Whitby;[2] Colman, then bishop of Northumbria, assisted by Chad, bishop

---

[1] *Sax. Chr.* 88.

[2] BROMPTON. *X. Scriptores.* Lond. 1652, col. 788. Whitby was then called Streaneshalch. This famous conference was holden there in 664.—WHARTON de Episc. Dunelm. *Angl. Sacr.* i. 692. Inett (*Hist. of the Engl. Ch.* i. 62) seems to think that the Roman party might have prevailed before, had it not been for the uncommon merit of Aidan and Finan; and that its eventual prevalence arose from some inequality to its predecessors on the part of Colman. The principal reason, however, there can be no doubt, was the influence of Eanfleda.

of Essex, conducted the British cause.[1] Wilfrid pleaded for that of Rome. The national divines insisted chiefly upon a tradition originating, as alleged, in St. John, our Lord's beloved disciple. The foreign party traced Roman tradition to St. Peter, who was intrusted by Christ with the keys of heaven. " Were they really intrusted to him?" asked Oswy. " Undoubtedly so," he was answered. " And can you allege the grant of any such privilege to an authority of yours?" Oswy then demanded. " We cannot," Colman replied. " I must leave your party, then," said Oswy; " for I should not choose to disoblige him who keeps the key of Heaven. It might be found impossible to get the door open when I seek admittance."[2] Unless

---

[1] Agilbert, bishop of the West Saxons, was the real representative of the Roman party; but he devolved the advocacy of his case upon Wilfrid, on account of his own imperfect acquaintance with the Saxon language.

[2] BED. iii. 25. p. 236. It is curious to observe how Romish partisans, eventually, expanded favourable hints into broad admissions. Oswy's concluding speech stands thus in Bede:—" Ego vobis dico, quia hic est ostiarius ille cui ego contradicere nolo, sed in quantum novi, vel valeo, hujus cupio in omnibus obedire statutis, ne forte, me adveniente ad fores regni cœlorum, non sit qui reseret, adverso illo qui claves tenere probatur." John of Tinmouth, an unpublished chronicler of the 14th century, gives the following version of these words:—" Ex quo, quod vos omnes in hoc consentitis, quod Christus tradidit Petro claves regni cœlestis, *una cum ecclesie principatu,* nec alteri alicui tale quid commisit, dico vobis quod tali ostiario contradicere non audeo, ne forsitan, cum venero, claudat mihi fores." (*Bibl. Lameth.* MSS. 12. f. 26.) It should be observed, that although Wilfrid appealed to the authority of the Roman see as deserving respectful attention, he did not claim for it any right of deciding the controversy.—See *Bampton Lectures,* p. 163.

one again remembered the chieftains of America, this language would seem like jest rather than earnest. But it was generally applauded, and the ancient usages of Britain were formally renounced. Colman, however, with many of his adherents, were disgusted, and retired to their brethren in Scotland.[1]

Probably this triumph of the Roman party involved little or no change in articles of belief. If we except prayers and offerings for the dead, we have indeed no sufficient evidence that papal peculiarities of doctrine were then established. Gregory the Great is known, from his epistles, to have repudiated the authority since claimed for his see,[2] and to have disapproved the adoration of images.[3] His Sacramentary shews him to have earnestly desired of God that departed saints should pray for the faithful, but to have lived before Christians had fallen into a habit of invoking them.[4] Of ceremonies he was a zealous patron; and upon the whole, undoubtedly, he bore no unimportant part in laying the foundations of Romanism both in England and elsewhere. Still the system established under his auspices was widely different from that eventually sanctioned at Trent. Ritually the two were very much alike; doctrinally very far apart. The earliest Anglo-Saxon Christians,

---

[1] BED. iii. 26, p. 239.

[2] GREG. PP. *Epist.* lib. iv. 32, 34, 38, 39. *Labb. et Coss.* v. 1182, 1189, 1192, 1195.

[3] *Ejusd. Epist.* 9. lib. ix.

[4] See a prayer from his MS. Sacramentary, formerly belonging to the church of Exeter, now in the Bodleian library.—*Bampt. Lect.* 218.

therefore, agreed essentially with their descendants since the Reformation in all but services for the dead. Reasons assigned for these are, however, so very far from satisfactory, that their discontinuance in the sixteenth century may fairly be considered, not only as allowable, but even as an exercise of sound discretion.[1]

---

[1] A priest, Gregory says, had received many attentions from an unknown person at a warm bath. By way of recompense he brought him one day some bread, which had been among the eucharistic oblations. "Why do you give me this, Father?" his attendant said. "This is holy bread: I cannot eat it. I was once master here, and am still bound to the place for my sins. If you wish to serve me, offer this bread in my behalf; and know that your prayers are heard, when you find me here no longer." The speaker then vanished. A week was now spent by the priest in fasting, prayers, and daily offerings of the Eucharist. When it was expired he went to the bath again, but he saw nothing of his former attendant."—GREG. *Mag. P. Opp.* tom. III. p. 304.

This idle tale is an instructive commentary upon prevailing notions as to the soul's posthumous condition. As it is only one among many such stories, long circulated in proof of purgatory and in support of services for the dead, our Reformers, having no scriptural warrant for such services, were fully justified in discontinuing them. Though of high antiquity they had been largely indebted for popularity to such contemptible inventions, and they had been latterly urged as undeniable evidences that primitive times held the Platonic doctrine of purgatory.

CHAPTER II.

FROM THEODORE TO ALCUIN.
669—804.

WILFRID'S APPOINTMENT TO THE PRELACY—THEODORE—COUNCIL OF HERTFORD—WILFRID'S DISGRACE—COUNCIL OF HATFIELD—BENEDICT BISCOP—ORIGIN OF A PAROCHIAL CLERGY—DEATH OF THEODORE—FINAL TROUBLES, AND DEATH OF WILFRID—LAWS OF INA—COUNCILS OF BAPCHILD, AND BERGHAMSTED—CHURCH-SHOT—TYTHES—MONASTERIES—PILGRIMAGES TO ROME—ALDHELM—BEDE—EGBERT—TRIPARTITE DIVISION OF TYTHES—ALCUIN—BONIFACE—COUNCIL OF CLOVESHOO—OFFA, AND THE ARCHBISHOPRIC OF LICHFIELD—COUNCIL OF CALCUITH—PETER-PENCE—IMAGE WORSHIP—RECEIVED WITH EXECRATION IN ENGLAND—THE CAROLINE BOOKS—EGBERT'S PENITENTIAL.

At Whitby, Augustine's ambitious designs were only realised in part. All England now, indeed, received religious usages from Italy; but no farther concession seems to have been intended. When, accordingly, Tuda, another of the revered Scottish divines,[1] was chosen to succeed Colman, he did not seek con-

---

[1] It was, probably, Tuda's connection with former bishops of Northumbria, joined to his early partiality for usages different from theirs, that procured his election to the episcopate. Something of a compromise might seem to have been intended in this appointment. Bromton bears the following testimony to the excellence of the three preceding bishops. "Hi autem tres episcopi Scotorum prædicti; scilicet, Aidanus, Finanus, et Colmannus, miræ sanctitatis et parcimoniæ extiterunt, nec enim potentes seculi suscipiebant, nisi qui ad eos causa orandi solummodo veniebant."—*X. Scriptores*, 789.

secration at Canterbury, but among the Picts, or southern Scots, a Christian body ever in communion with Rome.[1] His possession of the Northumbrian see lasting only a few months, Wilfrid, then about thirty,[2] was appointed bishop. He, too, disregarded Canterbury;[3] and crossing over into Gaul, obtained consecration at Compeigne from his friend, Agilbert, now removed from the West Saxon bishopric to that of Paris.[4]

In Wilfrid, real excellences were alloyed by levity and ostentation. He did not, accordingly, hasten to return after consecration, but thoughtlessly displayed his new dignity amidst the tempting hospitalities of Gaul. His royal patron, disgusted by this delay, conferred the Northumbrian see upon Chad, abbot of Lestingham, and brother to the East Saxon bishop.[5] The prelate elect would have been consecrated at Canterbury, had not Deusdedit, the archbishop, in-

---

[1] BED. III. 26. p. 239. " Ipsi australes Picti, qui intra eosdem montes habent sedes, multo ante tempore, ut perhibent, relicto errore idololatriæ, fidem veritatis acceperant, prædicante eis verbum Nynia episcopo reverendissimo et sanctissimo viro de natione Britonum, *qui erat Romæ regulariter fidem et mysteria veritatis edoctus.*"—*Ib.* III 4. p. 169.

[2] SIM. Dunelm. *X. Script.* 78.

[3] " Rex Alchfrid misit Wilfridum presbyterum ad regem Galliarum, qui eum sibi suisque consecrari faceret episcopum." (BED. III. 28. p. 246.) Wilfrid desired this, being unwilling to receive consecration " either from prelates not in communion with Rome, as the Britons and Scots, or from those who agree with schismatics: *qui schismaticis consentiunt.*" (Eddii Vita Wilf. *XV. Script.* Oxon. 1691. III. 57). This last clause is, probably, the key to his disregard of Canterbury.

[4] *Ib.* 247. Bromton, 789.

[5] STUBBS. Act. PP. Ebor. *X. Script.* 1689.

opportunely died. He repaired, therefore, to Winchester, and received consecration from Wine, the bishop there, assisted by two British bishops.[1] The two kings of Kent and Northumbria now thought of staying the progress of religious dissension, by sending a new primate to Rome for consecration. Their choice fell upon Wighard, a native priest, who was very kindly entertained at the papal court, but who died there before consecration.[2] This opportunity was not lost upon Italian subtlety. Vitalian, then pope, determined upon trying whether the Anglo-Saxons would receive an archbishop nominated by himself. He chose eventually Theodore, an able and learned monk of sixty-six, born at Tarsus, in Cilicia.[3] As former nominations to Anglo-Saxon sees had been domestic, some doubt would naturally arise as to Theodore's reception; and after consecration, he spent several months in Gaul. The insular princes, however, wearied by the animosities of contending parties, only sought an umpire likely to command respect; hence they did not merely receive Theodore, but also they conceded to him that primacy over the whole Anglo-Saxon church, vainly coveted by Augustine, and after his death apparently regarded as unattainable.[4]

---

[1] BED. III. 28. p. 247. Wine was then the only prelate in the island, whose conformity to Roman usages made him considered by that party as canonically consecrated.—*Ib.*

[2] *Ib.* III. 29. p. 249.

[3] *Ib.* IV. 1. p. 254. Theodore was consecrated, at Rome, by Pope Vitalian, in March, 668, and he came to Canterbury in May, 669. —WHARTON, de Vera Success. Archiep. Cantuar. *Angl. Sacr.* I. 93.

[4] BED. IV. 2. p. 258.

Theodore may be regarded as the parent of Anglo-Saxon literature. His exertions to illumine his adopted country were unwearied, and were crowned by the happiest success. Learned labours were not allowed, however, to trench unduly on his time. He made efficient use of his authority, by taking extensive journeys, and urging every where an uniformity with Rome. One of the earliest cases referred to him was that of Wilfrid. The superseded bishop represented Chad as an intruder, and begged for his own restitution to a see of which he had been so so unexpectedly deprived. At all events, Theodore decided Chad had been uncanonically consecrated. Upon this, however, that humble Christian felt no disposition to dispute: " He had been unwillingly drawn," he said, " from his beloved abbey at Lestingham, and thither he should again gladly retire."[1] He did not long enjoy there that religious obscurity which his mind so fondly coveted. Jaruman, the Mercian bishop, died soon after; and Chad, having consented to the imposition of Theodore's hands,[2] was placed in the deceased prelate's room at the Mercian king's desire. Wilfrid regained possession of the Northumbrian diocess, then extending beyond the confines of modern England into the country of Oswy's Pictish subjects.[3]

A national synod was now convened[4] by Theodore,[5] at Hertford, a frequent residence of the East

---

[1] Bed. 259. [2] *Ib.* 260. [3] *Ib.* iv. 3. p. 261. [4] A.D. 673.
[5] Baronius would have it believed that this council met under authority of the Roman see. English Protestants have understood it to have met under authority of the Saxon princes. The latter is

Saxon kings.¹ The bishops of East Anglia, Rochester, Wessex, and Mercia, were personally present, together with many well known canonists. Wilfrid, the Northumbrian prelate, sent two representatives. " My object," said Theodore, " is a solemn engagement by us all, to observe uniformly whatever the holy fathers have decreed and defined." He then asked his hearers, individually, whether they were willing; being answered affirmatively, he produced a body of canon-law,² and from it selected ten provisions, as especially demanding approbation. These prescribe the Roman Easter, some regulations for bishops, clergymen, and monks; the holding of synods twice in every year, and the due maintenance of matrimonial ties. The approval sought followed a sufficient examination, and was regularly signed. Refractory clergymen were to be disqualified from officiating, and utterly disowned.³

---

a more probable supposition than the former. But Bede, who is the only source of information, says merely *Theodorus cogit concilium.*

[1] CHAUNCY's *Hertfordshire.* 1826. p. 453. Bede's spelling is *Heorutford*, which has occasioned some speculation. Cambden, and after him, Chauncy, say that this means *The Red Ford*, and is a translation of *Durocobriva*, the ancient British name of Hertford. They proceed, however, upon the principle of taking *he* as identical in Saxon with *the*, which Spelman reasonably says *ego non reperio.* King Alfred's translation of Bede has *Heortford*, and so has the Saxon Chronicle. There can, in fact, be little or no doubt that Hertford is the place.

[2] Probably " the collection, or book of canons, which is mentioned in the thirteenth session of the Council of Calcedon, and was afterwards confirmed in a *novel* of the Emperor Justinian."— INETT. i. 77.

[3] BED. iv. 5. p. 271. The ten especial canons may be there

Theodore, after thus providing a national code of ecclesiastical jurisprudence, authorised two episcopal depositions. Winfrid, bishop of Mercia, having given some offence,[1] was driven from his bishopric, and the metropolitan approved.[2] He did the same in Wilfrid's case. Egfrid, the Northumbrian king, had married Etheldred, an East Anglian princess, bred a zealous Christian, and smitten with a superstitious trust in monastic austerities. A subject of high distinction had been her husband in early youth, but she repelled his embraces. As a queen, this pertinacity continued: vain were Egfrid's importunities, vain his promises and persuasions to her spiritual adviser, Wilfrid. At length her humour was indulged, and she gladly left the profusion of a court for the privations of a cloister.[3] The new queen, probably, found Egfrid prejudiced against Wilfrid, as an abettor of his late wife's mortifying repugnance. The Northumbrian prince, accordingly, became an attentive hearer, when she painted invidiously his extensive acquisitions and ostentatious habits.[4] Two prelacies, it was urged,[5] might be maintained upon his endow-

---

seen at length, and also in *Spelman* (i. p. 153.), *Wilkins* (i. 41.), and as translated in *Johnson's Collection*, and in *Chauncy*, i. 254.

[1] " Per meritum cujusdam inobedientiæ."—BED. IV. 6. p. 275.

[2] Wharton considers the Council of Hertford to have determined upon dividing the immense diocess of Mercia, and that Wilfrid's consent was found unattainable. (*Angl. Sacr.* i. 424.) This is, probably, the fact.

[3] BED. IV. 19. p. 304.

[4] MALMESBURY.—*Scriptores post Bedam*, 149.

[5] Two prelacies were actually founded, on his disgrace; those of York, and Hagulstad, the modern Hexham. Johnson says, (*Collection.* Pref. to the Rom. Counc. 679.), " Wilfrid, for opposing

ments, and the charge was too great for one. His own consent, however, for any division, appears to have been hopeless: hence the case was laid before Theodore, under whose deliberate sanction he was deprived of his bishopric. National authorities being all against him, he determined upon trying the effect of papal interposition. At Rome, he found some sort of council sitting, and before it he laid his case. The body pronounced his treatment uncanonical, and Pope Agatho furnished him with a letter, announcing this decision. Papal jurisdiction, however, being unknown to Wilfrid's countrymen, they spurned Agatho's interference, and angrily thrust the disgraced prelate into prison;[1] nor, when liberated, could he regain his bishopric. Under this disappointment he was driven to display the best parts of his character: he passed into Sussex, yet a neglected, heathen district; and his active, able mind, there found honourable employment in evangelising the country.[2]

That interminable folly of rash and conceited spirits, from which arises a succession of subtle speculations on the Deity, had lately agitated Christen-

---

this partition, was deposed, if not degraded." From the following words of Stubbs, it is plain that Wilfrid's disgrace was not a hasty measure, nor, probably, uncanonical." Quia rex pontificem de sede sua præter consensum Theodori archiepiscopi Cantuar. pellere nequibat, mandavit archiepiscopo ut adesset, auditisque quas accusatores ejus finxerant causis, pulsus est ab episcopatu sanctus Wilfridus, anno ab incarnatione Domini DC. lxxviij. qui est annus episcopatus sui xiij. et per decennium exulavit."—Act. PP. Ebor. X. Script. 1691.

[1] *Bampton Lectures*, 168. MALMESBURY de Gest. PP. Angl. — *Scriptores post Bedam*, 150.

[2] BED. IV. 13. p. 292.

dom by broaching *Monothelite* opinions. These had been approved, amidst the din of a bewildering controversy, even by Honorius, then Roman pontiff,—an indiscretion sorely embarrassing to advocates of papal infallibility.[1] Agatho, a successor of his, advised Constantine Pogonatus to enforce religious peace, in a general council. This met at Constantinople in 680, and condemned the Monothelites. For the same purpose, Theodore, archbishop of Canterbury, procured a meeting of the Anglo-Saxon church at Hatfield, in Hertfordshire,[2] then a portion of the royal patrimony.[3] This assembly solemnly received the first five general councils,[4] and a synod lately holden at Rome.[5] Thus was the foundation laid of that sound discretion in treating questions above human comprehension, from which the Church of England never has departed. Crude novelties respecting "the deep things of God"[6] have invariably been irreconcilable with her communion.

Among the divines at Hatfield was John the

---

[1] Mosheim, Cent. VII. ch. v. Berw. 1819. vol. ii. p. 191.

[2] Bed. iv. 17. p. 300. The Council of Hatfield met in September, 680.

[3] Chauncy, ii. 4. The Saxon kings continued in possession of his estate, until king Edgar bestowed it upon the monastery of Ely.—*Ib.*

[4] That of Nice, against the Arians; that of Constantinople, against Macedonius and Eudoxius; that of Ephesus, against Nestorius; that of Chalcedon, against Eutyches and Nestorius; and that of Constantinople, against Theodore, Theodoret, and the Epistles of Ibas.—Bed. *ut supra.* Spelm. i. 168. Wilk. i. 51.

[5] In 649, under Martin I. The particular object of this was to condemn the Monothelites.—See Labb. *et* Coss. vi. 354.

[6] 1 Cor. ii. 10.

Precentor, an illustrious foreigner, brought over by Benedict Biscop.[1] That noble Northumbrian had been designed in youth for a military life, but literature and religion made him their own. He travelled accordingly to Rome, and, on his return, amazed his countrymen by a considerable collection of books.[2] A collector in modern days would also have imported antiquities and works of art. Benedict, as might be expected, imported relics,[3] and valued them probably, intellectual as he was, even more highly than his volumes. For the whole collection a resting place was provided in a monastery, founded by Benedict's means, at the mouth of the Wear. To this retreat he also conducted the *Precentor*, whom he drew from Roman society, as a master for his rising community of monks, in chanting the service and in reading Latin.[4] Before John's departure, he was furnished by the pope with a copy of the decrees lately passed synodically at Rome against the Monothelites. It was also his charge to make particular observations upon the faith of England.[5] Although Theodore, by uncommon ability, zeal, and firmness, had brought the whole Anglo-Saxon people to a conformity with papal usages, yet leading Roman ecclesiastics were jealous and suspicious. He was a Greek, and re-

---

[1] BED. iv. 18. p. 302.

[2] "Librorum innumerabilem, ut legitur, omnis generis copiam, domum comportavit."—*Brit. Mus. MSS. Cotton. Nero. E.* 1. *Vita Venerabilis Bedæ*, f. 394.

[3] DUGDALE, *Monasticon*, 1. 96. " Quot vero Benedictus divina volumina, quantas beatorum apostolorum sive martyrum Christi reliquias attulit, quis annunciet ?"—SIM. *Dunelm. X. Script.* 92.

[4] BED. iv. 18. p. 303.   [5] *Ib.*

markable for independence of mind. Hence Pope Vitalian sent him originally into England with Adrian, a learned abbot, who aided him zealously in spreading literature through the country, but who was to be a spy upon his actions.[1] This espionage, the successor of Vitalian gladly renewed by means of the *Precentor*.

Besides providing for his adopted country an outline of ecclesiastical jurisprudence and terms of religious conformity, Theodore appears to have been guided by an usage of his native Asia in planning the establishment of a parochial clergy. Under royal sanction, he followed Justinian in offering the patronage of churches as an encouragement for their erection.[2] Opulent proprietors were thus tempted to supply the spiritual wants of their tenantry; and Bede records two instances in which this judicious policy proved effective.[3] Theodore's oriental system

---

[1] " Ne quid ille contrarium veritati fidei, Græcorum more, in Ecclesiam cui præesset, introduceret.—BED. iii. 1. p. 255.

[2] WHELOC. in Bed. p. 399. The authority is an extract from the *Codex Cantuariensis*, a MS. in the library of Trinity Hall, Cambridge. " There are some things also to be found in those laws (of Justinian), which shew that country churches had anciently been built and endowed in the East; since Justinian there begins about this time to settle the rights of patronage, giving to him who had built the church, the power to nominate a priest to officiate in it, but leaving the bishop authority to approve or reject the person so nominated."—COMBER's *Divine Right of Tythes*. Part 2. p. 79.

[3] The cases of Puch and Addi, both counts, in the north of England. (*Bed*. v. 4, 5. pp. 375, 388.) There can be no doubt that many other such cases of pious munificence had occurred when Bede wrote, for he does not mention these as extraordinary acts.

had been, however, in operation for ages before every English estate of any magnitude had secured the benefit of a church within its boundary. This very lingering progress has thrown much obscurity around the origin of parishes. The principle of their formation will, however, account sufficiently for their unequal sizes, and for existing rights of patronage.

At the great age of eighty-eight, Theodore was released from earthly labours.[1] His life had been no less honourable than long; and he must, undoubtedly, be ranked among the ablest of English primates. A Protestant may possibly regret that such eminent qualities laid the foundation of an insidious influence, which eventually adulterated sound religion, and insulted the national independence. The days of Theodore, however, were anterior to most Roman innovations, and he seems always to have looked upon the papal see under an Oriental feeling of independence. Far inferior persons in the religious history of ancient England have, accordingly, been canonised. The name of Theodore, although he was the corner stone of pontifical authority through all the British isles, will be vainly sought among the saintly rubrics in a Romish calendar: but his reputation stands on higher grounds. He first gave stability to the religious establishment of England, by defining principles of doctrine and discipline. He provided for the nation's intellectual growth, by a zealous and active patronage of learning. During the earlier years

---

[1] BED. v. 8. p. 398. Theodore died in 690. INETT. i. 117. *Sax. Chr.* 57.

of his English residence, instruction was indeed given personally, both by himself and by his friend, Adrian, in every branch of scholarship then known to students.[1] As a theologian, Theodore long maintained a high degree of importance. He had adopted a prevailing opinion, that every sin must be visited by some corresponding penalty.[2] For the just apportionment of this, he compiled his famous *Penitential*, an assumed authority for the modern Romish confessional, of extraordinary value from its antiquity and bulk. Theodore, however, has afforded Romanists considerable embarrassment, by pronouncing confession to God alone sufficient for spiritual safety.[3] His authority, therefore, is unfavourable to sacramental absolution, that scholastic lure, so ominous to attrite souls, but admirably fitted for a ready and powerful hold upon mankind.

When Theodore felt his end approaching, he thought of Wilfrid,[4] conscious, perhaps, of some harshness towards him, or merely anxious to render him a parting service. As usual, that vain and restless prelate had shone under adversity. On his first

---

[1] BED. IV. 2. p. 259.

[2] See *Bampton Lectures*. Sermon V.

[3] See the canon, as given in the published Penitential, *Bampt. Lect.* 289. It stands thus in an ancient copy, or fragment of Theodore's Penitential, in the British Museum (MSS. Cotton. Vespasian. D. 15, f. 100). " Confessionem suam dō soli, si necesse est, licebit agere."

[4] MALMESBURY de Gest. PP. Angl. *Script. post Bed.* 151. Malmesbury, as might be expected from his Romish prejudices, makes Theodore deeply repentant on account of his conduct to Wilfrid.

journey in quest of Roman interference, he had been driven by stress of weather into Friesland, and had nobly spent a winter there in evangelising the heathen population.[1] In his recent exile, he had rendered a like invaluable service to pagan Sussex.[2] Whatever, therefore, might have been Theodore's displeasure or disapprobation, he could not fail of considering the expatriated prelate a very meritorious labourer in the Gospel vineyard. He now wrote in his favour to the court of Northumberland, and Wilfrid was again tempted by prosperity, being restored to his bishopric. At first his jurisdiction did not reach its original extent; but, on the death of Cuthbert, he was once more invested with spiritual authority over the whole Northumbrian dominions. Unhappily, however, his intractable, haughty spirit, had not even yet been sufficiently disciplined: he could not bend himself to the canons enacted under Theodore, or endure the conversion of his own monastic foundation, at Hexham, into an episcopal see.[3] These new displays of turbulence induced the king to call several of the prelacy together; and under their sanction Wilfrid was once more driven into exile.[4] His age was now verging upon seventy, but anger and impatience yet roused him into activity. He again hastened to Rome; and regardless of the contempt poured by his countrymen upon papal interference before, he

---

[1] Bed. v. 20. p. 443.   [2] *Ib.* 444.

[3] " Secunda est (causa dissentionis) ut monasterium supradictum, quod in privilegium nobis donabatur, in episcopalem sedem transmutatur."—Eddii, Vit. Wilf. *XV. Script.* iii. 74.

[4] Bed. v. 20. p. 444.

laid his case before the pontiff, and pleaded strenuously for a favourable judgment. His exertions having prevailed, he made another experiment upon the authorities of Northumbria. He was partially successful: a synod assembled on the banks of the Nidd, allowing him the see of Hexham, which he held peaceably during the remaining four years of his agitated life.[1] His indefatigable zeal for Italian usages, and repeated calls for papal interference, were naturally thought, in the course of years, an ample title to Romish invocation. St. Wilfrid's tutelage was, accordingly, long implored in northern England.

In the time of Wilfrid, England legally became a Christian commonwealth. A legislative assembly, holden under Ina, king of the West Saxons,[2] imposed fines upon parents neglecting the timely baptism of their infants,[3] and upon labour on Sundays.[4] It also gave the privilege of sanctuary to churches, made perjury before a bishop highly penal,[5] placed epis-

---

[1] BED. 447. Wilfrid died in 709, at Oundle, in Northamptonshire, and was buried at Ripon, in Yorkshire.—WHARTON de Episc. Dunelm. *Angl. Sacr.* i. 695. *Sax. Chr.* 61.

[2] About the year 693.—JOHNSON, *sub. ann.*

[3] Unless a child were baptised within thirty days, the father was to be fined as many shillings; if it died before baptism, he was to forfeit all his possessions.

[4] A slave, working on Sunday by his lord's order, was to become free, and the lord was to pay thirty shillings; by his own will, he was to be whipped, or pay a pecuniary compensation instead.

[5] " This was one reason for the bishop's sitting on the temporal bench with the alderman, viz. to tender necessary oaths in the most

copal and royal residences upon the same footing as to housebreakers,[1] and recognised baptismal relationship by pecuniary satisfactions.[2] About the same time Wihtred, king of Kent, in two meetings of his legislature, one holden at Bapchild,[3] the other at Berghamsted,[4] confirmed churches in all properties

---

solemn manner; for the English, in this age, were under the greatest awe of falsifying an oath taken on the bishop's hand, or on a cross holden in his hand."—JOHNSON.

[1] 120 shillings was to be the satisfaction for this offence in either case. The next case mentioned is the breaking into an alderman's house. For this 80 shillings was the penalty.

[2] The compensation for killing a godson, or a godfather, was to be made to the survivor, just as if the parties had been related in blood.

[3] Becanceld, or Baccanceld, is the Saxon name of this place: " now called Bapchild, near to Sittingbourn, on the Canterbury side, being about midway between the coast of Kent and London, and therefore a very convenient place for a Kentish council. At this place, not many years since, were the visible remains of two chapels, standing very near to one another, on the right hand of the road from Canterbury to Sittingbourn. The present church stands on the opposite side, at no great distance from them. Dr. Plott, many years ago, observed to me, that this, and other circumstances, were good presumptions, that this was the old Baccanceld, the place for Kentish councils. The old Saxons very often wrote a simple *c*, where we now write and pronounce *ch*."—JOHNSON, *sub. ann.* 692.

The *Saxon Chronicle* assigns the council at Bapchild to 694, and this date has been adopted by Spelman. Bede, however (v. 9. p. 400), says that Brihtwald, Theodore's successor, was elected to the see of Canterbury July 1, 692, Wihtred being then king of Kent. Johnson makes it appear that Wihtred began his reign in that very year; and the *Saxon Chronicle* says, perhaps rather loosely, " as soon as he was king, he ordained a great council to meet in the place that is called Bapchild." Hence Johnson infers that 692 is the true date of this council.

[4] " Perhaps, now Bursted, or Barsted, near Maidstone." (*Johnson, sub. ann.* 696.) Chauncy, who assigns 697, the fifth

and immunities bestowed upon them; allowed a *veto* to the archbishop, on the election of bishops and abbots; inflicted penalties upon incontinence; lent solemnity to altars, by making them the places for manumitting slaves and taking oaths; and fined the profanation of Sunday,[1] idolatrous offerings, and the eating of flesh on fast days.

The laws of Ina record also England's earliest known enactment for supplying the exigences of public worship, anciently provided for by oblations upon the altar. When whole communities became Christian, such contributions would not only be precarious, but also often most unfairly levied. Ina's legislature wisely, therefore, commuted voluntary offerings for a regular assessment upon houses. Every dwelling was to be valued at Christmas; and the rate so imposed, called *church-shot*, was payable on the following Martinmas. Money being scarce, the payment was made in produce; usually in grain or seed, but sometimes in poultry. Defaulters were to be fined forty shillings, and to pay the *church-shot*

---

year of Wihtred, as the date of the council, supposes it to have been holden at Berkhamsted, in Hertfordshire, where "the kings of Mercia often resided and kept their court." A place within the bounds of Kent, however, seems more likely to have been chosen by a Kentish prince.

[1] Sunday was reckoned from sunset on Saturday, until sunset on Sunday. A remnant of this ancient reckoning is, perhaps, yet to be found in the half-holidays usual in schools, on Saturdays. Wihtred's council was not quite so strict as that of Ina, inasmuch as lords making their slaves work on Sundays did not thereby lose their property in them necessarily, being merely liable to pay a satisfaction of eighty shillings.

twelvefold.¹ This pious care of divine ministrations may be considered as the legal origin of *church-rates.* Thus, earlier than almost any of English written laws, appears on record a legislative provision for the sacramental elements, and like demands of our holy profession. Of titles to property, unless royal or ecclesiastical, no one approaches even an era so remote. It is true that Ina's laws were only legally binding within the limits of his own dominions; but, probably, such of them as bore upon religion, if not so confirmed already, were soon confirmed by the usage or express enactments of every petty principality around. *Church-scot* accordingly makes repeated appearances among the legislative acts of other Anglo-Saxon states; and even the latest of these is far earlier than any title to a private inheritance.

The sacred and inalienable right of God's ministers to maintenance — poverty's most important claim on opulence[2] — appears not among the laws of Ina; an omission understood as evidence, that provision for the souls of men was already made ordinarily, and not unwillingly, by means of tythes.[3]

---

[1] LL. INÆ, 4, 10. SPELM. I. 184, 185. WILK. I. 59. JOHNSON, *sub ann.* 693.

[2] Let any observer cast his eye upon a considerable country congregation, and he must feel that very few present either do, or can pay any thing in support of the public worship and instruction by which all are benefitting. To say nothing, therefore, of relief, local expenditure, and assistance of various kinds, which an endowed ministry confers upon rural districts, it is plainly the only means for securing to them a supply of sound religious knowledge.

[3] " We cannot doubt but tythes were paid in England, at this time, and before: Boniface, in the year 693, was twenty years of

These had, indeed, been rendered in every age, and under every religion.[1] Hence their origin, probably, ascends to that patriarchal faith, which ever shed a glimmering ray over even the most benighted

---

age (he was born 670); and he testifies that tythes were paid in the English church, in his letter to Cuthbert; and there is reason to believe that they were paid freely and fully, or else this king (*Ina*), who made so severe a law for paying the *church-scot*, would have made a severer for paying tythes, as some kings did, some hundred years after this, when the people's first fervours abated. The *church-scot* was a new taxation, and therefore not readily paid; tythes were from the beginning, and therefore paid without repining."—JOHNSON, *sub ann.* 693.

[1] " In *Arabia*, we find a law whereby every merchant was obliged to offer the *tenth* of his frankincense, which was the chief product and commodity of this country, to the god *Sabis*. (PLIN. *Nat. Hist.* l. XII. c. 14.) The *Carthaginians* sent the *tythe* of their spoils taken in the *Sicilian* war to *Hercules* of *Tyre*. (JUSTIN. l. XVIII. c. 7) The *Ethiopians* paid *tythes* to their god *Assabinus*. (PLIN. l. XII c. 19) The *Grecian* army which was conducted by *Xenophon*, in their memorable retreat after the death of Cyrus, reserved a *tenth* of their money to be dedicated to *Apollo* at *Delphi*, and *Diana* at *Ephesus*. (XENOPH. *de Exp. Cyr.* l. v.) When the *Greeks* had driven the *Persians* out of their country, they consecrated a golden tripod, made of the *tenths* of their spoils, to *Delphian Apollo*. (DIOD. SIC. l. XI.) The inhabitants of the isle *Siphnus* presented every year the *tenths* of the gold and silver digged out of their mines to the same god. (PAUSAN. *Phoc.*) The *Athenians*, and their confederates, dedicated a buckler of gold out of the *tenths* of the spoils taken at *Tanagra* to *Jupiter*. (*Ib. Eliac. á.*) And the *Athenians* dedicated a chariot and horses of gold, made out of another *tenth*, to *Pallas*. (HEROD. l. v. c. 77.) When *Cyrus* has conquered *Lydia*, *Crœsus* advised him to prevent his soldiers from plundering the goods of the *Lydians*, ὡς σφέα ἀναγκαίως ἔχειν δεκατευθῆναι τῷ Διι, because they were of necessity to be tythed to Jupiter. (*Ib.* l. 1.) The *Crotonians* vow to give a *tenth* of the spoils which they should take in their war with the *Locrians*, to *Delphian Apollo*. (JUSTIN. l. XX. c. ult.) *Sylla*, the *Roman* general, dedicated the *tenth* of all his estate to

branches of Adam's posterity.[1] Conversion to Christianity strengthened pagan prejudice in favour of this appropriation. It was the very provision, expressly enjoined by God, for that Levitical establishment

---

Hercules. (PLUTARCH. *Sylla.*) And the same was done by *M. Crassus.* (*Ib. Crasso.*) And we are told by Plutarch (*Roman. Quæst.*) that this was a constant custom at *Rome.* Hercules himself is said to have dedicated to the gods the *tenth* of the spoils which he took from *Geryon* (DIONYS. HALICARN. l. 1.) When *Camillus* sacked Veii, a city of Hetruria, the soldiers seized the spoils for their own use, without reserving the accustomed *tenth* for the gods. After this, the augurs discovered, by their observations on the sacrifices, that the gods were exceedingly offended; whereupon the *senate* of *Rome* required all the soldiers to account upon oath for the spoils which they had taken, and to pay a *tenth* of them, or the full value: all which, with a golden cup of eight talents, was conveyed to Apollo's temple at *Delphi* by three men of the first quality in Rome. (PLUTARCH. *Camillo*) And lastly, we are informed by Festus, that the *ancients offered to their gods the tythes of all things* without any exception."—(POTTER's *Discourse of Church Government.* Lond. 1707, p. 430.) From this general usage, the Greeks, we learn from Harpocration, understood δεκατεῦσαι, to tythe, as if it were καθιεροῦν, to consecrate; ἐπειδήπερ ἔθος ἦν Ἑλληνικὸν τὰς δεκάτας τῶν περιγινομένων τοῖς Θεοῖς καθιεροῦν, since it was the Grecian custom to consecrate the tythes of their acquisitions to the gods.—HARPOC. *in voc.* Δεκατεύειν. Ed. Maussac. Par. 1614, p 76. See also Sir HENRY SPELMAN's *Larger Treatise concerning Tythes* Lond. 1647, p 114, *et seq*—Dr COMBER's *Historical Vindication of the Divine Right of Tythes.* Lond 1685. Part I. ch. III. p. 29.

[1] " They who are guided by chance, or fancy, and act without any certain and fixed rule, cannot be supposed to agree in the same manner of acting : and, therefore, since the most distant nations, many of whom do not appear to have had any intercourse with one another, agreed in dedicating an exact *Tenth*, we can scarce derive this consent from any other principle, beside the tradition of *Adam*, or *Noah*, or some other *Patriarch*, who lived before the dispersion from *Babel*; and it can scarce be conceived, that any of the *Patriarchs* should enjoin the observation of this tradition upon the

which an evangelical ministry had superseded. Men were accordingly exhorted to consecrate the tenth of their substance as a religious duty, and tender consciences obediently heard a call so strong in Scriptural authority — so familiar even to heathen practice. The Anglo-Saxons had been, as usual, prepared for such appeals after conversion, by habit previously formed.[1] They seem also to have found the tenth esteemed God's portion among British Christians;[2]

---

whole race of mankind, without a Divine precept for it."—POTTER, p. 428.

[1] It appears from Sidonius Apollinaris, that the Saxon pirates were in the habit of sacrificing the *tenth* captive to their gods. (COMBER, 190.) Their captives were, in fact, merchandise. Malmesbury tells us (*de Gest. RR. Angl.* p. 6.) that Cedwalla, king of the West Saxons, baptised in 686, *tythed* all his warlike spoils taken even before baptism. " Inter hæc arduum memoratu est, quantum etiam ante baptismum inservierit pietati, ut omnes manubias, quas jure prædatorio in suos usus transcripserat, *Deo decimaret.*" This statement gives room for inferring that *tything* was familiar to the pagan Saxons, and hardly allows a doubt of its establishment among the Christians of Wessex in 686.

[2] This may be inferred from the following tale related of Augustine, the Kentish apostle. When preaching in Oxfordshire, a village priest addressed him thus :—" Father, the lord of this place refuses to pay tythes, and my threats of excommunication only increase his obstinacy." Augustine then tried *his* powers of persuasion, but the lord replied, " Did not I plough and sow the land? The tenth part belongs to him who owns the remaining nine." It was now time for mass, and Augustine, turning to the altar, said, " I command every excommunicated person to leave the church." Immediately a pallid corpse arose from beneath the doorway, stalked across the churchyard, and stood motionless beyond its boundary. The congregation, gazing in horror and affright, called Augustine's attention to the spectre. He did not choose, however, to break off the service. Having concluded, he said, " Be not alarmed. With cross and holy water in hand, we

it is highly probable, therefore, that the silence of Ina upon clerical maintenance merely resulted from general acquiescence in a system which immemorial usage prescribed, and Scripture sanctioned.[1]

---

shall know the meaning of this." He then went forward, and thus accosted the ghastly stranger :—" I enjoin thee, in the name of God, tell me who thou art ?" The ghost replied, " In British times I was lord here; but no warnings of the priest could ever bring me to pay my tythes. At length he excommunicated me, and my disembodied soul was thrust into hell. When the excommunicated were bidden to depart, your attendant angels drove me from my grave." Augustine's power was now exerted in raising the excommunicating priest from his narrow resting-place; and having thus a second spectre before him, he asked, " Know you this person ?" The unearthly clergyman replied, " Full well, and to my cost." He was then reminded by Augustine of God's mercy, and of the departed lord's long torture in hell; a scourge was put into his hand, the excommunicated party knelt before him, received absolution, and then quietly returned to the grave. His own return thither soon followed, although Augustine, desirous of his assistance in preaching the Gospel, would fain have prayed for a renewed term of life."—BROMTON. *X. Script.* 736.

Besides the inference to be drawn from this apocryphal story, Germanus and Lupus are said, on the authority of Giraldus Cambrensis, to have taught the Britons " to pay their tythes partly to the bishop, and partly to their baptismal church."—COMBER, 183.

[1] The Mosaical provision for God's ministers is obviously a reasonable precedent for the guidance of Christians. Express authority for this particular provision could hardly find a place in the New Testament, both because its several portions appeared as circumstances called for them, and because it was important to avoid all appearance of interfering with vested rights. Now, no questions as to the fixed maintenance of an established ministry could have arisen while the Apostles lived, and prospective claims to the endowments prescribed by Moses would only have given occasion for representing Christian principles as a mere device for spoiling the Jewish priesthood. The general right, however, of a Christian clergy to competent maintenance is established by the

Other facilities for spreading religion, and secular information also, were now generally provided by means of monasteries. Rarely was a prince converted, or awakened to a serious concern for eternity, without signalising his altered state by one or more of these foundations. This munificence was highly beneficial to society. An age of barbarism and insecurity required such cloistered retreats for nurturing, concentrating, and protecting the peaceful luminaries of learning and religion. It was from the convent-gate accordingly that heralds of salvation proceeded to evangelise the country.[1] Undoubtedly, monasteries also found for fanaticism both a nursery and an asylum: within their walls were trained and sheltered ascetic monks, perhaps even more abundantly than active teachers. These latter were however cheaply purchased at the price of moderate encouragement for the former. Religious enthusiasm arises, besides, from a mental unhealthiness, common in every age, and often far from unproductive of real good. A place of refuge, therefore, and regular control, for spirits impatient under sober piety, would frequently render important public service. In earlier portions of the Anglo-Saxon period, such monastic services were unalloyed by any approach towards that extensive system of organisation which eventually became so mischievous. Benedict of Nursia had in-

---

practice and express permission of Jesus, and by various texts in the Epistles.—St. Matt. xxvii. 55, 56   *Ib.* x. 9, 10.   St. Luke, viii. 2, 3.   *Ib.* x. 7.   *Ib.* xxii. 35.   Acts, iv. 37.   Gal. vi. 6. Phil. iv. 18.   2 Thess. iii. 9.   1 Cor. ix. 14.   1 Tim. v. 17, 18.

[1] Bed. iv. 27. pp 348, 349.

deed appeared,[1] and Wilfrid seems to have claimed the merit of introducing his regulations into England.[2] Such introduction must however have been incomplete and partial, for Dunstan was unquestionably the father of British Benedictines.[3] Earlier monasteries, therefore, were never even likely to offer facilities for the formation of that powerful confederacy which, in after ages, riveted the chains of papal domination.

That intellectual advance by which Theodore had obliged so deeply his adopted country, was undoubtedly promoted by the prevailing passion for pilgrimages to Rome. Man's natural thirst for novelty and variety intrenched itself under cover of Christian zeal, dignifying impatience of home, and a restless curiosity to visit foreign regions, as a holy anxiety for worshipping on the spots where apostles taught, and their bones repose. Persons of both sexes, accordingly, and of every rank, found religious excuses for journeying to the ancient seat of empire.[4] There, however, yet lingered a higher civilisation, and more extensive knowledge, than in any other city of western Europe. From constant intercourse, therefore, with a spot so favoured, could hardly fail of flowing considerable improvements in manners, understanding, and information. These benefits, however, were by no means unattended with counter-

---

[1] Benedict was born in 480, and died in 542 or 543.—CAVE. *Hist Lit.* Lond. 1688. p. 402.

[2] MALMESB. de Gest. PP. *Script. post Bed* f. 151.

[3] OSBERN. de Vit. S. Dunst. *Angl. Sacr.* II. 91.

[4] BED. v. 7. p. 395.

vailing evils: many of the pilgrims proved unequal to their own guidance in common decency, when removed completely away from domestic restraints. Females left their native shores, alleging an uncontrolable impulse of piety. In hardly any city on the way to Rome were not some of these unhappy women living by prostitution: even nuns were among the travelling devotees thus earning the wages of infamy. Serious minds became deeply scandalised by the frequency of such disgraceful spectacles; hence Boniface, archbishop of Mentz, recommended the prohibition of English female pilgrimages, by royal and synodical authority.[1]

Of Anglo-Saxons importantly benefitted by intercourse with Rome, no one obtained more credit in his day than Aldhelm, a near kinsman probably to the sovereigns of Wessex.[2] His education was chiefly conducted by Adrian, the learned friend of Archbishop Theodore, and his proficiency was highly honourable to both parties. Having gained a great literary reputation, he was chosen to write in favour of the Roman Easter, at a conference with the Britons on that much-litigated question: his arguments are said to have made many converts.[3] Afterwards he

---

[1] Epist. Bonif. ad Cuth. Archiep. Cantuar. SPELM. *Conc.* 1 241. WILK 1. 93.

[2] " Aldelmus Saxonum oriundus prosapia, familia haud dubie nobilissima. Ferunt quidam, incertum unde id assumpserint, fuisse nepotem Inæ regis West-Saxonum ex fratre Kentero."— MALMESB. de Vitâ Aldhelm. Episc. Scireburn. *Angl. Sacr.* ii 2.

[3] *Ib.* 15. This work of Aldhelm's appears to have been lost in Malmesbury's time; a deficiency which that author much regrets.

indulged himself in the prevailing pilgrimage to Rome; and a mind like his must have brought home stores of valuable information. Aldhelm was abbot of Malmesbury during a considerable period, and he spent the last four years of his illustrious life in the see of Sherborne. He has the credit of introducing his countrymen to Latin composition, both in prose and verse.[1] In addition to the appearance of such an author at a period little dignified by literature, the subject of his principal work long gained him extensive notice. Ages smitten with admiration of monastic life naturally applauded a genius who sang *the Praise of Virginity.* To later times, however, the muse of Aldhelm has appeared obscure and turgid.

A contemporary scholar has obtained more lasting celebrity. Bede, universally and justly called *the Venerable,* was born in the modern bishopric of Durham, upon an estate belonging to Benedict Biscop's

---

Its loss, in fact, is to be regretted, because the book, if extant, could hardly fail of throwing considerable light upon other points of difference between the British and Roman churches. There were many such points, for Malmesbury says of the Britons:— " Suis potius quam Romanis obsecundarent traditionibus. *Et plura quidem alia Catholica,* sed illud potissimum abnuebant; ne Paschale sacrum legitimo die celebrarent." (14.) A more extensive knowledge of *our own British traditions* would not only be very interesting, but also serviceable in refuting various pretensions of the Romanists

[1] " Primus ex Anglorum gente erat, juxta Cambdenum, qui Latine scripsit, primusque componendi carminis Latine rationem populares suos docuit."—(CAVE. *Hist. Lit.* 466.) Aldhelm was made Abbot of Malmesbury in 671, and chosen Bishop of Sherborne in 705.—*Ib.*

foundations at Wearmouth and Jarrow. In these two monasteries, learning, teaching, and writing, he passed agreeably the whole of his laborious, distinguished, and blameless life, from the age of seven years. His first instructor was the learned Biscop himself, at once founder and abbot, whose noble library proved a treasure from which he never ceased to draw happiness, occupation, and fame. That excellent person, so fortunate in furnishing a study for Bede, lived not, however, to complete his admirable pupil's education. The young scholar then passed under the tuition of Ceolfrid, abbot after Biscop.[1] The times were highly favourable for his proficiency; Theodore and Adrian, the lights of Britain, surviving through his earlier years.[2] At nineteen he was ordained deacon; at thirty, priest. When free from professional calls and monastic observances, his industry as a divine and general man of letters was inexhaustible. Scripture was his favourite study; but he seems to have explored most eagerly every branch of knowledge within his reach. Sergius, the Roman pontiff, would fain have had the personal assistance of so ripe a scholar upon some unknown emergency:[3] but Bede seems to have been untinctured by the prevailing rage for wandering over foreign countries. He remained steadily secluded in his monastery, attesting the diligent employment of his time by a long and rapid succession of literary works. Among these, the theological portions are

---

[1] BED. de seipso. *Eccl. Hist.* p. 492.
[2] STUBBS. *X. Script.* col. 1695.
[3] MALMESB. de Gest RR. Angl. *Script. post Bedam*, VI. 11.

little else than selections from the Fathers, especially from St. Austin. Englishmen, however, long considered Bede as their principal divine. The collections, therefore, stamped with his venerable name, form a copious repository of national religious tradition. In this view they are highly valuable, for they supply decisive evidence, in many particulars, against Romish claims to the ancient faith of England. Bede's fame has chiefly rested, in later ages, upon his *Ecclesiastical History*, an invaluable record of interesting events, compiled from ancient monuments, tradition, and personal knowledge.[1] A monastic author in the eighth century could hardly fail of intermingling his narrative with superstitious tales. The venerable monk of Jarrow accordingly presents many such indications of his profession and age. Fastidious moderns have excepted against this apparent credulity of Bede: objections have also been made to his loose and incidental mention of secular affairs; he professed, however, only to preserve the annals of religion. He had, probably, but little taste for investigating the mazes of selfish policy, and chronicling the outrages of licentious violence; he might even think such details unsuitable to the monastic profession, and to a Christian minister. Still he has preserved a great mass of civil information, and he may justly be venerated as the *Father of English History*. Nor is it among the least recommendations of his interesting annals, that in them appear so many traces of Britain's ancient church—

---

[1] BED. de seipso, *ut supra*.

such gratifying proofs that paganised England was more than half evangelised by the holy zeal of British missionaries. To Rome Bede was indebted for education, religious usages, and a library. She formed all his early prejudices, and filled him through life with grateful partiality. Yet, as a mere historian, it has been his fortune to weaken importantly the pleading of her advocates. On the verge of senility, Bede was attacked with asthma. The disorder became troublesome one year at Easter; and about dawn, on Ascension-day, he placidly observed his end approaching. When thus anticipating a speedy call to account for talents improved so nobly, he felt anxious to complete a vernacular version of St. John's Gospel.[1] As the sun rose, accordingly, his pupils collecting around, he entreated them to write diligently from his dictation. He was mournfully obeyed until afternoon, when all but one youth left him, to join the procession usual on that day. "A single chapter still remains," the lad remarked; " dearest master, will it distress you if I ask you to go on with its translation?" The dying scholar answered, " By no means; take your pen, but write quickly." As time thus wore away, the venerable translator said, " There are a few pleasing trifles in my desk; a little pepper, some handkerchiefs, and incense; run, bring them to me, and call my brother-priests; I would fain distribute among these friends such little marks of my kind regard as God has given me. Rich men's presents are gold and silver, or other costly things;

---

[1] MALMESB. *ut supra*, f. 12

mine must be recommended by the affectionate pleasure which I feel in bestowing them." The young amanuensis did as he was bidden, and the dim eyes of his admired instructor soon rested upon a circle of weeping friends. " You will see my face no more," Bede said, " on this side of another world. It is time that my spirit should return to him who gave it. My life has been long, and a gracious Providence has made it happy. The time of my dissolution is now at hand : *I have a desire to depart, and to be with Christ.*" Other such pious and affecting language the youth, whose writing had been broken off, thus abruptly terminated: " My dear master, one sentence has not even yet been written." He was answered, " Make haste and write it, then." This done, the sinking teacher said, " *It is finished.* Take my head, and turn my face to the spot where I have been used to pray. *Glory to the Father, the Son, and the Holy Ghost.*" His lips immediately ceased to move, and every saddened eye now saw that the most illustrious of Europe's luminaries was gone to his reward.[1] Bede's remains were first interred in his beloved monastery of Jarrow ; but each revolving

---

[1] SIM. DUNELM. *Epist. de Transitu Bedæ.* X. *Script.* col. 10. There is some discrepancy as to the exact year of Bede's death ; but it most probably took place in 735. He was born in 672. He died, therefore, in what is called the *grand climacteric.* (CAVE. *Hist. Lit.* p. 473.) The origin of *venerable,* affixed to the name of Bede, is not known ; but this designation seems ancient; for the second council of Aix-la-Chapelle, holden in 836, citing in its preface his mystical explanation of Solomon's temple, thus describes him : " *Venerabilis* et modernis temporibus doctor admirabilis Beda presbyter."—*Labb. et Coss.* vii. 1760.

year increasing the splendour of his fame, a grateful posterity demanded a more conspicuous tomb. His bones were accordingly transferred to Durham, and enclosed in the same coffin with those of saintly Cuthbert.[1]

Contemporaneous with Bede's death, or nearly so, was the consecration of Egbert to the see of York.[2] This admirable prelate's father was Eata, cousin to Ceolwulf, the victorious king of Northumbria.[3] The military fame, however, of that illustrious prince, proved no security against religious melancholy. He had frequently holden delightful converse with Bede; and, amidst the successful din of arms, he sighed for peaceful piety like his. Following, accordingly, no fewer than seven precedents among Anglo-Saxon kings, he buried his talents for active life under the monotonous austerities of a cloister.[4] His kinsman Eata had two sons, Eadbert and Egbert: of these, the former was probably educated for the royal dignity; the latter was placed in a monastery during infancy. When a youth, Egbert went to Rome with his brother, and there he was ordained deacon.[5] After his return home he was chosen to the see of York; and Ceolwulf, who yet filled the throne, de-

---

[1] STUBBS. *X. Script.* col. 1696.

[2] *Sax. Chr.* 66. The year 734 is the one mentioned. Bede's death, however, seems to have been deferred until the following year; and there is even reason for believing that Egbert's elevation to York did not occur before the year 743. See GODWIN. *de Præsul.* 656.

[3] SIM. DUNELM. *X. Script.* col. 11.

[4] HUNTINGDON. *Script. post Bedam*, f. 195.

[5] SIM. DUNELM. *ut supra.*

sired him to accept the complimentary pall,[1] a mark of deference to Rome paid by no one of his predecessors since Paulinus. Egbert, thus invested with a papal recognition of archi-episcopal dignity, became eminent for professional learning, and for a noble patronage of literature. He compiled some useful manuals of ecclesiastical discipline:[2] he prepared also, for the use of his clergy, a vernacular *Penitential*,[3] in which human iniquities are particularised, often with disgusting minuteness, and for every sin is prescribed a corresponding penance. Egbert's judicious munificence led him likewise to shed a lustre on York, by the formation there of an ample library,[4] always an important benefit, but especially so when literary appliances are scarce and costly. This invaluable prelacy was happily prolonged over more than thirty years,[5] a monument of superior abilities diligently used, and of ample wealth nobly viewed as an important public trust.

Among the *excerpts* of Egbert, is one prescribing

---

[1] " Regnante Ceolwulfo atque jubente, primus post Paulinum, accepto ab apostolica sede pallio."—SIM. DUNELM. *ut supra.*

[2] Dialogus Egberti de Ecclesiastica Institutione. (WILK *Conc.* i. 82.) Excerptiones D. Egberti, Ebor. Archiep. *Ib.* i. 101. SPELM. *Conc.* i. 258.

[3] WILK. *Conc.* i. 113. At the end of the table of contents of the first book is a paragraph thus translated: — *These capitulars Ecgbyrht, archbishop in Eoforwic, turned from Latin into English, that the unlearned might the more easily understand it.*

[4] Epist. Alc. ad Carol. August. ap. MALMESBURY de Gest. PP. Angl. *Script. post Bedam.* f. 153.

[5] Thirty-six years. (MALMESB. *ut supra.*) Simeon of Durham and Stubbs say thirty-two years. There is little or no doubt that Egbert died in 766.

a threefold division of tythes. From the first article in this collection, it appears that considerable progress had been already made in the settlement of a parochial clergy, but that popular eagerness for so great a benefit had outrun a sufficient provision for public worship.[1] Arrangements were probably made, in many cases, for appropriating a rural priest before a church was ready for his ministrations. Bishops might seem to have encouraged such arrangements, by surrendering their own portion of tythes. In Egbert's fifth *Excerpt*, accordingly, no mention is made of this portion. Clergymen are enjoined to expend one portion upon ornaments for their churches, another upon the poor and upon hospitality:[2] the third was to be their own.[3] This injunction, however, is obviously destitute of legal authority: at the most, it can only rank among recommendations in episcopal charges. Egbert's object was to lay before his clergy a code of instructions for their government, chiefly selected from foreign canonists,[4] and binding, as he thought, upon their

---

[1] "Let every priest build his own church with all diligence, and preserve the relics of the saints, watching over them by night, and performing divine offices."—JOHNSON's *Transl. sub ann.* 740.

[2] Clergymen were, in fact, the innkeepers, as one may say, of those ancient times. Hence the 25th *Excerpt* stands thus in Johnson: "That bishops and priests have an house for the entertainment of strangers not far from the church."

[3] Johnson is inclined to question whether this *Excerpt* may not be more modern than Egbert.

[4] That foreign books were not only used, but also very loosely, appears plainly from the following *Excerpt*, the 7th :—"That all priests pray assiduously for the life and empire of our lord the emperor, and for the health of his sons and daughters." This is

consciences; domestic legislation, therefore, he naturally overlooked.

In Egbert's episcopal city was born Flaccus Albinus, or Alcuin.[1] This eminent genius, illustrious eventually above all contemporary European scholars, received from the archbishop even personal instruc-

---

evidently a mere transcript from some book written abroad, without even the trouble taken of adaptation for domestic use. Many of the latter *Excerpts* are prefaced by a mention of the quarters which have supplied them. This is not the case, however, with that prescribing the threefold division of tythes; but probably Egbert had in his eye the fifth canon of the first Council of Orleans, holden in 511, which provides: " De oblationibus, vel agris, quos dominus noster rex ecclesiis suo munere conferre dignatus est, vel adhuc non habentibus Deo inspirante contulerit, ipsorum agrorum vel clericorum immunitate concessâ, id esse justissimum definimus, ut in reparationibus eccclesiarum, alimoniis sacerdotum, et pauperum, vel redemptionibus captivorum, quicquid Deus in fructibus dare dignatus fuerit, expendatur." (LABB. et Coss. iv. col. 1405.) It is, however, worthy of remark, that the Fathers at Orleans were very far from contemplating any such abuses as have pauperised and demoralised so extensively the lower classes of modern England. Their sixteenth canon stands thus : " Episcopus pauperibus, vel infirmis, *qui debilitate faciente non possunt suis manibus laborare*, victum et vestitum in quantum possibilitas habuerit, largiatur." (*Ib.* col. 1407.) Such, therefore, as would use the tripartite system to confiscate the generally slender maintenances of clergymen, for the payment of their own able-bodied servants, must not seek authority from the Council of Orleans. Such persons also may fairly be referred to the thirty-seventh canon of the first book of Egbert's Penitential. (WILKINS, 1. 123.) From this it might seem, that people paid every tenth *sceat* (about equal to a groat), at Easter for religious purposes. A revival of this practice would probably answer all the calls for which a certain class of antiquaries would fain make provision from predial tythes alone.

[1] " Vos fragiles infantiæ meæ annos materno fovistis affectu." —ALCUIN, *Epist. ad Fratres Eboracenses.* Acta SS. Ord. Benedict. iv. 163.

tion; and he was left by him, when dying, in charge of his library.[1] Another trust, at least equally honourable and useful, devolved upon him, in the direction of Egbert's school. The learned and princely metropolitan of Northumbria was thus no less fortunate than Benedict Biscop, in meeting with a Bede. He, too, has the glory of enabling a brilliant luminary to shed extensively some humanising rays over a period of grossness and illiteracy. The fame of Alcuin resounded on every side; and students, however distant, eagerly sought in York that instruction which no other master could supply. His labours, however, were unexpectedly transferred from the ancient city for which they had gained so much celebrity. He had gone to Rome, a suitor for the pall, desired as usual by Eanbald, formerly his pupil, now promoted to the see of York. In his way homeward, passing through Parma, he saw Charlemain, and that enlightened prince immediately became anxious to retain him. The learned Anglo-Saxon, won by a desire so flattering, promised to return, if the king of his native land, and his friend, Eanbald, would admit of his departure. Their permissions gained, Alcuin reappeared before the Frankish conqueror. In that wonder of his day, as in Xenophon, Cæsar, and our

---

[1] "Laus et gloria Deo, qui dies meos in prosperitate bonâ conservavit, ut in exaltatione filii mei carissimi gauderem, qui laboraret vice meâ in ecclesiâ, ubi ego nutritus et educatus fueram, et præesset thesauris sapientiæ, in quibus me magister meus dilectus Egbertus archiepiscopus hæredem reliquit."— *Epist. Alcuini ad Eambald. Archiep. Ebor.* apud MALMESBURY, de Gest. RR. Angl. *Script. post Bedam,* f 12. See also *Acta SS. Ord. Benedict.* ut supra.

own immortal Alfred, the glare of splendid military talents was tempered by the mild lustre of literary taste. Charlemain, accordingly, had no sooner secured the services of Alcuin, than he sought profit from them personally. The potent and victorious chief astonished his rude and imperious officers, by becoming an attentive pupil: listening also to Alcuin's judicious counsel, he rendered monastic foundations, under his control, efficient schools for disseminating useful knowledge. Thus, all his extensive territories felt most beneficially the peaceful influence of a foreign scholar. Charlemain gratefully acknowledged, in grants of conventual dignities, the services thus rendered to his people and himself. But Alcuin pined for home: his humble spirit merely sighed for pious exercises and learned labours, which he would fain have plied amid scenes familiar to his youthful eye. At length he was allowed the pleasure of revisiting his native isle, to negociate a treaty between Charlemain and the Mercian Offa. The justly-celebrated Frank urged repeatedly his quick return; Alcuin, however, was no less eager to remain, and three years elapsed before he crossed again the sea, to live in splendour, yet in exile. Never afterwards could he gain permission to behold his beloved country: Charlemain even felt impatiently his absence from the court. At last he was gratified by an unwilling license of retirement to his abbey of St. Martin, at Tours, where soon assembled, from every quarter, but especially from England, a crowd of students.[1] On the termination of his religious and

---

[1] *Acta SS. Ord. Benedict.* iv. 169, 179.

industrious career, he had attained the summit of literary fame.[1] The far more extended information of later times has, it is true, rendered his works valuable only as evidences and monuments. Long after his own day, however, Alcuin's name shone with a lustre that knew no eclipse, and which it could justly challenge. Nor ought it ever to be forgotten, that his powerful talents, directed to every known branch of learning, his unwearied industry, his holy piety, dispelled importantly the intellectual darkness of a barbarous age.

A zealous missionary, born at Crediton, in Devonshire, acknowledged his intellectual obligations to Rome, by an active and unusual assertion of the papal supremacy. This eminent ecclesiastic, originally named Winifrid, received a monastic education in his own country. When more than thirty, a noble impulse of piety led him to emulate his countryman, Willibrord, in preaching the Gospel among the continental pagans.[2] Considerable success having waited on his labours in Batavia, he sought allowably the favourite recreation of a pilgrimage to Rome. He was greeted there with most gratifying applause, and sent back to the scenes of his former usefulness with

---

[1] Alcuin died in 804, at Tours. Hence it is not likely that he should have been the disciple of Bede, deceased in 735, as it has been sometimes said that he was.—CAVE, *Hist. Lit.* 496.

[2] BED. v. 11. p. 407. Willibrord, after several enterprising journeys with his brother missionaries, returned into Friesland, where his preaching had already been very successful, in 693. He was consecrated afterwards to the see of Utrecht, and he died among the Batavians advanced in age.—MOSHEIM, *Cent.* 7. ch. i. vol II. p 155.

recommendatory letters from the pope. In a subsequent visit to the pontifical city, he found his vanity further tempted, being consecrated bishop of the Germans, and distinguished by the name of Boniface.[1] Afterwards he was complimented by the pall, and appointed papal legate. In filling this latter office he displayed all his wonted ardour and activity, even going so far as to procure a synodical submission of Germany to the papal see—an unexpected return for their flattering civilities, highly delightful to the Romans.[2]

Boniface now seems to have become bent upon lowering the tone of his native country's independence, by winning it over to a similar submission. He was a personal friend of Cuthbert, archbishop of

---

[1] Boniface passed over into Friesland in 715. He was consecrated bishop by Gregory II. in 723, and made archbishop in 738. In his old age he returned to Friesland, being desirous of ending his days amid a people now relapsing, yet endeared to him by early success. He was, however, murdered there by the barbarous inhabitants in 755. He has been canonised, and commonly designated as the *Apostle of Germany*. His archiepiscopal see was Mentz.— MOSHEIM, *Cent.* 8. ch. 1. vol. II. p. 206. CAVE, *Hist. Lit.* 481.

[2] " Decrevimus autem in nostro synodali conventu, et confessi sumus fidem catholicam, et unitatem, et *subjectionem Romanæ ecclesiæ*, fine tenus vitæ nostræ velle servare Sancto Petro, et *vicario ejus velle subjici*, synodum per omnes annos congregare, metropolitanos pallia ab illâ sede quærere, et per omnia præcepta Petri canonicè sequi desiderare, ut inter oves sibi commendatas numeremur. Et isti confessioni universi consensimus, et subscripsimus, et ad corpus S. Petri, principis apostolorum direximus; *quod gratulando clerus et pontifex Romanus suscepit.*"—*Epist. Bonifacii, Archiep. Mogunt. ad Cuthb. Archiep. Cantuar.* SPELMAN, *Conc.* 1. 237. WILK. 1. 91. LABB. et COSS. *Conc.* VI. col. 1544.

Canterbury, and to that prelate he transmitted a copy of the canons enacted by his own obsequious synod, together with a letter. In this, like too many religious reformers, he paints the profligacy of those whom he was anxious to convert. An epistle of like import was also addressed by him to Ethelbald, king of the Mercians. From these communications, it is plain enough that the Anglo-Saxons were abundantly tainted by the gross impurities of a barbarous age; nor do ascetic pretensions among them seem frequently to have been much else than a cloak for lasciviousness. Intercourse between the sexes appears to have been most imperfectly regulated by matrimonial ties; and the chastity of nuns was evidently not more inviolable than that of their countrywomen generally.[1] For the formal condemnation of such offensive and pernicious immorality, solemn synodical authority was probably desirable. Cuthbert accordingly procured the meeting of a numerous council at Cloveshoo,[2] in which the Mercian Ethelbald acted as president.[3] Before this assembly, two

---

[1] " Et adhuc, quod pejus esset, qui nobis narrant, adjiciunt, quod hoc scelus ignominiæ, *maximè cum sanctis monialibus, et sacratis Deo virginibus, per monasterium commissum sit.*"—*Epist. Bonif. ad Æthelbald.* R. Spelm. *Conc.* 1. 233. Wilk. i. 88.

[2] " Cliff, at Hoo, Kent."—Dr. Ingram's *Index to the Sax. Chr.* 433. The *Saxon Chronicle* refers this council to 742, as also do the *Evidences of Christ-church, Canterbury.* Spelman, however, refers it to 747, which is most probably the correct date, being that standing in the preamble to the acts of the council.

[3] " Præsidente eidem concilio Ethelbaldo, rege Merciorum, cum Cuthberto, archiepiscopo Dorobermiæ." (*Evidentiæ Ecclesiæ Christi Cant.* X. *Script.* 2209.) The *Saxon Chronicle* merely says that Ethelbald was there, which is also said in the *Preamble.*

admonitory writings of Pope Zachary were read, and then explained in the vernacular tongue :[1] the deliberators abstained, however, from any submission to the Roman see. In several particulars his countrymen indeed consented to follow Boniface; but they patriotically disregarded his example when it would have led them to compromise their dignity as a nation, by professing submission to a foreign ecclesiastical authority.[2]

The canons of Cloveshoo are, in fact, adapted chiefly for the correction of existing irregularities in morals and discipline. Their general tenor is highly favourable to the Roman church, because they enjoin a strict uniformity with her offices and usages: they establish, however, a strong case of inexpediency against such uniformity, by directing priests to learn the construction of the creed,* the Lord's prayer, and

---

He probably acted as a sort of chairman; but as the business was entirely ecclesiastical, the lead most likely was taken by Cuthbert, the archbishop.

[1] " Malmesbury saith, that this council was opened with the letters of Pope Zachary; but it does not appear what were the contents, if any such were; but by the archbishop's despatch of the canons of this council to Boniface, and not to Zachary, it seems most likely that these were some epistles of Zachary to Boniface; and most probably those congratulating the union of the French bishops to the see of Rome."—INETT. *Hist. Engl.* Ch. 175.

[2] " The French Benedictine monks ingenuously confess that Boniface was an over-zealous partisan of the Roman pontiff, and attributed more authority to him than was just and fitting. Their words, in their *Histoire Littéraire de la France*, tom. IV. p. 106, are as follow : " *Il exprime son dévouement pour le S. Siège en des termes qui ne sont pas assez proportionés à la dignité du caractère épiscopal.*"—MOSHEIM, *Cent.* VIII. ch. 1. vol. II. p. 206, note.

of the offices of baptism, and the mass, for the sake of explaining these forms vernacularly.[1] At that period, Latin probably was far from unintelligible, even among the populace in southern Europe; but all of Teutonic origin, unless travelled or highly educated, must have been utterly unable to receive from it any accurate impression. Thus, it could hardly fail of being deplored by serious and intelligent observers, that ignorant persons, even among the clergy, evidently regarded religious offices rather as powerful charms, than as a reasonable service. It is lamentable, upon many accounts, that experience here was not allowed its natural operation in freeing northern Europe from the pernicious absurdity of a foreign ritual. It was a price rather dear, even for such solid advantages of information and refinement, as naturally flowed from constant intercourse with the ancient capital: it was an extravagant compensation for amusing rambles over Italy, under the sanctimonious guise of pilgrimages.

Another conspicuous evil of Anglo-Saxon deference for papal authority, was the liability to abuse by artful men, inseparable from such a principle. Crafty spirits, though foremost in spurning alien interference when hostile to their own selfishness, would eagerly use it under any temporary difficulty. To such a politician thus embarrassed, England owes the first public encouragement of papal assumptions. Offa, king of the Mercians, won an arduous way to superiority over every domestic impediment and neigh-

---

[1] *Can. Conc. Cloves,* 10. SPELM. I. 248. WILK. I. 96.

bouring power, through a remorseless career of sanguinary wars and crimes. Among his victims was the king of Kent, who perished in battle amidst a frightful carnage.[1] This decisive victory, however, failed of satisfying Offa : his vindictive spirit now fastened upon Lambert, archbishop of Canterbury, who had negotiated for assistance from abroad, while his unfortunate sovereign was preparing for the fatal conflict :[2] nor could he rest without making the offending prelate feel the bitterness of his resentment. He determined upon curtailing importantly that extensive jurisdiction which Lambert and his predecessors had hitherto enjoyed, by establishing an archbishopric at Lichfield, in his own dominions : but such arrangements demand an acquiescence, often baffling very powerful sovereigns. Hence Offa turned his eyes to Italy, shrewdly calculating that recognition there would prove effective nearer home. He was duly mindful to give his application pecuniary weight ;[3] and he thus established a precedent for

---

[1] *Vita Offæ Secundi.* MATT. PARIS. Ed. Watts. Lond. 1639, p. 16.

[2] " Ante contracta fœdera, promiserat idem Lambertus Karolo, quod si hostiliter ingressurus Britanniam adveniret, liberum in archiepiscopatum suum introitum inveniret, favorem et adjutorium."—*Ib.* 21.

[3] " Misit igitur ad Papam Adrianum hinc præsidentem, cui rex Offa, fuerat propter suam supereminentem sanctitatem amicissimus, nuncios discretos et facundos, honore atque favore condignos, *insuper donativis conferendis præmunitos. Noverat enim Rex desideria Romanorum.*" (*Ib.*) " Simul regnum Merciorum archiepiscopatu insignire affectans, epistolis ad Adrianum Papam, et *fortassis muneribus egit*, ut pallio Licetfeldensem episcopum, contra morem veterum efferret."—MALMESB. de Gest. PP. *Script. post Bedam*, f. 113.

stamping that mercenary character upon Rome, which Englishmen reprobated as her conspicuous infamy, even under the blindest period of their subserviency.[1] The recognition sought in a manner so discerning was not refused, a pall arriving, testifying papal approbation of Offa's wish to seat a metropolitan at Lichfield.[2]

From the vengeance of this imperious Mercian arose another injurious innovation upon English polity. Since the days of Augustine, no agent bearing a papal commission had ever set his foot on British ground;[3] but under a recent exigency, domestic approbation had been sought through Roman influence. Two legates soon appeared to improve the opening thus afforded by a selfish and shortsighted policy. Whether these Italians, Gregory, bishop of Ostia, and Theophylact, bishop of Todi, were invited expressly by Offa, is not known; he received them, however, most courteously,[4] and they

---

[1] " Datâ pecuniâ infinitâ, a sede Apostolicâ, *quæ nulli deest pecuniam largienti*, licentiam impetravit." (MATT. PAR. *Hist. Angl.* p. 155.) " Ut quid ad nos se extendit *Romanorum insatiata cupiditas?*" (*Ib.* 278.) Matthew Paris affords many similar passages.

[2] " Rex vester præcellentissimus Offa, suis literis testatus est, ut in id omnium vestrum una voluntas et unanima esset petitio, vel propter vastitatem terrarum vestrarum, et extensionem regni vestri, nec non et aliis quam plurimis causis et utilitatibus. Pro his præcipuè causis honorem Pallii Merciorum episcopo Dominus Adrianus Apostolicus direxit."— *Epist. Leonis III. Papæ ad Kenulphum Regem. Angl. Sacr.* i. 460.

[3] *Prœmium ad Adrianum Papam I. Conc. Calchuth.* SPELM. i. 293. WILK. i. 146.

[4] " Cum ingenti gaudio suscepit."—*Ib.* 292.

travelled over England as accredited agents of the papal see. Their mission led to a solemn ratification of the Mercian ecclesiastical arrangements. A council was holden at Calcuith,[1] in the presence of these foreigners, and there Lambert was driven to acquiesce under the mutilation of his archiepiscopal dignity,[2] Lichfield being placed over all the Mercian suffragans of Canterbury.[3] The legates also produced a body of canons, to which the council gave assent. It thus yielded a solemn affirmation to the faith professed in the first six general councils, condemned various heathen practices, and regulated several points of ecclesiastical discipline. From one of these canons it appears, that although tythes were customarily paid, yet such payment was popularly considered a discharge from alms-giving. The legates reprobate this view, enjoining men to surrender not only God's tenth, but also to seek his blessing by

---

[1] " Challock, or Chalk, in Kent."—Dr. INGRAM's *Index to the Sax. Chr.* The *Saxon Chronicle* writes this place *Cèalchythe*, and places the council in 785. There is, however, some difference of opinion both as to place and date. Spelman's date is 787.

[2] " Jambertus in synodo litigiosâ quæ apud Chealchite celebrata est, non modicam suæ parochiæ perdidit portionem." — GERVAS. *Act. PP. Cantuar. X. Script.* col. 1641.

[3] " Quorum hæc fuerunt nomina, *Denebertus*, Wigornensis episcopus, *Werenbertus*, Legecestrensis episcopus, *Edulphus*, Sidnacestrensis, *Wlpheardus*, Herefordensis ; et episcopi Orientalium Anglorum, *Alheardus*, Elmanensis, *Tidfrid*, Dommucensis."— (MALMESB. de Gest. RR. *Script. post Bedam*, f. 15.) After Offa's death, Canterbury recovered her ancient jurisdiction, Lichfield having been complimented by no more than a single pall. Her archiepiscopal honours ended about the year 800. (WHARTON. *Angl. Sacr.* i. 430.) See also *Bampton Lectures*, p. 175.

charitable gifts out of the nine portions remaining for themselves.[1]

When Offa felt his agitated and guilty life wearing fast away, he became, as is common with such men, a superstitious devotee. Some remains of mortality, discovered miraculously, as it was said, at Verulam,[2] were pronounced the relics of Alban, the British proto-martyr, and a splendid abbey was founded to receive them. Not contented with this royal display of penitence, Offa visited Rome, a suitor for papal approbation upon his extraordinary munificence. Being fully gratified, he settled upon the English college at Rome a penny from every family, not absolutely destitute, within his dominions, excepting tenants under his abbey of St. Alban's.[3] From this donation arose the payment of *Rome-scot,* or the *Rome-penny,* afterwards called *Peter-pence,* which continued to be remitted, with occasional interruptions, to the papal treasury, until the Reformation.

But although in Offa's days the national dignity was first impaired by a request of papal recognition for English acts, yet his reign exhibited Italian influence under a most signal and mortifying defeat. A policy deep, indeed, but fatal and infamous, was threatening to paganise the Church of Rome. She

---

[1] *Conc. Calc. can.* 17. SPELM. i. 298. WILK. i. 150.

[2] MATT. PAR. *Vita Offæ II.* p. 26.

[3] *Ib.* 29. Offa has been said to have followed here the liberality of Ina, who is the reported grantor of the same contribution from Wessex; but there is no sufficient authority for Ina's grant. — INETT. i. 220.

had gloriously ridden superior to all the storms of oriental heresy; but seduction from the east had been found irresistible, when inviting to defile her purity by a base alliance with Gentile superstition. This glaring departure from Scriptural authority, drew such reproaches from Israelitish and Mahometan revilers, as galled severely, because their seasoning was unpalatable truth. Stung by this just pungency of rebuke, the imperial court of Constantinople ordered images to be removed from churches. It was a wise provision against a temptation found an overmatch for unwary Christians; but it was unworthily requited by the loss of Italy. The Roman bishop, pandering to their inveterate affection for heathen vanities, encouraged his flock in raising the standard of rebellion. Thus he sowed the seeds that eventually ripened in the sovereignty of his see.[1] This dexterous patronage of a fascinating worship

---

[1] " Tum vero Leo tertius imperator, cum apertè invehi in pontificem (GREG. II.) non posset, edictum proponit, ut omnes qui sub imperio Romano essent, sanctorum omnium, martyrum, et angelorum statuas atque imagines e templis abraderent, et auferrent, tollendæ, ut ipse dicebat, idololatriæ causâ : qui vero secus fecisset, eum se pro hoste publico habiturum. Gregorius autem tantæ impietati non modo non obtemperat, verum etiam omnes catholicos admonet ne in tantum errorem timore vel edicto principis ullo modo dilabantur. Quâ cohortatione adeo certè animati sunt Italiæ populi, ut paulum abfuerit, quin sibi alium imperatorem deligerent. Quo minus autem id fieret, autoritate suâ obstare Gregorius annixus est. Ravennæ tamen tanta seditio orta est, cum alii imperatori, alii pontifici obtemperandum dicerent, ut in ipso tumultu Paulus hexarchus cum filio occideretur."—PLATINA *de Vit. PP.* 87.

was confirmed at Nice, under an artful empress, with a minor son, by synodical authority. Pope Adrian now fain would have won western acquiescence in Italian degeneracy, by transmitting the decrees of this popular synod to Charlemain. The Frankish conqueror communicated them to Offa, by whom they were laid before the Anglo-Saxon clergy: that body pondered them with strong surprise and rising indignation. It is true that England had long sought pleasure and improvement from intercourse with Rome: she had also looked upon the papacy with filial deference; nor was she any stranger to imitative arts in ornamenting churches. No habit or authority was however powerful enough to make her invest with a sacred character any of those heathen superstitions that she saw with pain yet clinging tenaciously to her ignorant population. The papal court was now therefore placed under cover of a ceremonious reserve: English ecclesiastics affected to overlook its connection with the second Council of Nice: they treated this assembly as merely oriental, and hence made no scruple of pronouncing its decrees a grievous disgrace to Christianity, *the worship of images being that which God's church altogether execrates.* As this language must have sounded in Roman ears very much like an ironical attack, and was in fact no less than an open defiance of papal authority, the Anglo-Saxon divines anxiously desired an advocate, whose powerful pen might repress the rising displeasure of their Italian friends. Alcuin, the most illustrious of contemporary scholars, undertook this delicate task, and his execution of it excited unqualified admiration.[1] The work produced by him has not been preserved with his venerated name, but it can hardly be any other than the celebrated *Caroline Books*. These were prepared as an authentic declaration of Charlemain's opinions and policy upon the worship of images, and they are among the most valuable monuments that time has spared.

All worship of images is represented in these important *books* as an insidious relic of paganism,[2] identical even in origin, heathen images at first being merely commemorative, but eventually adored by popular superstition.[3] Iconolatry among Christians is accordingly treated as a Satanic[4] device, by which

---

[1] For authorities, see *Bampton Lectures*, p. 170. The evidence of England's rejection of the deutero-Nicene decrees is so decisive, and confirmed so completely by the *Caroline Books*, that it is needless to examine some tales, once current, about Egwin, bishop of Worcester, and a council, said to have been holden in London early in the eighth century, for the establishment of image-worship. Particulars may be seen in INETT. i. p. 145.

[2] " Imaginum usus, qui a gentilium traditionibus inolevit."— *Opus. Illustriss. Car. Mag.* 1549. p. 253.

[3] " Simulacrorum itaque usus exortus est, cum ex desiderio mortuorum quorumlibet virorum fortium, aut regum, aut quarundam urbium conditorum, aut quarumlibet artium inventorum imagines vel effigies ab his qui eos dilexerant conderentur, ut posterorum vel dilectorum dolor haberet aliquod de imaginum contemplatione remedium : sed paulatim hunc errorem persuadentibus dæmonibus ita in posteros irrepsisse, ut quos illi pro solâ nominis memoriâ pingendos censuerant, successores deos existimarent atque colerent, et in his sibi dæmones sacrificare inlectos quosq; miseros percenserent."—*Ib.* 581.

[4] " Omnium malorum suasor, et e contrario omnium bonorum dissuasor, idcirco homines persuasit creaturas colere, ut eos a Creatore averteret."—*Ib.* 392.

triumphs gained in open field are likely to be lost within the city walls.[1] It is also directly charged with novelty,[2] and attempts to shelter it under Mosaical commands, for sculptured *cherubim* and the brazen serpent are sufficiently exposed:[3] nor are various nice distinctions overlooked, by which discerning advocates fain would obviate objections.[4] No use indeed whatever is conceded to images, or pictures, in religious worship, beyond mere ornament and commemoration: hence the lighting of tapers, or the burning of incense before them, honours paid to

---

[1] " Sollicitè ergo præcavendum est, et summâ industriâ procurandum, ne dum quidam nostrorum quasdam res ultra quam ordo exposcit sublimare adfectant, vetustissimi illius et cariosi erroris redivivi illis cineres convalescant, et victoriam quam in campo adepti sunt, intra urbis mænia perdant."—*Opus. Illustriss. Car. Mag.* 1549. p. 583.

[2] " Majores eorum qui eas non adoravêre."—(*Ib.* 277.) " Quæ non ad adorandum ab antiquis positæ fuerant."—*Ib.* 610.

[3] " Quantum ita sint absurditatis, quantæque dementiæ illi qui his sacratissimis, et summo honore dignis rebus, præcipiente Domino, a legislatore conditis, imagines æquiperare conantes, illarum adorationem his exemplis stabilire moliuntur, nec ferrea vox explicare, nec nostri sensus existimatio poterit indagare."—(*Ib.* 91.) " Nam dum æneus serpens, præcipiente Domino, a Moyse conditus, et in sublimi fuerit, non ut adoraretur positus, sed ut ad tempus ignitorum serpentium vriosis obsisteret morsibus, falsè spei ludificatione deluduntur, qui ita se manufactarum imaginum inspectione sanandos arbitrantur."—*Ib.* 114.

[4] " Non sunt imagines cruci æquiperandæ, non adorandæ, non colendæ."—(*Ib.* 248.) " Isti autem quasdem res insensatas adorandas, sive colendas esse absurdissimâ deliberatione percenseant."—(*Ib.* 360.) " Aliud namque est hominem salutationis officio, et humanitatis obsequio adorando salutare, aliud picturam diversorum colorum fucis conpaginatam, sine gressu, sine voce, vel cæteris sensibus, nescio quo cultu adorare."—(*Ib.* 67.) " Nec tenuiter quidem adorare."—*Ib.* 68.

them by a kiss, or a salutation of any kind, are all condemned as unauthorised and superstitious:[1] their utility, however, as monuments and decorations, is fully admitted. Former imperial orders, accordingly, to remove and destroy them are pointedly reprobated.

But although the *Caroline Books*, in their general tenor, are highly favourable to Protestant views of theology, Romanists may gather from them several useful testimonies. Their author's evident anxiety to spare the feelings of his Roman friends, keeps him studiously from collision with any but Oriental names. Allusion to the papal see is very rare, but always,

---

[1] " Hæc præterea et hujusmodi superstitiones quas se quidam putant ob amorem Dei facere; sicut hi qui ob sanctorum amorem imaginibus luminaria accendunt." (*Opus. Illustriss. Car. Mag.* 1549. p. 117.) " Nunc mentis oculo sollicite intuendum est, quantum, in supra memoratarum imaginum abolitione vel veneratione, filium error à parentum errore dissentiat. Illi eas mancipavêre crepitantibus ignibus: isti honorant odoriferis thymiamatibus." (*Ib.* 281.) " Osculor et adoro imagines. O mira confessio episcopi!" (*Ib.* 329.) " Imagines, quæ rationis expertes sunt, nec salutatione nec adoratione dignæ." (*Ib.* 228.) These passages are inconsistent with Dr. Lingard's representation, an echo of Baronius (*Antiquities of the Anglo-Saxon Church*. Fr. Transl. p. 351.), that the *execration* of England on receiving the deutero-Nicene decrees arose from the mistranslation of a sentence uttered by Constantine, bishop of Cyprus, which makes him say that he adored images as he did the Trinity. That he was so understood in the West is evident from the *Caroline Books* (p. 382); and, most probably, this exaggerated view of his meaning tended to increase the *execration* so embarrassing to well-informed Romanists. But it is evident, sufficiently from our ancient chroniclers, and abundantly from the *Caroline Books*, that no *single* sentiment aroused Anglo-Saxon abhorrence. The truth is, that in Britain, Gaul, and Germany, pictures and images were then looked upon merely as church-furniture; hence no more fit for religious notice of any kind than a bench or a door.—See COLLIER, *Eccl. Hist.* i. 141.

when occurring, profoundly respectful.[1] To relics, and apparently to the cross, outward acts of veneration are allowed, under alleged sanction from antiquity;[2] this concession, however, is inconsistent with principles advanced elsewhere, forbidding all adoration of senseless things.[3] Prayers, masses, and almsgiving for the dead, are also maintained; and the intercession of saints is represented as important.[4] Still, it does not appear that the author thought omniscience to reside any where but in the Godhead: he renders, therefore, very slender service to the principle of invoking departed spirits. His work, indeed,

---

[1] " Sancta Romana Ecclesia cæteris Ecclesiis à Domino prælata." (*Opus. Illustriss. Car. Mag.* 50.) " Sicut igitur cæteris discipulis apostoli, et apostolis omnibus Petrus eminet: ita nimirum cæteris sedibus apostolicæ, et apostolicis Romana eminere dinoscitur."—*Ib.* 51.

[2] " Honor itaque dignè sanctorum corporibus, reliquiis sive basilicis, exhibetur, et omnipotenti Deo et sanctis ejus manet acceptus." (*Ib.* 378.) " Restat ut nos sanctos in eorum corporibus, vel potius reliquiis corporum, seu etiam vestimentis veneremur, juxta antiquorum patrum traditionem." (*Ib.* 381.) From the whole of the twenty-seventh chapter in the second book, it seems reasonable to infer, that in the author's time some sort of outward veneration was paid to the cross, and that he approved it. He does not, however, expressly say so, nor from his rhetoric and mysticism can it be affirmed certainly that he meant so.

[3] " Res insensatas contra divinarum scripturarum instituta adorare."—*Ib.* 340.

[4] " Saluberrimus namque à sanctis patribus Ecclesiis traditus usus est pro defunctorum spiritibus Dominum deprecari." (*Ib.* 278) " Nos nostris quietem exposcimus per missarum solennia. Nos nostris secundum ecclesiasticum usum per orationum et eleemosynarum instantiam deposcimus veniam." (*Ib.* 279.) " Revertantur ad Dominum, et per sanctorum intercessionem ab eo sanitatem se accepturos credant."—*Ib.* 117.

is chiefly valuable as a decisive testimony upon one important question, as a record of contemporary theological principles, and as an evidence that the passage was very gradual from primitive simplicity to a religion extensively destitute of Scriptural authentication.

Another interesting monument of contemporary theological principles, is the *Penitential* of Egbert. From this work plainly appears, what is also evident from a canon enacted at Cloveshoo, that penances were merely regarded as compensatory medicines for sins.[1] Hence, from ecclesiastics was expected an accurate acquaintance with all the niceties of penitential discipline, as an indispensable professional qualification. Egbert's provision for supplying his illiterate clergy with this information, prescribes penitential medicine for many cases most grossly obscene. Such loathsome pictures reveal a depraved, brutish age; and they could hardly fall under clerical scrutiny without communicating or confirming a taint of impurity. This compilation also reminds us of barbarous times, in the insecurity of life and liability to personal outrage which it strikingly displays: it is however plain, that ecclesiastical authorities were

---

[1] "*How can he preach sound faith, or give a knowledge of the word, or discreetly enjoin penance to others, who has not earnestly bent his mind to these studies?* Here you see for what purpose men in this age confessed their sins to the priest, viz. because he alone knew what penance was to be enjoined for every sort and degree of sin, not in order to obtain absolution. Petit's *Collections*, published with Theodore's *Penitential*, are full of proof as to this point."—JOHNSON's *Collection. Canons at Cloveshoo*, 747.

anxious to stem this torrent of violence. The *Penitential* provides penance even for justifiable homicide,[1] and for false oaths ignorantly taken;[2] but the murder of a priest or monk is more severely visited than that of another man.[3] Such a protection for the clerical order was not perhaps unfair, when its members were the only persons of superior condition likely to be found unarmed. Upon the whole, this system of clerical police is but imperfectly calculated for benefitting public morals, because opportunities are afforded for mitigating the rigour of fasting by psalm-singing and alms-giving.[4] This latter substitute was naturally very acceptable to wealthy sinners, and such, accordingly, seem even to have given alms in advance as it were of some projected iniquity.[5]

---

[1] "*If a man slay another in a public fight, or from necessity, where he is defending his lord's property, let him fast forty nights.*" JOHNSON's *Collection*, b 1. can. 24. WILKINS, 1. 120.—*Author's MS. Transl.*

[2] "*He who is led on to an oath, and knows nothing therein but right, and he so swears with the other men, and afterwards knows that it was false, let him fast three lawful fasts.*"—*Ib.* can. 34. WILK. 1. 122.

[3] "*Whatever man slays a priest or a monk, that is the bishop's decision, whether he give up weapons and go into a monastery, or he fast seven winters.*—*Ib.* can. 23. WILK. 1. 120

[4] "*A man should do penance for capital sins a year or two on bread and water, and for less sins a week or a month. But this is with some men a very difficult thing and painful; wherefore we will teach with what things he may redeem it who cannot keep this fast: that is, he shall with psalm-singing and with alms-deeds, make satisfaction a very long space.*"—*Ib.* can. 2. WILK. 1. 115.

[5] " *Let not alms be given according to the new-invented conceit of men's own will, grown into a custom, dangerous to many,*

Of religious peculiarities incidentally discovered in Egbert's *Penitential,* no one is more striking than Anglo-Saxon reception of that compromise with Jewish prejudices which apostolical authority established early in the Christian era. Our forefathers were enjoined a rigorous abstinence *from blood, and from things strangled:*[1] nor did they disregard Levitical distinctions between the clean and unclean among animals.[2] They seem to have been taught,

---

for the making an abatement or commutation of the satisfactory fastings and other expiatory works enjoined to a man by a priest of God. Monsieur Petit observes, that this canon does not condemn the practice of giving alms by way of penance, with a purpose of leaving sin, but giving them in hopes to purchase license to sin." —JOHNSON, *ut supra.*

[1] Acts, xv. 29. This text is cited in the thirty-eighth canon as a reason for the remarkable prohibitions occurring in that canon, and in some of those connected with it. In these, fish is allowed to be eaten, though met with dead, as being different from land animals. Honey might not be eaten if the bees killed in it remained a whole night. Fowls, and other animals suffocated in nets, were not to be eaten, even although a hawk should have bitten them. Domestic poultry that had drunk up human blood were not to be eaten until after an interval of three months A man knowingly eating blood in his food was to fast seven days; any one doing this ignorantly was to fast three days, or sing the Psalter. Such provisions naturally made scrupulous persons uneasy whenever they swallowed blood accidentally. Hence an assurance is given that swallowing one's own blood in spittle incurs no danger. —*Can.* 40. WILK. I. 124.

[2] Especially the weasel and the mouse were considered unclean. A layman giving to another even water in which one of these animals had been drowned was to fast three nights; a minster-man was to sing three hundred psalms. A large quantity of water in which one of these animals had been drowned was not to be used until sprinkled with holy water. Hare, however, it is expressly said, might be eaten (can. 38); and so, plainly, might swine's flesh

however, nothing decisive, in Egbert's time, upon the value to departed souls of services intended for their benefit by survivors; it is expressly said, that fasting for such purposes is of uncertain efficacy :[1] a declaration rendering it probable, that masses and almsgiving for the dead also occasioned hesitating speculation. It is plain, likewise, that modern Romish purgatorial doctrines were then only in their infancy at furthest. Men are enjoined to confession and penance, lest they should be consigned hereafter to eternal torments.[2] A divine would hardly have used such language who believed in the sufficiency of confession alone upon earth, and the safety of deferring satisfaction for purgatory.

(can. 40); yet, it might seem from can. 39, the pig was thought to labour under some sort of uncleanness.—WILK. 123, 124. *Levit.* xi. 29.

[1] *He who fasteth for a dead man, it is a consolation to himself, if it helpeth not the dead. God alone wot if his dead are benefitted.*—JOHNSON's *Collection,* can. 41. WILK. I. 124.

[2] *It is better to all men that they amend* (bete) *their sins here than that they should continue in eternal torments* —B. ii can. 5. WILK. I. 126.

CHAPTER III.

FROM ALCUIN TO DUNSTAN.

804 — 928.

DARKNESS OF THE AGE SUCCEEDING ALCUIN — COUNCIL OF CELYCHYTH — INCIDENTAL EVIDENCE AGAINST TRANSUBSTANTIATION — SECULAR MONASTERIES — NOTICE OF THE ANCIENT BRITISH CHURCH — ETHELWULF — HIS DECIMATION — HIS LIBERALITY TO ROME — ALFRED'S VISITS TO ROME — HIS EARLY IGNORANCE OF LETTERS — HIS ACCESSION TO THE THRONE — HIS CONCEALMENT IN THE ISLE OF ATHELNEY — HIS VICTORY OVER THE DANES — HIS LITERARY WORKS — HIS PHYSICAL INFIRMITIES — HIS ECONOMY OF TIME AND OF MONEY — HIS ECCLESIASTICAL LAWS — HIS TRUNCATED DECALOGUE — HIS RELIGIOUS BELIEF — ERIGENA — ALLEGED PAPAL EXCOMMUNICATION UNDER EDWARD THE ELDER — ATHELSTAN — COUNCIL OF GRATELEY — DOCTRINES.

THE era between Theodore and Alcuin was that of Anglo-Saxon intellectual eminence. Modern times, drawing invidious comparisons, may charge it with ignorance and barbarism: it justly held a very different estimation among contemporaries. The successive appearances of Aldhelm, Bede, Egbert, and Alcuin, bore ample testimony to admiring Europe, that the able monk of Tarsus, and Adrian, his no less gifted friend, had requited nobly their adopted country. The literary fame of ancient England reached its height when Charlemain listened eagerly to Alcuin; and some of the church's brightest luminaries proudly owned him for a master.¹ He proved, however, the immediate precursor to a dark and stormy night of ignorance. In political institutions his native land soon attained, indeed, a maturity that he had never witnessed. No longer did unceasing struggles for ascendancy, among several petty princes, find only an occasional respite in the general acknowledgment of a *bretwalda*. The eighth and last bearer of that title,² Egbert, king of Wessex, contrived to render its prerogatives hereditary in his family, thus laying the foundations of a national monarchy. But England had already smarted under a ruinous counterpoise to any domestic advantage. Anglo-Saxon cruelty and injustice to the British race were frightfully retaliated by hordes of pirates, issuing from their own ancestral home. A succession of Danish marauders, fired with hope of abundant booty, condemned several generations to a constant sense of insecurity, and the frequent endurance of bitterest suffering. In a country so harassed, every peaceful art necessarily languished, especially literature; both fanaticism and cupidity directing the ferocious Northmen to monasteries, where alone books were stored, and scholars found a home.³

---

[1] See *Bampton Lectures*, 375, 377.

[2] *Sax. Chr.* 88. Egbert's pre-eminence is there assigned to the year 827, when, by the conquest of Mercia, he became sovereign, or chief of all England, south of the Humber.

[3] " The cruelties exercised by Charlemain against the Pagan Saxons in Nordalbingia had aroused the resentment of their neighbours, and fellow-worshippers of Odin, in Jutland, and the isles of the Danish archipelago. Their wild spirit of adventure, and lust of plunder, were now wrought up to a pitch of frenzy by religious

A period of such absorbing public uneasiness can afford but few materials for ecclesiastical history, though it is obviously favourable to the stealthy progress of religious corruptions. Earlier years of the ninth century are naturally identified in principles with a happier age. A council holden at Celychyth, in 816, under Wulfred, archbishop of Canterbury, in presence of Kemulf, king of Mercia, and his more distinguished laity, makes, however, a slight advance towards Roman innovation. It enjoins, on the consecration of a church, that the saint in whose honour it was built should be commemorated on its walls :[1] but the canon is so obscurely worded as to render it uncertain whether a picture or an inscription was intended; probably the question was designedly left open for individual discretion. Even, however, if a picture were exclusively the object, it is enjoined in a spirit very different from that grovelling superstition and arrogant intolerance which Nice lately

---

fanaticism. Hence the ravages of the Northmen were directed with peculiar fury against the monasteries and churches in France and England, and against the priests of a religion rendered doubly hateful to them in consequence of the attempts made by the successors of Charlemain in the empire to force it upon them as a badge of national slavery."—WHEATON's *History of the Northmen.* Lond. 1831. p. 146.

[1] " Seu etiam præcipimus unicuique episcopo, ut habeat depictum in pariete oratorii, aut in tabula, vel etiam in altaribus, quibus sanctis sint utraque dedicata." (*Syn. Celych.* cap. 2. SPELM. i. 328. WILK. i. 169.) Johnson thus renders this clause: " And we charge every bishop, that he have it written on the walls of the oratory, or in a table, or also on the altars, to what saints both of them are dedicated."

saw displayed upon such questions.[1] Deposition had been also there awarded against any bishop who should consecrate a church without relics.[2] In case, however, these could not readily be gotten, the council of Celychyth expressly sanctioned such a consecration. Under this deficiency, prelates were to deposit the sacramental elements alone in a coffer, ordinarily containing both them and relics.[3]

Attention has been drawn to this permission, as an incidental testimony against transubstantiation, the great distinctive doctrine of modern Romanism:[4] nor, indeed, can discerning believers in that principle fail of regretting, at the very least, that an assumed incarnation of the Deity should be denied even a level with relics of the saintly dead. In this canon, however, as in many other ancient authorities alleged against the corporal presence, expressions are employed which qualify the dissatisfaction of Romish minds. The consecrated elements are allowed to be

---

[1] " Ei, qui non salutat *sanctas* imagines, anathema."—*Conc. Nicæn. II. Actio* 8. LABB. et COSS. vii. 591.

[2] *Ib.* can. vii. col. 603.

[3] " Postea eucharistia, quæ ab episcopo per idem ministerium consecratur, cum aliis reliquiis, condatur in capsulâ, ac servetur in eadem basilica. Et si alias reliquias intimare non potest, tam hoc maximè proficere potest."—SPELM. WILK. *ut supra.*

[4] " Much less would they have spoken of the holy elements as an inferior sort of relics, and have given them place accordingly, if they had believed that the elements which they appointed to be deposited in a chest among their relics was the same body that was glorified in heaven." (INETT. *Hist. Engl. Ch.* i. 256.) " Here the eucharistical symbols are set on a level with the relics of saints, and scarce that neither."—JOHNSON, *in loc.*

sufficient of themselves, *because they are the body and blood of Christ.* For speaking thus, the synod of Celychyth undoubtedly could plead antiquity. The reason why such precedents abound in early monuments of theology may readily be conjectured : primitive worshippers received the eucharist constantly, even daily. Scoffing and thoughtless observers must have often represented this as a superstitious habit, adopted by a peculiar society, of taking mere bread and wine together. Now, no considerable number of preachers and writers ever seek to correct a prevailing error, without supplying many rhetorial expressions, obviously favourable to misinterpretation in a subsequent age : such a fate has naturally attended speculations upon the holy supper. Believers in transubstantiation would fain establish its title to implicit faith upon many passages of the fathers, and of other ancient ecclesiastical remains : those who deny that doctrine entrench themselves behind plain declarations, the general tenor, and the expressive silence of the very same monuments. The last proof is little needed by Protestant controversialists, when appealing to Anglo-Saxon evidence. The great eucharistic peculiarity of modern Rome attracted general attention in ante-Norman times ; hence the luminaries of ancient England were called eventually to speak decidedly upon this interesting question, and their voice has inflicted a vital injury upon belief in the corporal presence. Whenever their testimony, therefore, has, as at Celychyth, an aspect of some ambiguity, it may, notwithstanding, be fairly cited to disprove the eucharistic opinions now maintained by Rome.

Another canon[1] brings under observation a point in theological antiquities, little generally understood. Monachism has been for ages an immense organised association, marshalling and controlling certain orders of ecclesiastics and female recluses: it is natural to regard it under the same aspect from the first. Such a view is, however, inaccurate. Many of the earlier monks and nuns were merely the stricter sort of religious professors, identical, substantially, with similar devotees variously designated among Christians. For the reception of such ascetics opulent individuals often opened their houses, assuming themselves the character of abbot or abbess. These lay or secular monasteries[2] naturally offered considerable impediments to the exercise of ecclesiastical authority; they were, besides, loudly taxed with immorality. Another objection to them were the claims of their superiors to immunities conferred ordinarily upon monastic foundations. Their enemies, accordingly, represented them as little better than receptacles of hypocritical profligacy, established by crafty proprietors, to escape from the liabilities of other men. Severe as were these representations, and no doubt often unjust, sufficient truth was in them to bring

---

[1] *Syn. ap. Celych.* can. 8. SPELM. I. 329. WILK. i. 170.

[2] These monasteries are thus mentioned (JOHNSON's *Transl.*) by the council of Cloveshoo, A.D. 747: "It is necessary for bishops to go to the monasteries (if they can be called monasteries, which in these times cannot be in any wise reformed according to the model of Christianity, by reason of the violence of tyrannical covetousness,) which are, we know not how, possessed by secular men, not by divine law, but by presumptuous human invention."— *Conc. Cloves.* can. 5 SPELM. I. 247 WILK. i. 95.

discredit on the system: hence public opinion powerfully seconded arguments upon the necessity of suppressing religious establishments in private houses: monks and nuns, it was extensively admitted, ought hereafter to reside only in abodes inalienably devoted to them by fixed endowments, and regularly under ecclesiastical discipline. The synod of Celychyth provided for these objects, and thus laid the foundation of that discord upon monastic questions which long agitated England. Among great numbers of ostentatious professors, charges of sanctimonious licentiousness could always be successfully retorted; advocates for secular monasteries might also plausibly designate objections urged by their opponents as a mere veil for priestly ambition. Thus, when Italian monachism sought public favour, at a later period, it was encountered by inveterate habits of commenting invidiously on monastic pretensions.[1]

It may be collected also from one of these canons,[2]

---

[1] INETT, *Hist. Engl. Ch.* 1. 261.

[2] " 5. That none of Scottish extract (*de genere Scottorum*) be permitted to usurp to himself the sacred ministry in any one's diocess; nor let it be allowed to such an one to touch any thing which belongs to those of the holy order, nor to receive any thing from them in baptism, or in the celebration of the mass, or that they administer the eucharist to the people, because we are not certain how, or by whom, they were ordained. We know how 'tis enjoined in the canons, that no bishop or presbyter invade the parish (*parochiam, i. e.* diocess) of another without the bishop's consent. So much the rather should we refuse to receive the sacred ministrations from other nations, where there is no such order as 'that of metropolitans, nor any regard paid to other (orders.") JOHNSON's *Transl.* SPELM. 1. 329. WILK. 1. 170.) The last clause is obscure, standing thus: *Cum quibus nullus*

that ancient Britain had not yet lost her influence upon the people indebted so largely to her Christian zeal. Europe is often loosely viewed as under papal vassalage, from the period of her conversion down to that of the Reformation. On a closer inspection, however, appear very early traces of the faithful, unconnected with Rome, in most western countries: in England, such professors assume a foremost rank among the national apostles. Nor, although depressed by a long course of unfavourable events, was the Romish party able to look upon them without jealousy, even after more than two centuries from Augustine's arrival. The synod of Celychyth, accordingly, strictly forbids any of the Scottish race to minister in England: uncertainty as to the ordination of such ministers is assigned as the reason for this prohibition, their native country being without metropolitans.[1] This objection would wear the semblance of a reasonable precaution, had any opening been left at Celychyth for verifying the ministerial character of divines from Scotland; but the prohibition is absolute, as if intended for crushing a rival party. Posterity may store it among evidences against Romish claims to antiquity and universality.

It was fortunate for the progress of papal ascen-

---

ordo metropolitanis, nec honor aliis habeatur. Johnson reads *metropolitanus*, and supplies *orders* to explain the last word.

[1] " It is well known there was no metropolitan in Scotland till after the middle of the fifteenth century, when St. Andrews was created into an archbishopric. Nay, their bishops had no distinct diocesses before the middle of the eleventh century."—JOHNSON, *in loc.*

dancy, that England had scarcely taken the form of a single state before her sceptre devolved upon a sovereign, called into active life from a cloister, and fitted only for one. Egbert's early prosperity was alloyed in his declining age by domestic disappointment: an elder son preceded him to the tomb,[1] and his later hopes were consequently centred in Ethelwulf, a younger child. One of this prince's instructors was Swithin, bishop of Winchester,[2] whose name is yet familiar to English tongues, from its proverbial association with rainy summers. By the generations immediately succeeding his own, the memory of this illustrious prelate was profoundly venerated: eagerly did sickly pilgrims crowd around his tomb, and implicitly did they rely upon leaving their maladies behind. This posthumous reputation evidences a high contemporary character; but it is remarkable that admirers, even before the Norman conquest, vainly sought authentic particulars of Swithin's life:[3]

---

[1] TURNER, *Hist. Angl. Sax.* 1. 486. note. On the authority of an ancient fragment preserved by Leland. Upon no other principle, indeed, is it easy to account for Ethelwulf's monastic education and habits.

[2] RUDBORNE, *Hist. Mag. Wint. Angl. Sacr.* 1. 199.

[3] Þe ne funðon on bocum hu ꝼe biꞃceop leoꝼoðe on ðyꞃne populðe æn þan þe he ȝepenðe to Cꞃiꞃte. (*Hom. in S. Swith.* Brit. Mus. MSS. COTTON. JULIUS. E. 7. f. 94.) *We have not found in books how the bishop lived in this world ere that he departed to Christ.* This omission of Swithin's contemporaries as to his biography, is thus blamed as a mark of their carelessness. Ðæt ƿæꞃ þæꞃa ȝymeleaꞃt þe on liꝼe hine cuþon ꝥ hi nolðon aꝼꝼitan hiꞃ peoꝼc ⁊ ꝺꞃohtnunȝe þam topenðum mannum ðe hiꞃ mihte ne cuðon. *It was their carelessness who knew him in life, that they would not write his works and conversation for future men who knew not his excellence.* (*Ib.*)

his character of saintship is, however, sufficient attestation that his tastes were monastic and Roman. Under such an instructor, Ethelwulf, a prince apparently of peaceful, inactive habits, and of moderate capacity, could hardly fail of imbibing a partiality for monachism and the papacy. So decidedly religious, indeed, was his destination at one time, that, not contented with becoming a monk, he appears to have been also ordained sub-deacon:[1] nay, it has been represented, that he was actually appointed to the see of Winchester.[2] This, however, wants confirmation, though it is not unlikely that Egbert might have intended him for that see, during the lifetime of his elder brother: but that young man's premature decease raised Ethelwulf to higher prospects, though to such as were, probably, far less congenial to his natural disposition. Instead of the cloister or the mitre, he was urgently taxed for superior qualities, both as a statesman and a soldier.

In such endowments he discovered all that defi-

Again, Elfric ingenuously confesses that Swithin's known claims upon the veneration of posterity rested entirely upon his posthumous fame as a worker of miracles. Nu næɼ uɼ hıɼ lıf cuð ɼpa ɼpa pe æɲ cpæðon· butan þ he pæɼ bebynʒeð æt hıɼ hıɼceop-ɼtole be peɼtan þæɲe cyncan· ⁊ oɼeɲ-poɲht ɼyððan· oð ðæt hıɼ punðɲa ʒeɼputeloðon hıɼ ʒeɼælða mıð Loðe. (*Ib.* f. 95.) *Now, his life is not known to us, even as we ere said, but that he was buried at his bishop's see, on the west of the church, and overwrought* (enshrined) *afterwards, when his wonders manifested his happiness with God.*

[1] RUDBORNE, *ut supra*.

[2] Diceto speaks of Ethelwulf's episcopate as if he did not credit it. "Hic in juventute, *sicut legitur*, fuit episcopus Wintoniæ." (*X. Script.* 450.) Bromton speaks positively. "In primævâ ætate episcopus Wyntoniensis factus fuerat."—*Ib.* 802.

ciency which was naturally to be expected from a peaceful spirit with an ecclesiastical education. Unhappily, this unfitness was more than ordinarily injurious to his native country. Nothing, however, could weaken the force of his religious impressions. An agitated reign, accordingly, made him anxious to secure the favour of heaven by a conspicuous display of piety. The most remarkable instance, perhaps, of this anxiety has been attributed to the advice of St. Swithin, and has been often represented as the charter under which England became legally subject to tythes.[1] This interpretation, however, appearing hardly warranted by the document as now extant, has generally lost ground.[2] Ethelwulf seems, indeed,

---

[1] This view is, accordingly, adopted by Hume; and from the popularity of his history passes, probably, among the generality of readers, as indisputable. Had he found, however, in ecclesiastical questions, a call for thought and inquiry, instead of an irresistible temptation to scoff and sneer, it is likely that he would have entertained a different opinion of Ethelwulf's donation. Rudborne attributes this act of Ethelwulf to St. Swithin.—*Hist. Maj. Winton. Angl. Sacr.* i. 200.

[2] Ingulf of Croyland, William of Malmesbury, and Matthew of Westminster, have recorded this document; but their versions of it do not exactly agree. Their discrepancies are stated by Mr. Turner in a note. (*Hist. Angl. Sax.* i. 494.) The document, after reciting the miseries of Danish invasion, sets forth that the king, with a council of his bishops and chiefs, has granted " some hereditary portion of land to all degrees before possessing it, whether male or female servants of God, serving him, or poor laymen; always the tenth mansion: where that may be the least, then the tenth of all goods." (TURNER's *Transl.*) *Aliquam portionem terrarum hæreditariam antea possidentibus omnibus gradibus, sive famulis et famulabus Dei, Deo servientibus, sive laicis miseris; semper decimam mansionem: ubi minimum sit, tum decimam par-*

merely to have obtained legislative authority for dedicating to religious uses, free from all secular bur-

---

tem omnium bonorum. (INGULF, *Script. post Bedam,* 491.) Mr. Turner well observes that "*famulis et famulabus Dei,*" mean usually monks and nuns."

The recent historian of the *Anglo-Saxon Commonwealth* has thus treated this memorable grant :— " It has been considered as the legislative enactment by which the lands were first subjected to the payment of tythes to the clergy. But the right of the church had already been recognised in the most unequivocal manner; and the grants, many of which are extant, do not afford any voucher for the opinion which Selden erroneously entertained. The general statute expressly points out a decimation of the land by metes and bounds, to be held free from all secular services, exonerated from all tributes to the crown, and from the charges to which, of common right, all lands were subjected, namely, the *fyrd,* the *brycg-bote,* and the *burh-bote;* and this exemption was made to the end that the grantees might sedulously, and without intermission, offer up their prayers for the souls of Ethelwulf, and of those who had concurred in the donation: the land was, therefore, to be held in *frank-almoign.* Proceeding upon his general enactment, Ethelwulf carried his intentions into effect by the specific endowments, which he conferred upon the various churches and their ministers, of lands, which may be termed ecclesiastical benefices, rendering no service except at the altar. By some historians the grant has been construed into an enfranchisement of all the lands which the church then possessed; an interpretation not altogether void of probability; yet, if adopted, we must admit that the exoneration only affected the lands which the church possessed when the decree was made."—PALGRAVE. I. 159.

" A Frankish *mansus* was the allotment sufficient to maintain a family."—*Ib.* II. 448.

The contemporary authority of Asser might lead us to consider, that Ethelwulf's grant was merely one of immunities, and was co-extensive with his dominions. " Venerabilis rex decimam totius regni suî partem ab omni regali servitio et tributo liberavit." (*De Reb. Gest. Alfred.* Oxon. 1722. p. 8.) Ethelwerd, almost a contemporary, is more obscure. " In eodem anno decu-

thens, a tenth of the royal domains.[1] He was then contemplating, probably, an extensive foundation of monasteries, and other pious establishments. Ecclesiastical rights to tythes of produce had been acknowledged as indefeasible long before his time.

The religious King of Wessex appears to have

---

mavit Athulf rex de omni possessione suâ in partem Domini, et in universo regimine suî principatûs sic constituit." (*Script. post Bedam*, 478.) The *Saxon Chronicle* (Dr. INGRAM's *Transl.* 94) says, " King Ethelwulf registered (ʒebocuþe *booked*) a tenth of his land over all his kingdom, for the honour of God and for his own everlasting salvation." From this it seems reasonable to infer, that he formally surrendered, by means of regular written instruments, a tenth of all the crown lands for pious uses. Such an alienation was not valid without the consent of his *witena-gemot*, and, probably, the act, giving this consent, is the document found in states more or less complete by some of our ancient chroniclers, and yet preserved in their works.

[1] This is distinctly stated by an anonymous annalist of the church of Winchester, printed in the *Monasticon* (i 32), " Rex Ethulfus, a Româ reversus, totam terram de dominio suo decimavit, et decimam quamq; hidam contulit conventualibus ecclesiis, per regionem." The following is Rudborne's view of this grant : " Ecclesias regni suî ab omni tributo regali liberavit. Decimam *rerum suarum* domino obtulit." (*Angl. Sacr.* i. 202.) Ethelred says of Ethelwulf, " Eleemosynis sanè sic operam dabat, ut totam terram suam pro Christo decimaret, et partem decimam per ecclesias monasteriaque divideret." (*X. Script.* 351.) These words might reasonably lead to a belief that Ethelwulf set apart a tenth of the crown lands as endowments for monasteries, and glebes for parochial churches. Bromton also represents Ethelwulf's donation as consisting in land, not in tythes of produce; but his words might be so taken as to give the grant an appearance strictly eleemosynary. " Iste Rex Ethelwolfus contulit Deo et ecclesiæ sanctæ decimam hidam terræ totius Westsaxiæ, ab omnibus servicius secularibus liberam et quietam, ad pascendum et vestiendum pauperes debiles et infirmos."—*X. Script* 802.

made the donation which has attracted so much attention, immediately before he undertook a journey to Rome.[1] During a year's residence in that celebrated city he displayed abundant liberality. The English school there, founded by Ina, had been destroyed by fire in the preceding year. Ethelwulf rebuilt it, and provided for its permanent utility, by renewing or confirming the grant of Peter-pence. He gratified, also, the Pope, by splendid presents and a pension of a hundred mancuses. Besides which, he promised two annual sums of the same amount, for supplying with lights the churches of St. Peter and St. Paul.[2] Before he

---

[1] Bromton (*ut supra*) places Ethelwulf's Roman journey after his decimation; as also do Asser, Ethelwerd, and the *Saxon Chronicle*. Ingulf, Huntingdon, and others, place the decimation after the journey to Rome. The year 854 is assigned to Ethelwulf's act by the *Saxon Chronicle*, the following year by Asser, and most probably by Ethelwerd; but that author's chronology is marginal.

[2] ASSER, 13. MALMESB. *Script. post Bed.* 22. RUDBORNE. *Angl. Sacr.* i. 202. Both Malmesbury and Rudborne state Ethelwulf's benefactions in *marks*. *Mancus* the term used by Asser, however, was the name ordinarily given among the Anglo-Saxons to their gold currency of less value than a pound. Mr. Turner (*Hist. Angl. Sax.* ii. 495) coincides in an opinion of older writers that the *mancus*, like the *pound*, was the name of no coin, but only of a certain quantity of uncoined metal. If it were otherwise, indeed, some Saxon gold coins could hardly fail of being yet found. The *mancus* was equal to thirty pennies, each worth a modern threepence; it amounted, therefore, to seven shillings and sixpence of our present money. (*Notes to the Will of King Alfred.* Lond. 1828. p. 31. *De Nummis Saxonum Dissert. præfix. Alfr. M. Vit* A.D. JOH. SPELMAN. Oxon. 1678.) In a note to this latter work (p. 6) is a citation from the contemporary authority of Anastasius *Bibliothecarius*, detailing Ethelwulf's splendid presents on his visit to Rome.

shewed himself, however, again among his own subjects, he had effectually provided for lessening their admiration of all this pious munificence. On his way through France, he became enamoured of Judith, daughter to Charles the Bald; and his people were disgusted in seeing their sovereign, who left them an elderly widower upon a pilgrimage, return home a bridegroom, with a young and handsome wife. Popular discontent was heightened by Ethelwulf's determination to have Judith crowned, and invested with all the honours of royalty. The Anglo-Saxons had long denied such privileges to the wives of their princes, and an intention to revive them came with a grace peculiarly ill from one who had abandoned a cloister for a throne.[1] The king's absence had given rise to a conspiracy; the uxorious weakness displayed on his return rendered it irresistible; and he was compelled to resign the chief of his dominions to Ethelbald, his eldest son. He survived this humiliating compromise only two years.[2]

---

[1] Asser says, that the West-Saxons had been used to deny the wives of their sovereigns a seat on the throne, or any other designation than that of the *king's spouse*. This usage, arising from the gross misconduct of a former queen, Ethelwulf appears to have been peremptory in breaking through, on his marriage with Judith, refusing to hear any expostulation to the contrary. " Juthittam, Karoli regis filiam, quam a patre suo acceperat, juxta se in regali solio, sine aliquâ suorum nobilium controversiâ et odio, usque ad obitum vitæ suæ, contra perversam illius gentis consuetudinem, sedere imperavit." (*De Reb. Gest. Alfr.* 10.) The coronation service used for Judith is still extant.—SPELM. *Alfr. M. Vita.* p. 8. note.

[2] ASSER, 8, 12. MALMESB. *Script. post Bed.* 22. The *Saxon Chronicle* says that Ethelwulf reigned eighteen years and a half.

Ethelwulf took with him to Rome his youngest and favourite son, eventually and permanently known as Alfred the Great. The royal child, now seven years old, had already visited Europe's ancient and illustrious capital: his father's fond partiality having sent him thither, with a large and splendid retinue, two years before. Upon this former visit Alfred was welcomed by the Pope with some distinguished compliment; but posterity has found it far from easy to decide exactly upon its nature. Asser, Alfred's personal friend, literally, but rather darkly, states, that Leo, then pontiff, *anointed him for king; and, taking him to himself as a son of his adoption, confirmed him.*[1] The *Saxon Chronicle* here, probably, written by Plegmund,[2] another of his personal

---

His death, however, cannot have happened much before the close of 857, and his father Egbert died in 836. His name, meaning *noble aid*, is variously spelt, and often appears in the contracted form of *Athulphus*; it is evidently the *Adolphus* of later times.

[1] " Quo tempore dominus Leo quartus apostolicæ sedi præerat, qui præfatum infantem Alfredum oppido ordinans unxit in regem, et in filium adoptionis sibimet accipiens confirmavit."—ASSER, 7. See also *Bampt. Lect.* 246.

[2] " The first chronicles were, perhaps, those of Kent, or Wessex; which seem to have been regularly continued, at intervals, by the archbishops of Canterbury, or by their direction, at least, as far as the year 1001, or even 1070; for the Benet MS., which some call the Plegmund MS., ends in the latter year; the rest being in Latin. From internal evidence, indeed, of an indirect nature, there is great reason to presume that Archbishop Plegmund transcribed, or superintended this very copy of the Saxon annals to the year 891, the year in which he came to the see; inserting, both before and after this date, to the time of his death in 923, such additional materials as he was well qualified to furnish from his high station and learning, and the confidential inter-

friends, uses nearly the same words. From such language it is, at least, undeniable, that more than a single compliment was received by the infant Alfred. Nor does it seem hardly less doubtful, that one of the ceremonies by which Leo greeted him was intended as a solemn destination to his country's throne. Kingly power, among the Anglo-Saxons, though strictly confined within a royal *caste*, was not equally limited by primogeniture. Ethelwulf might argue, therefore, that papal sanction would afford authority sufficient for naming his favourite child as the successor to himself. From their acquaintance with such an intention, perhaps, arose the undutiful conduct of his elder sons, and the strong party that espoused their cause.[1] Much posi-

---

course which he enjoyed in the court of King Alfred. The total omission of his own name, except by another hand, affords indirect evidence of some importance in support of this conjecture."— DR. INGRAM's *Preface to the Saxon Chr.* xii.

[1] " Ethelwulf's visit to Rome without having resigned his crown, may have begun the discontent. Two of the preceding sovereigns of Wessex, who had taken this step, Cadwalla and Ina, had first abdicated the throne, though Offa retained it during his journey. But Ethelwulf had been in the church, and had not the warlike character of Offa to impress or satisfy his thanes and earls." (TURNER, *Hist. Angl. Sax.* i. 497.) Asser (8) darkly makes the conspiracy against Ethelwulf to originate in *quâdam infamiâ*. The *Saxon Chronicle* makes no mention of it, nor does Ethelwerd. Under this dearth of direct information, it may, perhaps, allowably be conjectured, that one cause of Ethelwulf's discredit among his people, was his known partiality to the infant Alfred, to the prejudice of his elder sons. It was, most probably, no secret that the pope had already anointed that favourite child; and it might be represented that his doting father had now sought the consummation of his injustice in taking him personally to the most venerated of spiritual authorities.

tive improvement could hardly be reaped by any child of five years old, or of seven, from foreign travel. But a reminiscence, delightful, though indistinct, must have been permanently established in the mind of an Alfred from two such journeys as his. He could hardly fail, through life, of associating with Rome and the papacy all that was gratifying, venerable, polished, and magnificent. A clue is thus found for understanding a weak and sinful compliance which mortifies a Protestant inquirer into the history of this admirable king. Had any political encroachments upon him been attempted, he was far too wise, firm, and patriotic for enduring them. It is his fate, nevertheless, to fill no unimportant place among Anglo-Saxon builders of that Italian system which gradually undermined scriptural religion, and eventually degraded English policy. Nothing short of some strong seduction, like that of Alfred's early Roman predilections, might seem capable of winning so much piety and wisdom to break down the barrier nobly raised in England against the semi-pagan canons, by which Nice had astonished Western Europe. In this fatal abandonment of a holy cause, his name, however, stands painfully prominent. Posterity is driven to qualify its veneration for his character, by admitting that he must find a place among corruptors of the national religion.

Alfred was born at Wantage, in Berkshire, then a portion of the royal domains, in the year 849. His mother, Osburgh, a person of excellent abilities and conspicuous piety, was daughter to the royal cup-bearer, and descended from a family long pre-

eminent among Anglo-Saxon nobles.[1] This parent
it was Alfred's misfortune to lose in infancy; his extraordinary talents, therefore, owed but little to her
culture. Nor does any degree of scholarship appear
to have entered into the plans of those who directed
his earlier education. He was trained in the habits
of a sportsman and a warrior;[2] but his twelfth year
overtook him while yet unable to read.[3] He had
shewn, however, a considerable taste for literature, in
his keen attention to the poems commonly recited in
the royal presence.[4] By one of these, beautifully written, his mother-in-law, Judith, who had disgraced
herself by an incestuous marriage with his eldest
brother,[5] endeavoured to shame the gross illiteracy
of her new connexions. " I will give this," she said,
" to that one of you, young people, who shall first
learn it by heart." Alfred gazed eagerly upon the
manuscript, fascinated particularly by an illuminated
capital. " Now, will you really give this?" he asked.
Judith declared herself in earnest. Nothing more
was needed by the resolute and intelligent boy. He
applied himself instantly to learn his letters; nor
did he rest until able to repeat accurately the poem
that had so happily captivated his eye.[6] He now
found his eager thirst of knowledge met by a mortifying repulse. Reading to any extent, or to much
advantage, required a knowledge of Latin. Upon
overcoming this new difficulty he soon, accordingly,

---

[1] ASSER, 4.   [2] *Ib*. 16.
[3] *Ib*. Asser leaves it even doubtful whether Alfred's illiteracy
did not extend beyond his twelfth year.
[4] *Ib*.   [5] *Ib*. 13.   [6] *Ib*.

determined. But instruction was not easily obtained, even by a prince.¹ The taste for learning, and the facilities for its cultivation which England once owed to Theodore, had become extinct under the protracted horrors of Scandinavian piracy. Alfred, however, feeling ignorance insupportable, was impelled by a generous energy to set ordinary obstacles at defiance, and he diligently sought instructors.² How effectually he profited by their aid, his literary labours most nobly testify. These evidences of learned industry are, indeed, sufficient for immortalising any name in a dark and tempestuous age. As the works of an author, unable even to read until fully twelve years old, and who grew into manhood before he had mastered Latin, they claim a distinguished place among victories of the human intellect.

On reaching maturity, Alfred served gloriously and incessantly in the armies of his brothers. Of these, the two eldest, Ethelbald and Ethelbert, reigned concurrently; the latter holding a subordinate authority over Kent, Sussex, and Essex; the portion of his paternal dominions left for their father's administration during his last two years. Both these princes quickly followed Ethelwulf to the tomb; and his third son, Ethered, became head

---

¹ Asser, 17.

² Alfred's principal instructors in Latin, were, according to his own account, Plegmund, Asser, Grimbald, and Erigena. (*Preface to* Gregory's *Pastoral.* Spelm. *Vit. Alf. M. Append.* 3. p. 197.) He was, probably, not acquainted with one of these four scholars during his youth.

of the royal family.¹ Alfred appears now to have had an opportunity, either of assuming the subordinate eastern sovereignty, or of being recognised as King of Wessex.² He contented himself, however, with a secondary place under Ethered. Rarely, indeed, has a sceptre been less tempting. But Alfred was unable to decline it long; Ethered, like former sons of Ethelwulf, being released early from an uneasy throne. An elder brother had left children,³ whose prior claims Alfred, probably, would have willingly admitted. Any such forbearance was, however, so manifestly unsuitable to a time of urgent difficulty and danger, that these infant claimants were unhesitatingly set aside. The nation would hear of no reluctance in their uncle, now in the very flower of manhood, but called him loudly to the royal dignity.⁴ Alfred's reign opened with a

---

[1] Ethelbald died in 860, three years after his father. Ethelbert then added to the kingdom of Wessex his former dominion over the kingdoms of Kent, Sussex, and Essex. He governed this united kingdom with considerable success, during six years, and died in the year 866. Ethered succeeded in that year. Mr. Turner calls him Ethelred, as does Malmesbury; and there can be no doubt that this is the correct form of his name. But King Alfred's Will, Asser, the *Saxon Chronicle,* and Ethelwerd, write it *Ethered,* which, probably, comes more nearly to its ordinary pronunciation. It seems to be the *Edridge* or *Etherege* of later times.—*Sax. Chr.* 96, 97. *Script. post Bed.* f. 479. ASSER, 14. 24.

[2] ASSER, 24.

[3] Alfred left estates to Æthelm and Athelwold, each of them designated " my brother's son." Ethelbert appears to have been the father of both.—*King Alfred's Will,* 16, 17.

[4] Asser (24) says that Alfred began to reign *quasi invitus.* His accession is placed in 871 by Asser and the *Saxon Chronicle.* Mr. Turner adopts this date; but the Editor of *King Alfred's*

serious disaster, undergone at Wilton, where the Danish arms gained a decided victory.[1] Various ill successes followed, which were constantly aggravated by a weak and temporising policy. Thus unfortunate, Alfred naturally became unpopular, and he completed the alienation of his people by haughtiness and tyranny.[2] His kinsman, St. Neot, rebuked him sharply for these intolerable defects, and foretold their sinister operation on his happiness.[3] The youth, even of an Alfred, was, however, proof against unpalatable warnings. The young king of Wessex found himself, accordingly, as little able to gain any mastery over his own impetuous passions, as any respite from the fierce rovers of Scandinavia. At length public affairs were apparently overwhelmed

---

Will (6) refers Ethered's death to Apr. 23, 872. This is the year to which it is referred by Ingulf. (*Script. post Bed.* 494.) Malmesbury also places Alfred's accession in that year. *Ib.* 23.

[1] Asser, 25.

[2] *Ib.* 31. From Alfred's conduct, his friend and biographer, Asser, honestly admits that adversity came upon him *non immeritò*. To the stern severity of his rule, striking testimony is borne by the *Miroir des Justices*, a production of Edward the First's reign, well known among legal antiquaries. Thence we learn that Alfred hanged forty-four judges in one year, for errors and malversations in the exercise of their functions. (Spelm. *Alf. M. Vit.* note, p. 80.) Considerable severity was, no doubt, necessary to overawe a barbarous people, during a season of extraordinary public difficulty; but severity like this was cruel, and must have been grossly unjust in several instances.

[3] Asser, 32. A speech to this effect, attributed to St. Neot, is to be found in a Saxon homily. (*Brit. Mus. MSS.* Cotton. *Vespasian.* D. 14. f. 146.) This homily is printed in Gorham's *History and Antiquities of Eynesbury and St. Neots.* Lond. 1824. ii. 257. Part of St. Neot's speech is also given by Mr.

by hopeless ruin, and his lofty spirit was all but broken under a mortifying sense of general desertion. Unable farther to resist aggression, or to rally his own dejected, offended people, he crouched indignantly before the storm, and wholly disappeared from public observation.

His place of retreat was a small thickly wooded spot in Somersetshire, surrounded so completely and extensively by waters and morasses as to be almost inaccessible. In this deep and safe seclusion, the memorable isle of Athelney, he sought shelter and concealment with one of the royal herdsmen. By the mistress of his humble refuge he appears to have been unknown: probably, with her husband it was otherwise. The woman's ignorance of his quality may fairly be presumed from that very ancient and fascinating tale, which represents her as expecting him to watch some cakes baking by the fire, and venting angry verse, when she found him to have negligently let them burn. *So, man!* her irritated measures run:

> *What? Slack and blind when the cakes want a turn!*
> *You're greedy when they smoke upon the board.*[1]

Turner (*Hist. Angl. Sax.* 1. 549). Mr. Gorham says of St. Neot, "The precise year of his death is not stated by any ancient authority, and can only be collected from circumstantial evidence: the most probably date is 877. (1. 44.) Mr. Turner places Alfred's retirement in 878.

[1] *Heus, homo!*
Urere quos cernis panes, gyrare moraris?
Cum nimium gaudes hos manducare calentes?
ASSER. 31.

It has been thought by many that the paragraph which contains

But whatever might have been precisely the circumstances of Alfred's retirement, undoubtedly they were not such as to cut off communication with his confidential friends. Hence he soon organised small but courageous bands of trusty followers, by whom the Danes were severely harassed in a quick succession of such incursions as mocked every calculation. Thus his people's ardour rapidly revived. Vigour, ability, and success, gave an importance to every sally from his lurking-place, which forbade remembrance of his late reverses and unpopularity. When ready for striking the decisive blow, early tradition paints him disguised as a wandering minstrel, and unguardedly admitted into the Danish camp. Its hostile inmates, enchanted by his matchless music, and by the rich profusion of his legendary lore, could not fail of greeting eagerly such a harper wherever

---

this distich, and the whole story of Alfred with the neatherd's wife is an interpolation. It is not found in the Cotton MS. of Asser; and the printed text of that author would read quite as well without it. The woman's speech, too, being verse, is rather a suspicious circumstance. Mr. Turner, however, appears to consider it genuine (*Hist. Angl. Sax.* i. 561.), influenced probably by finding the tale in the *Homily on St. Neot.* (*Brit. Mus. MSS.* COTTON. *Vespasian.* D. 14. f. 146.) But this MS. is in a *Normanno-Saxon* hand. The several pieces in it, of course, were transcribed from older MSS. Mr. Gorham conjectures, with considerable probability, that the *Homily on St. Neot* was written about the middle of the eleventh century, and the tale of Alfred and the cakes interpolated from it into Asser.—(*Hist. of Eynesbury and St. Neots.* Suppl. ii. cii. Vol. i. 39.) Against this tale the silence of the *Saxon Chronicle* is also a presumption. In fact, that venerable record might lead us to consider Alfred's condition something less desperate than it has commonly been represented. Ethelwerd likewise has nothing of the tale, nor even Ingulf.

his inquiring eye directed him.[1] Thus he must have entered on the field which saw the crisis of his fate, with such information as a general very rarely can command. It proved an obstinate and sanguinary fight; but Alfred's military skill, admirably seconded by the desperate valour of his troops, at length gladdened him with victory. His brave but baffled foe sought safety within the ramparts of an impregnable fortification. Around its base, Alfred maintained a strict blockade, leaving the consummation of his hopes to privation and alarm. In fourteen days these irresistible auxiliaries proved him to have decided wisely. The Danish army surrendered; agreed to receive baptism, and to settle as a peaceful colony in the eastern counties.[2] Henceforth Alfred, although never free from apprehensions of invading Northmen, shone uninterruptedly the father of his people, and the glory of his age.

Among proofs of his title to contemporary gratitude and posthumous admiration, few are more conclusive than his literary labours. It is commonly said of professed scholars once embarked in active life, that future opportunities for learned industry are hopeless. Alfred, however, though a soldier and a

---

[1] INGULF, *Script. post Bed.* 494.
[2] ASSER, 34. Ethandum, supposed to be Yatton, near Chippenham, was the place of Alfred's decisive victory. The date of it is 878. Alfred himself stood godfather to Godrun, or Guthrum, the Danish chieftain. The Danish colony was to possess the country north of the Thames from its mouth to the mouth of the Lea, thence to the source of that river, thence it was to be bounded by the Watling Street to Bedford, thence the Ouse was to be its boundary to the sea.—SPELM. *Vit. Ælf. M.* 36. note.

statesman from education, office, and stern importunate necessity, yet found ample time for convincing the world that he was a student also. He conceived the noble design of founding a vernacular literature, and by his own personal exertions he realised very considerably that wise and generous intention. No author had thrown so much light upon the national affairs as Bede: but he wrote in Latin. Unwilling that all but scholars should be denied access to the annals of their country, Alfred rendered into Anglo-Saxon the venerable Northumbrian's *Ecclesiastical History*.[1] For dispensing information respecting foreign countries, he translated also the *Geography of Orosius*, with additional matter from other sources.[2] To diffuse a taste for literary gratification of a higher order, he presented his countrymen with a free version of *Boëthius on the Consolation of Philosophy*,[3] a work then highly valued by the few who read. He was not even contented without attempting to remedy the gross illiteracy of his clergy. For their use he became a translator of Pope *Gregory's Pastoral*, a text-book in the apportionment of penance.[4]

---

[1] Alfred's *Bede* was first published by Whelock, at Cambridge, in 1643, afterwards by Smith, in 1722. It is not a servile translation, some things being omitted in it, and others abridged.

[2] The *Orosius* was published by Mr. Daines Barrington in 1773. Mr. Turner has given a long and interesting account of this work.—*Hist. Angl. Sax.* ii. 79.

[3] Published by Mr. Rawlinson, in 1698, and again by Mr. Cardale, in 1829. The work contains much not in the original. Mr. Turner has given numerous extracts from it.—ii. 25.

[4] There are MSS. of this work in the British Museum, the Bodleian, the Public Library at Cambridge, and the Library of

Alfred's name has also been inserted among those of scholars who provided ancient England with a Bible in her native tongue.[1] But his versions of Scripture generally did not extend probably beyond such portions as appeared, from time to time, peculiarly suited for his own comfort and instruction.[2] He seems, however, to have been employed upon a regular translation of the Psalms when overtaken by a summons to eternity.[3]

He had then only attained his fifty-second year,[4] an age apparently very insufficient for laying solidly the foundations of national security, legislation, and literature. Alfred, however, accomplished all these

---

C. C. C. there. It is hardly creditable to England that this work has never been printed.

[1] SPELM. *Vit. Ælf. M.* 167. The authority for this is an ancient *History of Ely.*

[2] "Hic aut aliter, quamvis dissimili modo, in regiâ potestate Sacræ rudimenta Scripturæ divinitûs instinctus præsumpsit incipere in venerabili Martini solemnitate; quos *flosculos undecunque collectos* à quibuslibet magistris discere, et in corpore unius libelli, mixtim quamvis, sicut hinc suppetebat redigere, usque adeo protelavit, quousque propemodum ad magnitudinem unius psalterii perveniret; quem Enchiridion suum, id est, manualem librum, nominari voluit, eo quod ad manum illum die noctuque solertissimè habeat: in quo non mediocrè, sicut tunc aiebat, habebat solatium."— ASSER, 57.

[3] MALMESB. *Script. post Bed.* 24. There is reason also to believe that Alfred made translations from the *Fables of Æsop,* compiled a book of proverbs, and wrote a treatise on falconry.— (SPELM. *Vit. Ælf. M.* 166. TURNER, *Hist. Angl. Sax.* ii. 95, 96.) Some select versions from St. Austin by King Alfred are preserved among the Cotton MSS.

[4] The *Saxon Chronicle* (124) places Alfred's death in 901, and it is probably a contemporary authority. Other ancient authorities place it a year earlier.

mighty ends. Nor were incessant and sanguinary struggles against piratical invasion the only difficulties that taxed his ingenuity, consumed his time, and wore away his spirits. His towering intellect and indomitable energy were imprisoned in a most unhealthy frame. He seems to have been a sickly and a suffering child. As manhood opened on his view, he became oppressed by a dread of leprosy, or blindness, or some other such conspicuous infirmity, as must drive him hopelessly from the haunts of men. His generous ambition shrank before this mortifying prospect, and earnestly did he desire that no physical affliction should render him unfit for the public eye, and exclude him from active duties. Having once gone into Cornwall with a hunting party, he came near the burial-place of a British saint. His pious mind had ever viewed such spots as hallowed ground, and this was devoutly visited. Long was he prostrate, offering urgently humble suit to Heaven, that an unhappy constitution might not realise his most insupportable apprehensions. On his homeward journey he thought himself relieved; and some real or imaginary change freed him soon after from the fear of becoming politically dead.[1] If his pains, however, lost any portion of their intensity, he found it nothing more than a temporary respite. The gross and prolonged festivity that celebrated his nuptials, effectually doomed him to a life of misery.[2] His natural infirmities were hopelessly aggravated by that fatal blow; henceforth, he was racked habitually by

---

[1] Asser, 40.   [2] *Ib.*

agonising pain, and often thought himself on the verge of dissolution: nor, when intervals of ease allowed him to recruit his strength, could he shake off a horrid apprehension of impending torture.[1] Vainly did he seek the most approved medical advice: the physicians were at a loss even to name his malady.[2] In this respect, probably, they would have been surpassed by the more skilful and learned practitioners of later times; but it may well be doubted, whether any proficiency in the healing art could have ministered effectual relief to Alfred. His constitution appears to have been radically bad; and internal cancer, or some other such incurable disease, might seem to have thriven, with malignant luxuriance, in a soil that early sickliness had most effectually prepared.

A principal secret for benefitting society and attaining eminence, is economy of time. Deeply sensible of this, Alfred provided a specific employment for every coming hour. The natural day he seems to have divided into three equal portions: one of these was reserved for sleep and refreshment, another for public duties, and a third for God's especial service.[3] Under this last head were included not

---

[1] ASSER, 42.

[2] *Ib.* 40. Alfred appears to have suffered, in early life, under the excrescence called *ficus* by surgeons. (*Ib.*) Mr. Turner suggests that the sufferings of Alfred's mature life arose, probably, either from internal cancer, or from some derangement of the biliary functions.—*Hist. Angl. Sax.* II. 155. note.

[3] MALMESB. *Script. post Bed.* 24. Asser (65) states that Alfred devoted the *half* of his time to God, but he gives no particulars. His account, therefore, if presented in detail, might be found to differ very little from that of Malmesbury.

only religious exercises, in which no monk was more unsparing and regular than Alfred, but also those literary labours, which he wisely ranked among the most powerful instruments for dispensing heavenly light. His country possessed, however, no other measurement of time than close observation of the sun's progress. This was far too incomplete and unexact for Alfred: hence he caused wax candles to be made of equal weight, and each twelve inches long, every inch being distinctly marked and numbered. Six of these were provided for every twenty-four hours, and by their successive combustion Alfred could ascertain how far the day was gone. Upon this contrivance, however, he quickly found himself unable to rely, unless the air was perfectly serene. It was but rarely so, even in the rude, unglazed apartments of an Anglo-Saxon palace; much less so in a tent: hence arose a new demand on Alfred's ingenuity. He now fitted thin plates of horn into a wooden frame-work, and thus protected his waxen clocks from every blast, while the semi-transparent case enabled him to watch their progress. Posterity may smile to learn that *stable lanterns* are an invention, or an importation, which it owes to the immortal Alfred.[1] It must admire that industry and

---

[1] Alfred's clock-cases appear to have excited the *wonder* of his rude subjects and associates. Asser thus mentions them (69):—
" Quæ itaque laterna *mirabiliter* ex lignis et cornibus, ut ante diximus, facta." Alfred, however, might not have drawn this *wonderful* invention from the unassisted resources of his own genius, but only have refined somewhat upon a convenience that he had seen in Italy, and have applied it to a more dignified use. It

perseverance which could effect so much, when these humble instruments were the best within a king's command for maintaining a strict economy of time.

Alfred was no less liberal and strict in economising money. The rude hospitality of his court was maintained by the royal domains, which were not let to tenants, but merely managed by bailiffs.[1] Our ancient kings were thus the largest farmers in their dominions; and, like other occupiers of land, they drew the necessaries of life directly from the soil: their pecuniary resources must necessarily have been extremely scanty. Of these, however (such was his magnanimous piety), Alfred strictly devoted one-half to religion and learning.[2] One-fourth of this liberal appropriation was regularly distributed in alms, another fourth was remitted to the monasteries of Athelney and Shaftsbury, founded by himself,[3] another was disbursed in promoting education at

---

appears from Plautus, that horn-lanterns were known to the ancient Romans:—

"Quo ambulas tu, qui Vulcanum in cornu conclusum geris?"
Amphitr. act i. sc. 1, l. 185.

Nor was glass absolutely unattainable in Alfred's time, Benedict Biscop having brought some, long before, to his monastery at Wearmouth. It was however very rare, probably, and expensive: hence, as horn would answer his purpose, Alfred might not think of such costly materials for his lanterns.—SPELM. *Vit. Ælf. M.* 162.

[1] SPELM. *Vit. Ælf. M.* 161.   [2] ASSER, 66.

[3] Athelney was for men, Shaftsbury for women. In the latter, Alfred's own daughter became abbess. Asser says (61), that the monastic profession was then at a very low ebb in England, no particular rule being ordinarily observed with any strictness.

Oxford,[1] and the last was reserved for monastic establishments, either abroad or at home. The remaining half of his revenues Alfred divided into three portions only. Of these, the first paid his officers, the second was expended upon buildings and mechanical arts, the third upon learned foreigners, whom his judicious patriotism anxiously sought for his own ignorant and unpolished country.[2]

As an ecclesiastical legislator, Alfred appears to have done little more than confirm the sanctions of his more approved predecessors. Having made a digest from the laws of Ina and Offa, kings of Mercia, and from those of Ethelbert, the first Christian sovereign of Kent, he submitted it to his legislature, and obtained a solemn confirmation of it.[3] Under him, accordingly, the privilege of sanctuary was again legally recognised, and especial protection was extended to churches and ecclesiastics. His treaty with Godrun, which planted a Danish colony in the

---

[1] Asser does not mention Oxford, but he mentions only *one* school: *tertiam scholæ, quam ex multis suæ propriæ gentis studiosissimè congregaverat.* Brompton (*X. Script.* 818), evidently writing with Asser before him, places the *school* at Oxford: *tertiam scolaribus Oxoniæ noviter congregatis.* Oxford's obligations to Alfred are indeed indubitable. The only question is, whether he did not rather restore and augment that venerable seat of learning, than found it. If a paragraph in Asser be genuine (52), the former service was that rendered by the great king of Wessex; but this paragraph is wanting in some of the MSS.; and hence Cambridge men, desirous of denying superior antiquity to the sister university, have pronounced it an interpolation.

[2] Asser, 66.

[3] Præf. Al. M. ad LL. suas. Spelm. *Conc.* i. 363. Wilk. i. 190.

eastern counties, throws further light upon ecclesiastical affairs. Alfred stipulates in this, for the payment of tythes, *Rome-shot, light-shot,* and *plough-alms,* providing by pecuniary fines against disobedience.¹ The two last named of these dues now appear (at least under those particular designations), for the first time among the legislative records of England.² Another testimony is thus borne to the very high antiquity of a payment for the exigencies of public worship, independently of tythes. What private owner of an estate can produce a title for his property, so old by many centuries, as this enlightened monarch's constitutional recognition of the Church's title to a rent-charge upon it for the due celebration of divine offices? It is observable, too, that Alfred's legislation leaves no room for pleading that ecclesiastical dues were ordinarily rendered upon grounds merely religious. Civil penalties protected the clergy in their maintenance,³ the Church in her dues, and Rome in her claims upon every householder's penny.

---

¹ *LL. sub Alf. et Guth.* SPELM. *Conc.* i. 377.

² The *light-shot* of Alfred's code may answer, perhaps, to the *church-shot* made payable, under a heavy penalty, by the laws of Ina. The *plough-alms* are thought to have been an offering made to the church, in proportion to the number of plough-lands holden by the payers. This due is not mentioned by name in Alfred's own treaty with Godrun as now extant: we find specified there only tythes, *Rome-fee, light-shot,* and " Dei rectitudines aliquas." In the renewal of this treaty, however, under Edward the Elder, *plough-alms* are inserted.—SPELM. i. 392. WILK. i. 293.

³ Of civil penalties guarding the right to tythes, probably no earlier record is known. Such might, however, have been provided by the laws of Offa, to which Alfred appeals, but which are lost.

Alfred's appearance as an ecclesiastical legislator has, however, inflicted a severe wound upon his memory, even with such as can feel the danger of allowing individual selfishness to tamper with religious duty. He prefaces his laws by the Decalogue, and many other sanctions, drawn from the sacred text of Moses; but his Decalogue offers not a trace of the second commandment in its proper situation: a slight hint of it only is thrust down to the tenth place, and this is worded so as to give an iconolater ample room for subterfuge and evasion.[1] Evidently, therefore, Anglo-Saxon divines reprobated no longer the second council of Nice, and Alfred was contented to naturalise among his countrymen its insidious decrees. Rome had, indeed, gained early upon his affections; and the centre of civilisation was but little likely to lose its hold upon such a mind: his venerated relative, also, St. Neot, was smitten so deeply by attachment to that celebrated city, that he journeyed to it no fewer than seven times.[2] Alfred himself, too, entertained a high regard for relics,[3] the superstitious merchandise of Rome. Nor among the compliments that he received, was any one, probably, more acceptable than a fragment of some size, presented by the pope, as a portion of our Saviour's cross.[4] The whole stream of contemporary theology,

---

[1] See *Bampton Lectures*, 248.

[2] Þe ʒeneoroðe Rome-buph ɼeoɼe ɼiðen xpe to loɼe ⁊ ɼemte Petɼe. (Hom. in S. Neot. *Brit. Mus. MSS.* Cotton. Vespasian, D. 14. f. 143.) *He visited Rome-city seven times, in honour of Christ and St. Peter.*

[3] Asser, 41.   [4] *Ib.* 39.

and his own translation of Pope Gregory's *Pastoral*, attest sufficiently his belief in the necessity of a strict personal satisfaction for sin. His friend and biographer, Asser, accordingly represents the unpopularity that tried him so severely in early life, as mercifully sent by Providence, to exact a penalty which he must have paid, but which could never fall so lightly as while he continued in the body.[1] It is probable that Alfred's own view is here detailed; and that, reasoning upon this principle, he found some consolation under the wearing intensity of bodily distress. His authority, therefore, might be colourably pleaded, in favour of the penitential doctrines eventually prevailing among schoolmen, and solemnly confirmed at Trent. Alfred, however, in common with other luminaries of his age, only lent an unconscious aid in the foundation of a system, essentially different from their own, and much more seductive. Their penitential doctrines had no reference to that perilous anodyne, technically termed in after ages, sacramental absolution. Hence Anglo-Saxon views of man's reconciliation with his God, although not exactly Protestant, varied importantly from those of modern Rome.[2] Nor were those extravagant assertions of papal supremacy, which have occasioned so many offensive acts and acrimonious debates among subsequent generations, known to the days of Alfred. Had such been advanced, however, it is far from likely, that any veneration for the papacy would have led him into such concessions as tarnish

---

[1] Asser, 32. [2] See *Bampton Lectures*, Serm. 5. p. 255.

the honour of a nation, and outrage reason. Roman pretensions, when fully before the world, were never admitted by our ablest sovereigns. But English royalty can boast no abler name than that of Alfred. That illustrious prince, it should also be remembered, must have dissented from transubstantiation, the great distinctive feature of modern Romanism. His age first saw eucharistic worshippers invited formally to deny the evidence of sense; and Alfred patronised Erigena, a celebrated opponent of that startling novelty.[1] Plainly untenable, therefore, are Romish claims to the only English sovereign whom posterity has dignified as the *Great*. Alfred lived in a superstitious age, and before many theological questions, afterwards debated fully, had called for critical examination. His belief, therefore, cannot be identified strictly and accurately with that of the modern church of England. He knew nothing, however,

---

[1] Collier mentions Alfred's remittances to Rome of Peter-pence, by the hands of bishops and other great men; and he mentions the return made by the pope, of an alleged fragment from our Saviour's cross, and of an exemption from taxes to the English school at Rome. He then adds: "But notwithstanding these civilities, we meet with no letters of compliment or submission: we find no learned men sent from Rome to assist the king in his scheme for the revival of arts and sciences; there is no intercourse of legates upon record; no interposings in the councils and regulations of the church; no bulls of privilege for the new abbeys of Winchester and Athelney; and which is more, King Alfred, as we have seen, entertained Johannes Scotus Erigena, and treated him with great regard, notwithstanding the discountenance he lay under at Rome. From all which we may conclude, the correspondence between England and Rome was not very close; and that this prince and the English Church were not servilely governed by that see."—*Eccl. Hist.* i. 171.

of sacramental devices for speaking peace to a conscience, merely attrite; and he denied, in common with all his countrymen, the rising principle of transubstantiation. Now these two doctrines are essential to the Romish belief of later times, and are the main pillars of its hold upon mankind. English Romanists, therefore, are egregiously mistaken in taking credit for the profession of a creed identical with that of Alfred.

Of his most illustrious literary friend, John Scotus Erigena, the birthplace has been disputed. That scholar's ordinary designation, however, which is no other than *John the Irish-born Scot*, renders it hardly doubtful that he was born in Ireland, of the Scottish race long seated there. Many of his earlier years were spent in France, where he stood foremost among learned men. Charles the Bald esteemed him highly, and admitted him to the most familiar intercourse. By that enlightened prince he was desired, together with Ratramn, to examine critically those eucharistic doctrines by which Paschasius Radbert had recently amazed the world. Erigena, like Ratramn, vindicated the evidence of sense, assigning a figurative character to our Lord's words at the last supper.[1] That numerous class which is ever eagerly upon the watch for something new and surprising, was probably very little pleased with scholars, however eminent, thus employed. Radbert's theory was one upon which ephemeral conceit could fix triumphantly as an undoubted discovery of its own improving age; it

---

[1] See *Bampton Lectures*, 418.

was one, too, which could hardly fail of making a powerful impression upon lovers of mystery and paradox. Erigena seems also to have given offence by some of his writings upon the predestinarian controversy.[1] He gladly, therefore, accepted an invitation from Alfred to pass over into England, and his patron provided for him by a professorship at Oxford. After some stay there he removed to the abbey of Malmesbury, still undertaking the instruction of youth. In this employment Erigena rendered himself hateful to his pupils, who, rushing upon him tumultuously, murdered him with their penknives.[2] This outrage

---

[1] CAVE. *Hist. Lit.*, 548. This controversy was excited by Godeschalc, a monk of Orbais, about the middle of the ninth century. (See MOSHEIM. ii. 344.) Collier, after mentioning Alfred's invitation to Erigena as a presumption against England's belief at that time in transubstantiation, thus proceeds, " Cressy seems apprehensive of this inference, and endeavours to fence against it. He affirms, in the first place, from Hoveden, that Scotus had brought himself under a *just infamy* in France, upon the score of his heterodoxy. This imputation made him desire to retreat into England. But in this relation Cressy misrepresents Hoveden; for this historian asserts no more than that Scotus was eclipsed in his reputation, which is no wonder, considering the letter Pope Nicholas wrote to Charles the Bald, to his disadvantage,—where he taxes him with unsound opinions, but without naming any particulars. 'Tis true Hoveden does say he laid under an ill report, but, that this historian thought he deserved it, we have no reason to conclude." (*Eccl. Hist.* i. 165.) Nor, probably, have we any reason to conclude that Erigena had given so much offence by his writings upon the eucharist as by those upon predestination.

[2] MALMESB. *Script. post Bed.* 24. SIM. DUNELM. *X. Script.* 149. Fuller, Collier, and Inett, make *penknives* to have been the instruments of Erigena's death. *Graphiis*, however, is the word used by Malmesbury, and Simeon of Durham, a word by

appears to have been provoked by the moroseness of his manners and the sternness of his discipline. In happier times, however, Erigena had been famed for a ready playfulness of wit.[1] But his sportive sallies appear to have been always tinged by satire, and, probably, the most discerning of those who had enjoyed his talent for enlivening society, would have named acerbity of temper among the exciting causes to which they were indebted for amusement. Erigena's violent death long caused him, rather strangely as it seems, to be venerated as a martyr. Berenger, however, effectively obscured his posthumous reputation. By appealing to his work upon the eucharist, he procured its formal condemnation.[2] Thus, Erigena,

---

which Du Cange, with every appearance of probability, understands iron *styles* used in writing. Fuller supposes (*Ch. Hist.* 119.) but seemingly with no great reason, that the murder of Erigena is attributable to the rancour of controversy: " Indeed Scotus detested some superstititions of the times, especially about the presence in the Lord's Supper; and I have read that his book, *De Eucharistiâ*, was condemned in the Vercellian Synod for some passages therein by Pope Leo. This makes it suspicious that some hands of more age, and heads of more malice, than schoolboys, might guide the penknives which murdered Scotus, because of his known opposition against some practices and opinions of that ignorant age."

[1] Simeon of Durham has preserved the following specimen of his wit. Sitting one day at table opposite Charles the Bald, and being rather severe upon a nobleman present, the king asked him, " *What is there between a Scot and a sot?*" (*Sot*, Fr. *a fool*.) " *Only this table!*" was Erigena's free and caustic reply.

[2] At the Council of Vercelli, in 1150. (LABB. et Coss. IX. 1056.) Mosheim (ii. 342) considers Erigena to have been by far the clearest and most powerful of Radbert's opponents, shewing no appearance whatever of any leaning towards a belief in the cor-

whom Alfred valued among writers as a theological authority, has long been condemned by Romanists to wear the brand of heresy.

Under Alfred's son and successor, Edward the Elder, occurred, according to Malmesbury, a very remarkable and successful exercise of papal power. Formosus, the Roman pontiff, we are told, sent an epistle into England, cursing and excommunicating the king with all his people, because the whole of Wessex had been destitute of bishops fully seven years. On receiving this Edward might seem to have convened a synod, and Plegmund, archbishop of Canterbury, to have presided over it. In that assembly it was determined, we learn, to supply the vacancies and erect three new sees. The primate is then represented as proceeding to Rome with honourable presents, laying the synod's decree before the pope, obtaining his approbation, and consecrating seven bishops in one day.[1]

This fulminating epistle came from Formosus, we learn, in the year 904.[2] That pontiff, however, died in the year 896.[3] Undoubtedly he did not rest quietly in his grave. His successor, Stephen, not contented with rescinding his decrees, procured his corpse to be

---

poreal presence. Perhaps quite so much cannot be safely said of Ratramn, and this may be the reason why Berenger rested so much upon the former author, and why his work has wholly disappeared; nothing less could be expected of any work synodically condemned in the eleventh century. Erigena's extraordinary acuteness, indeed, could hardly fail of leading him into very precise and guarded language.

[1] MALMSB. *Script. post Bed* 26.   [2] *Ib.*   [3] INETT, i. 297.

disinterred, arraigned before a council, stripped of the pontifical robes, and buried ignominiously among laymen. Nor were the two fingers chiefly used in consecration deemed worthy even of this interment. They were cut off and thrown into the Tyber.[1] These contumelies overtook the body of Formosus in the year 897, and it seems afterwards to have lain undisturbed in its unhonoured grave. Baronius, accordingly, is driven to admit some chronological mistake in Malmesbury's relation; but he is naturally unwilling to forego a case so useful for establishing the ancient exercise of papal authority over England. Hence, he suggests an earlier date by ten years as the proper one for this transaction.[2] Alfred, however, was then upon the throne, and not Edward the Elder. Two of the vacancies also, said to have drawn down papal excommunication in 904, did not occur until five years afterwards.[3] Although, therefore, it may

---

[1] PLATINA, 114. Boniface VI. is placed by Platina between Formosus I. and Stephen VI. But this intermediate pontiff appears not to have lived a month after his elevation.

[2] INETT, i. 297.

[3] *Viz.* the vacancy made by the death of Denewulf, bishop of Winchester, and that made by the death of Asser, bishop of Sherborne, Alfred's biographer. Denewulf is said to have been the identical neatherd, under whose roof Alfred sought concealment at Athelney. Denewulf's promotion to the see of Winchester, however, took place in 879. It was only in the preceding year when Alfred lay hidden at Athelney. He is said, of course, to have found his host possessed of extraordinary abilities, but still it is any thing rather than credible that Alfred should have considered a man, whom he had known as a neatherd one year, qualified for the see of Winchester in the next.—WHARTON, *Angl. Sacr* i. 208, 554

be true that Plegmund consecrated seven bishops in a single day,[1] yet there is no reason for believing the act to have been extorted by any pontiff's malediction. Had such, indeed, been the truth, allusions to it at least would most probably have been found in earlier authorities than Malmesbury. It is, however, likely that a council was really holden for partitioning the western dioceses, as deaths allowed facilities for such a change. Nor is it surprising that subsequent authors, finding a simultaneous effect given to some new arrangement, should have drawn upon their imaginations to make it square exactly with their own prejudices, and the habits which they saw established.

Edward the Elder was succeeded by Athelstan, his eldest son, but illegitimate. He proved a prince who nobly obliterated the stain of discreditable birth. By

---

[1] Wharton (*ut supra*) expresses himself unwilling to reject the tradition of Plegmund's seven-fold consecration, and therefore he suggests, as the best mode of obviating difficulties, that a council was probably holden in 904, or in the next year, for partitioning the western dioceses, and that its provisions were not carried into execution until 909, when Denewulf and Asser died. The seven consecrations appear to have been for Winchester, Wells, Crediton, Sherborne, St. Petrock's in Bodmin, Dorchester, and Chichester. (*Antiqu. Brit.* 112.) Collier, after mentioning Malmesbury's relation, thus proceeds: " The Register of the Priory of Canterbury speaks much to the same purpose, but with this remarkable addition, —that there was a particular provision made for the Cornishmen to recover them from their errors; for that county, as the Record speaks, *refused to submit to truth, and took no notice of the pope's authority.*" (*Eccl. Hist.* 1. 171.) The original words are, *nam antea in quantum potuerunt, veritati resistebant, et non decretis apostolicis obediebant.*—SPELM. I. 388. WILK. I. 200.

his vigour and ability, indeed, he really became monarch of England. In the decisive battle of Brunanburh he crushed the Danish sovereignty, to which Northumbria and the eastern counties had hitherto owned obedience.[1] By taking Exeter from the Welsh he laid securely the foundations of Anglo-Saxon dominion over the western extremity of England.[2] A reign of so much military activity, and of no long continuance,[3] is naturally deficient in materials for ecclesiastical history. Athelstan was, however, a religious prince, and eminent for liberality to monasteries.[4] Nor was he unmindful of a provision for the ordinary exigencies of piety. In a legislative assembly, holden at Grateley,[5] it was enacted that tythes should be strictly paid, not only upon the crops, but also upon live stock.[6] Another account of the decrees passed in this assembly, provides also for the payment of *church-shot*.[7] In both records is found an injunction to the royal stewards for charging every crown estate with a certain eleemosynary contribution.

---

[1] The site of this important battle has not been ascertained. TURNER, *Hist. Angl. Sax.* ii. 185.

[2] " Urbem Excestriam Cornwallensibus abstulit, quam turribus, et muro munivit, et quadratis lapidibus.—JOHAN. TINMOUTH, *Historia Aurea. Bibl. Lameth.* MSS. 12. f. 74.

[3] Athelstan was chosen king in 925, and he died in 941. (*Sax. Chr.* 139, 145.) Malmesbury places Athelstan's accession in 924, as also does Mr. Turner.

[4] MALMESB. *Script. post Bed.* 26.

[5] The name of this place does not appear in the body of the record, nor is it stated that any other advice was taken than that of Wulfhelm, the archbishop, and the bishops.

[6] SPELM. *Conc.* i. 396. WILK. i. 205.

[7] SPELM. *Conc.* i 402.

These documents likewise provide against violation of churches and profanation of Sunday; and, moreover, for the due management of ordeals. Another constitution of Athelstan's acquaints us with a judicious anxiety, long prevalent, for the general foundation of village churches. We learn from it that our Anglo-Saxon ancestors were free from the dangerous injustice of making rank in society a mere matter of *caste*. The dignity of thane, or gentleman, was open to every one possessed of a certain property, and admitted among the royal officers. But then one of such a person's qualifications was a church with a belfry upon his estate.[1] A wealthy aspirant of inferior origin would be careful to prevent any deficiency in this particular from crossing his ambitious views.

As the whole period from the death of Alcuin to that of Athelstan is remarkably deficient in literary monuments, its doctrinal character is necessarily rather a matter of inference than of direct evidence.

---

[1] SPELM. *Conc.* i. 406. " If a churl thrived so as to have five hides of his own land, *a church*, and kitchen, a bell-tower, a seat, and an office in the king's court, from that time forward he was esteemed equal in honour to a thane." (JOHNSON's *Transl.*) " It has been observed that a *Triburg*, that is, ten or more families of freemen, eat together. But it will appear that every thane's, or great man's family, was of itself esteemed a *Triburg* by law, 14 of *Edw. Conf.* 1065; therefore, at that time for a man to have a kitchen for the dressing of his own meat might well be esteemed the mark of a thane. Yet let the Saxonists judge whether we ought not to read Kyṛicena Bell-huɼ, that is a *Church-steeple* (to distinguish it from a common Bell-tower), instead of *Kitchen, Bell-tower*."—*Ib.* Note.

From Alfred's mutilated decalogue, however, a triumph must have been gained by image-worship. In the train of this insidious usage could hardly fail of following some disposition for invoking angelic and departed spirits. But that practice was not yet established. Alfred's friendship for Erigena, and the decisive testimony borne by a subsequent age against transubstantiation, prove sufficiently that England still continued completely free from the main distinction of modern Romanism.

CHAPTER IV.

FROM DUNSTAN TO THE CONQUEST.
928—1066.

THE MONASTIC SYSTEM—BIRTH OF DUNSTAN—HIS EDUCATION—INTRODUCTION TO COURT—EXPULSION THENCE—DISINCLINATION TO A MONASTIC LIFE—SUBSEQUENT ADOPTION OF ONE—FOUNDATION OF GLASTONBURY ABBEY — THE BENEDICTINES FIRST ESTABLISHED — LEGISLATIVE COUNCIL OF LONDON — ARCHBISHOP ODO—HIS CANONS — ETHELWOLD—EDWY—DUNSTAN'S EXILE — HIS RETURN—HIS ADVANCEMENT TO THE SEE OF CANTERBURY—EDGAR—LEGISLATIVE COUNCIL OF ANDOVER—CIVIL PENALTIES AGAINST THE SUBTRACTION OF TYTHES—OTHER LEGISLATIVE ENACTMENTS UNDER EDGAR—OPPOSITION TO THE MONASTIC SYSTEM—OSWALD — MONKISH MIRACLES—LEGISLATIVE COUNCIL OF WINCHESTER—OF CALNE—EDWARD THE MARTYR—ETHELRED THE UNREADY—DEATH OF DUNSTAN—HIS INDEPENDENT REPLY TO THE POPE—PRETENDED TRANSFER OF HIS REMAINS TO GLASTONBURY—LEGISLATIVE COUNCIL OF EANHAM—OF HABA—ECCLESIASTICAL DUES — ELFRIC, ASCERTAINED PARTICULARS OF HIS LIFE—HIS WORKS—OBSCURITY OF HIS HISTORY—PROBABLE OUTLINE OF IT—MENTION OF HIS NAME BY MALMESBURY AND OSBERN—APPARENT CAUSE OF THE INJUSTICE DONE TO HIS MEMORY—CANUTE—LEGISLATIVE COUNCIL OF WINCHESTER UNDER HIM—EDWARD THE CONFESSOR—STIGAND—HAROLD'S FOUNDATION FOR SECULAR CANONS—DOCTRINES.

ANGLO-SAXON Ecclesiastical History between Athelstan and the Conquest, is distinctly marked by a controversy that agitated every branch of society. From various and obvious causes, ascetic principles are likely to become popular, at any time, among religious professors. Oriental Christians had early been smitten with admiration of monkish devotees.[1] By this example of her elder sister, the western Church was readily infected; and the fifth century produced in Benedict, an Italian monk, a monastic patriarch of her own. The system of this eminent recluse had gained extensive celebrity abroad, before England bestowed upon it any great attention. Wilfred, indeed, took credit to himself for introducing it among his countrymen. Even a single Benedictine monastery does not, however, seem to have attested any such importation. England, it is true, was early and abundantly supplied with conventual foundations, liberally endowed. But these were generally rather colleges than regular monasteries. In them were provided accommodation for ordinary clergymen, education for youth, and a home for some few ascetics bound by solemn vows.[2] Such establishments were obviously unfavourable to the strict discipline of a cloister, and monks had consequently sunk in popular estimation. When Alfred, accordingly, founded his religious house at Athelney, he was driven to seek a motley group of monkish inmates for it from every quarter.[3] Scandinavian piracy was assigned as a reason why the Anglo-Saxons possessed

---

[1] See *Hist. Ref.* ii. 51.

[2] WHARTON, *Angl. Sacr.* ii. 91. " Siquidem a temporibus antiquis, ibidem et episcopus cum clero, et abbas solebat manere cum monachis, qui tamen et ipsi ad curam episcopi familiariter pertinerent."—MARSHAM, *Propyl. Monasticon*.

[3] " In quo monasterio diversi generis monachos undique congregavit."—ASSER, 61.

so little taste for monachism.[1] But England, probably, had never offered, in societies exclusively and uniformly ascetic, any sufficient facilities for nurturing such a disposition. The munificence which had consecrated so many spots by religious houses, appears, indeed, usually to have been stimulated by palpable deficiencies of religious instruction. In raising and endowing a *minster*, the vernacular form of *monasterium*, Anglo-Saxon piety had apparently little else in view than a church for ordinary worship, surrounded by a body of clergymen, who might both serve it and itinerate in the neighbourhood. Eventually many of these establishments became monasteries, in the sense affixed to that word by after ages. But one part of the generation, witnessing this change, condemned it as an injustice based upon delusion. The other part, probably, thought not of inquiring into the truth of such a charge. It assumed, unhesitatingly, that an ecclesiastical foundation of any magnitude would most completely answer the pious donor's meaning, in the hands of professed ascetics, regularly bound to certain mortifications. Innovations upon established usage and

---

[1] " Per multa retroacta annorum curricula monasticæ vitæ desiderium ab illâ totâ gente, nec non a multis aliis gentibus funditus desierat; quamvis perplurima adhuc monasteria in illâ regione constructa permaneant: nullo tamen regulam illius vitæ ordinabiliter tenente (nescio quare), aut pro alienigenarum infestationibus, quæ sæpissime terrâ marique hostiliter irrumpunt, aut etiam pro nimiâ illius gentis in omni genere divitiarum abundantiâ, propter quam multo magis id genus despectæ monasticæ vitæ fieri existimo."—ASSER, 61.

vested interests, require, however, time and perseverance. A complete monastic triumph was accordingly delayed until after the Norman Conquest.[1]

It was one celebrated individual, from whose talents, energy, and address, arose the Benedictine struggle for ascendancy. Dunstan was born, we learn upon contemporary authority, in the reign of Athelstan;[2] but this seems hardly reconcilable with his early prominence. Hence his birth has been referred to the very year of Athelstan's accession. Probably even this date is posterior to the event. Dunstan's father was named Herstan; his mother, Kynedrid. They held a high rank among the nobility of Wessex, and lived near Glastonbury. Such a residence was remarkably calculated for making a powerful and permanent impression upon the expanding mind of an intelligent and imaginative child. Glastonbury drew a character of solemn and pictu-

---

[1] W. Thorn informs us, that the secular canons were not expelled from the cathedral church of Canterbury until the year 1005. (*X. Script.* 1780.) Nor did this expulsion, then, meet with a ready acquiescence. On the contrary, the intrusive monks were not firmly established in possession until the primacy of Lanfranc. —INETT, i. 329.

[2] " Hujus (Æthelst.) imperii temporibus oritur puer strenuus in West-Saxonum finibus, cui pater Heorstanus, mater verò Cynethrith vocitatur." (*Brit. Mus. MSS. Cotton, Cleopatra.* B. 13. f. 60.) Osbern softens these names into Herstan and Kynedrida. He also places Dunstan's birth in the first year of Athelstan. (*Angl. Sacr.* ii. 90.) This year is not certainly fixed, but it can hardly be earlier than 924. Even this date, however, would only make Dunstan seventeen at Athelstan's death. Hence Wharton conjectures that he was born towards the close of Edward the Elder's reign.—*Angl. Sacr.* iii. 116. Note.

resque seclusion from the fishy waters that guarded its approach on every side. The most venerable tradition had marked it as a holy isle. It was now a royal domain;[1] it possessed a church erected long before the Saxon conversion;[2] its established sanctity was attested strikingly by Irish pilgrims, to whom its facilities for study and religion were doubly grateful, because tradition marked it as their own Patrick's burial-place.[3] The ancient Cimbric race, yet lingering, probably, throughout the west of England, and sole inhabitants of Cornwall, looked upon the glassy isle with profound respect. It seems to have been honoured as the cradle of their ancient church;[4] and Arthur, the most glorious of their warriors, was eventually found entombed within its hallowed boundaries.[5] The fame of Glastonbury

---

[1] " Erat autem quædam *regalis* in confinio ejusdem præfati viri (Heorstan.) *insula*, antiquorum vicinorum vocabulo Glestonia nuncupata." (*Cleop.* B 13. f. 31.) " Glastonia, regalibus stipendiis addicta."—OSBERN, 91.

[2] See *Introduction*.

[3] " Maximè ob beati Patricii senioris honorem, qui faustus ibidem in Domino quievisse narratur."—*Cleop.* B. 13. f. 63.

[4] " Quatenus ecclesia Domini nostri, Jesu Christi, et perpetuæ Virginis Mariæ, sicut in regno Britanniæ est prima, et fons et origo totius religionis." (*Carta Inæ, R. Monast.* i. 13.) To many of these charters, claiming very high antiquity, but little credit is due. They are, however, likely to embody some ancient traditions. Probability is given to this tradition from the interment of Arthur, and from the veneration for Glastonbury that was so widely and deeply spread. Hence we may reasonably conjecture that the Isle of Avalon contained the earliest British establishment for the accommodation of Christian ministers.

[5] After the burning of the church, in 1184, Henry de Sully, then abbot, was recommended to search for the remains of Arthur

depended, however, chiefly on tradition. Of any monastery existing there in British times, few traces had survived. Pious and well-informed minds, dwelling on the ancient sanctity of Avalon, must have regretted such desecration. English intercourse with foreigners was highly favourable to this cast of thought. Fleury had gained a splendid reputation as the main seat and seminary of Benedictine discipline. Hence that boast of Gaul was now the talk and envy of religious Europe. Prepared, not improbably, by hearing occasional conversations upon Fleury, Dunstan was taken by his father to spend a night at Glastonbury. The senior's principal object in this visit, appears to have been the satisfaction of offering up his prayers on a spot so highly famed for sanctity. There can be no doubt, however, that Herstan was mindful of drawing his interesting boy's attention to the various claims upon popular veneration that Avalon possessed. A mental eye, acquainted with the kindling imagination of thoughtful childhood, will readily discern young Dunstan's eager and delighted survey of the ancient church— the still solitude around — the devotees from distant Ireland. Impressions, deeply made in the early spring of life, are prolific in visions awaiting manhood for accomplishment. Of such delightful dreams Dunstan felt the full enjoyment on retiring for the

---

between two stone pillars, ornamented with carved work. At a great depth was found a coffin, containing bones and a leaden cross, the latter thus inscribed: *Hic jacet sepultus inclitus Rex Arthurus in insulâ Avalloniâ.* The cross was afterwards preserved in the treasury.—USSER, *Brit. Eccl. Antiq.* 62. 272.

night. His muscular energies were firmly locked in sleep: but an imagination highly excited, and a mind teeming with projects for the future, defied the influence of bodily fatigue. Before him rose an aged figure, clothed in white, who led him, majestically, about the very spots that had absorbed his interest while awake. They were not now, however, mere open spaces, with here and there, perhaps, a remnant of hoar antiquity. A splendid monastic pile lent them the dignity for which they had long seemed to call. Partial credulity was fain to represent the spacious erections, then captivating the sleeping boy, as the very prototypes of those which his influence eventually raised.[1] But the dreams, even of adult, informed, and accurate minds, are usually wanting in precision. The crude conceptions of a slumbering child, however highly gifted with imagination, must necessarily be confused, indistinct, and, in detail, impracticable.

Dunstan's early predilections for Glastonbury were confirmed by his education there. The pilgrims who sought Avalon from Ireland, finding no establishment, were wholly thrown upon their own resources, and tuition was their ordinary refuge.[2] Among this band of learned strangers Herstan selected an instructor for his intellectual boy. As the

---

[1] " Eo scilicet ordine quo nunc statuta referuntur fore demonstrantem."— *Cleop.* B. 13. f. 61.

[2] " Cum ergo hi tales viri talibus de causis Glastoniam venissent, nec tamen quicquid sibi necessarium erat sufficientissimè in loco reperissent, suscipiunt filios nobilium liberalibus studiis imbuendos.—Osbern, *Angl. Sacr.* ii. 92.

youthful student advanced in age, he rapidly realised the promise of his infancy, leaving the proficiency of every equal very far behind. But no talent will become thus effective without close application: Dunstan's thirst of knowledge seems, accordingly, to have undermined his health. A violent fever seized him, and delirious transports, of long continuance, overclouded the hopes of his doting parents with anguish and despair. As a last resort, they sought assistance from a female, famed for skill in medicine. Under her treatment Dunstan's illness became daily more alarming, and at length he sank upon his couch, to all appearance dead. As such, indeed, he seems to have been abandoned. He was, however, only labouring under complete exhaustion. Hence his bodily energies, after a short interval, were sufficiently recruited. He then sprang from the bed, seized a club, accidentally at hand, and rushed wildly into the fields, driven onwards by the fancied baying of savage hounds, that morbidly tingled in his ears. He long fled in horror before this imaginary chase, alike regardless of hill and dale. But as the sun declined, his frenzy felt again the sedative influence of lassitude. Half unconsciously, perhaps, he then turned his weary steps toward Glastonbury, and reached its venerable fane.[1]

---

[1] This incident is cautiously introduced by *ut ferunt*, in the contemporary life of Dunstan. It is, however, far from improbable; and its age, accordingly, appeared a sufficient warrant for its insertion. All these very natural particulars of Dunstan's illness are most absurdly exaggerated, and, indeed, caricatured by Osbern, who has made them vehicles for introducing what he,

A new panic seems now to have assailed him, which summoned up every energy once more. He placed his foot in some steps provided for workmen employed on a repair, mounted to the church's roof, and paced madly to and fro along its dangerous height. After a time his eye rested upon an aperture, and through it he pushed his way. It led into the church, though by a dangerous descent. Nothing could, however, stop his heedless frenzy; and he came safely down. He now found two guards fast asleep. Without making any noise he lay down between them, and sank exhausted into a most refreshing slumber. When morning broke, the men were astonished on finding their companion, especially when they thought upon the peril that he must have undergone to reach them.[1] Dunstan's disorder was now spent. Yesterday's excitement and fatigue having, eventually, plunged him in a sound and healthy sleep, had purged his morbid energies away. He remained master of himself, and youth soon repaired all the ravages of his late disease. A warning, however, so severe, could not fail of making a permanent impression on a mind like Dunstan's. Nor was the general character of his malady such as to leave him without augmented veneration for the isle of Avalon.

---

probably, considered a very pious and sublime machinery of angels and devils. An opportunity of thus comparing more modern representations with their ancient originals, is interesting and important. It tends to shew that Romish peculiarities, deemed objectionable by Protestants, are not the most ancient parts of the system, but that, in fact, antiquity is much more completely on the anti-papal side than superficial observers imagine.

[1] *Cleop.* B. 13. f. 62.

His pious disposition and studious habits naturally inclined him to the sacred profession. He was, accordingly, tonsured, and admitted into inferior orders, with the full approbation of his parents. He then retired to his favourite Glastonbury, and led the life of a religious recluse.[1] His mind, however, was too energetic, and his talents too versatile, for the mere monotony of ascetic observances. Hence he not only continued a diligent and multifarious reader, but also he relieved the severity of intellectual exertion by application to music and mechanics.[2] In both he soon excelled. His mastery over the harp attracted general admiration, and the fame of his mechanical skill yet survives in some of those tales that monkish credulity eventually circulated as an honour to his memory, and which are so ludicrous as to defy popular oblivion.

An individual so highly recommended by virtue, ability, and attainments, will generally make his way to the abodes of greatness, even from a humble rank; but Dunstan had no such obstacle to surmount. His family was noble, and his paternal uncle was Athelm, Archbishop of Canterbury. By this prelate he was introduced to Athelstan,[3] and that monarch soon treated him with unequivocal partiality. This flattering success appears to have

---

[1] *Cleop.* B. 13. 62.   OSBERN, *Angl. Sacr.* ii. 93.   MALMESB. *Script. post Bed.* 145.

[2] *Cleop.* B. 13. 63.   OSBERN, *ut supra.*   GERVAS, *X. Script.* 1646.

[3] OSBERN, *Angl. Sacr.* ii. 94.   MALMESB. *Script. post Bed.* 114.   GERVAS, *X. Script.* 1646.   BROMPT. *Ib.* 837.

altered his views. He had always been ambitious: most men are so, especially the young, and those who are conscious of commanding intellect. Dunstan's ambition, probably, had hitherto led him to calculate upon naturalising among his countrymen a system of monachism like that attracting so much notice and applause at Fleury. New hopes and new designs, however, were awakened by his success at court, and he began to build the airy castles of secular distinction. As usual, also, in youth, his mind became susceptible of female blandishment, and of a regard for personal appearance. The jealousy that so often embitters relationship brought all these delightful visions to a violent and sudden termination. It was represented to his royal patron that the youthful student's piety had been grossly overrated; much of his time being really spent over the pernicious vanities of exploded heathenism, from which he sought a proficiency in magic.[1] Dunstan's mechanical genius had given, probably, some colour to this ridiculous charge, in the estimation of ignorant minds, and Athelstan was not proof against it. He was induced, accordingly, though with difficulty, to desire his young friend's retirement from court. Dunstan's enemies could not rest satisfied with mortifying him by this galling disappointment. As he mournfully bent his course away from the scene of greatness that had lately smiled so bewitchingly upon him, they overtook him in all the wanton insolence

---

[1] " Dicentes eum ex libris salutaribus et viris peritis non saluti animæ profutura, sed avitæ gentilitatis vanissima didicisse carmina, et histriarum colere incantationes."—*Cleop.* B. 13. 63.

of savage triumph, bound him hand and foot, and kicked him prostrate into a fetid, miry marsh. This inexcusable violence may have been provoked by the sufferer's haughty, overbearing temper; and his assailants, probably, defended their barbarous revenge by representing it as treatment quite good enough for a confederate with infernal powers. On the departure of his persecutors, Dunstan struggled from the noisome fen, and made for the residence of a neighbouring friend. Blackened, however, with mud, and drenched with wet, his appearance was hardly human; and the fierce dogs that watched around the gate, shewed a strong determination to deny him entrance. A manner, at once kind and firm, having overcome their opposition, Dunstan found his way within the mansion, told his tale, and was hospitably received.[1]

Soon afterwards he visited one of his relations, Elphege the Bald, bishop of Winchester. That prelate appears to have been deeply smitten with admiration of monachism,[2] and he earnestly exhorted his youthful kinsman to consider late disappointments as a warning to adopt finally that monastic life which he had so happily begun at Glastonbury. But Dunstan's hope of courtly advancement, though severely checked, was far from extinguished. When Elphege, accordingly, painted the magnanimity of burying worldly ambition amid the austerities of a cloister, and the immortal rewards awaiting such a sacrifice, the impatient listener answered, " Much

---

[1] *Cleop.* 64.   [2] MALMESB. *Script post Bed.* 138.

greater self-denial is displayed by him who wears life away, professedly a secular, but careful to practise all the virtues of a monk. The habit once taken, a man has renounced his liberty; and future strictness of deportment flows not so much from choice as from necessity." Vainly did Elphege argue against the plain sense of this reply, and entreat of Dunstan to ponder the difficulty of escaping the fatal snares of concupiscence, unless completely removed from temptation.[1] His youthful relative heard all this eloquence in vain. He was violently in love, and his imagination wandered over delightful scenes of connubial bliss. He seems even to have found the monastic dress repulsive;[2] viewing it, probably, as at once the livery of odious celibacy, and a defiance to that eye for exterior grace which females usually possess. Dunstan's ancient biographer is wholly at a loss to explain this anxiety for marriage, and such aversion for the cloister, without attributing them to the temporary ascendancy of Satan. He soon has, however, the satisfaction of relating his hero's complete victory over this anti-monastic feeling. The disappointed courtier again fell dangerously sick, and his spirits were completely broken. As the fever left

---

[1] OSBERN, *Angl. Sacr.* II. 95.

[2] " Primum enim mulierum illi injecit amorem, (*diabolus sc.*) quo per familiares earum amplexus mundanis oblectamentis frueretur. Interea propinquus ipsius Ælfheagus, cognomine Calvus, præsul quoque fidelis petitionibus multus et spiritalibus monitis eum rogavit ut fieret monachus. *Quod ille instinctu præfati fraudatoris renuncians, maluit sponsare juvenculam, cujus cotidie blandiciis foveretur, quam more monachorum bidentinis indui pannis.*—*Cleop.* B. 13. 65.

him, he bade farewell to love, and hastily acquainted Elphege with his fixed intention to become a monk.[1] The prelate was delighted; and, after a short interval, ordained him priest.[2] The monkish habit he seems to have taken at Fleury,[3] then so famed among aspirants after monastic sanctity, and even revered as the spot in which the bones of Benedict himself had, by some very questionable management, found a resting-place.[4]

Dunstan's high connexions and qualities of unquestionable value, easily procured him again admittance into the royal palace. Athelstan, however, was dead, and his brother Edmund had ascended his throne. To this young prince the illustrious Benedictine appears to have been appointed chaplain.[5] The current of his ambition was now completely changed. Henceforth it flowed steadily along the channel provided for it by early predilections. Edmund was induced to build and endow a regular

---

[1] *Cleop.* 13. 65.
[2] MALMESB. *Script. post Bed.* 138.
[3] INGULPH. *Ib.* 496.
[4] EADMER, de Vitâ S. Osw. Archiep. Ebor. (*Angl. Sacr.* ii. 194.) " Cum in castro Cassino vasta solitudo existeret, corpus S. Benedicti ab Agilulfo monacho inde delatum est in cœnobium Floriacense, a Leopoldo abbate, nuper fundatum in Aurelianensi territorio." Of this *furtive deed*, however, as a pope justly styled it, Agilulfus was found to have been guiltless. In 1066, Benedict's bones were discovered in their original grave.—*Propyl. Monasticon.*
[5] " Rex autem Edmundus Dunstano sancto, *hinc presbytero suo,* monasterium Glasconiæ tunc in desolatione a paucis clericis occupatum, cum omnibus pertinentiis contulit restaurandum."— INGULPH. *Script. post Bed.* 496.

monastery at Glastonbury, under the superintendence of his gifted chaplain. Thus the visions of Dunstan's youth were realised. Monastic piles rose from the very soil on which the teeming imagination of his infancy had painted them. Around himself as a superior, was assembled a community of monks, emulating the regularity of Fleury. This was the first establishment of the kind ever known in England, and Dunstan was the first of English Benedictine abbots.[1] He was, in fact, the father of English monachism, a venerable institution, that long nobly patronised both arts and literature. It had, however, a fatal tendency to nurture idleness, fanaticism, imposture, and hypocrisy. These inherent evils of the system, joined to its close alliance with a hostile foreign power, made even thinking and honourable men admit its overthrow to be desirable. While the wealth accumulated by it during ages of popularity effectually secured the concurrence of those mercenary spirits who view political support, and every thing besides within their power, as mere instruments of private gain. Thus, the extraordinary success of the system that Dunstan planted proved eventually the main-spring of its ruin; and his zeal, that so many generations had admired, came to be represented as a national misfortune and dis-

---

[1] " Unde primum, eliminato quicquid oculos superni inspectoris offendebat, monachus et abbas effectus, monachorum ibi scholam primo *primus* instituere cœpit" (ADELARD. Vit. Dunst. ap. Wharton. *Angl. Sacr.* II. 101. note.) " Saluberrimam S. Benedicti sequens institutionem, *primus abbas Anglicæ nationis enituit*."—*Cleop.* 13. 72.

grace. There can be no doubt, however, that Dunstan, though fanatical and ambitious, was able and sincere. Nor can it be denied that the Benedictine order has amply merited respectful consideration. It stands upon far higher ground than that heterogeneous mass of friars, and of discordant monastic sects which gradually overspread the papal reign.

Under Edmund was holden in London[1] a legislative assembly, very fully attended. In this appeared the operation of Dunstan's favourite principles, the first enactment passed being to restrain ecclesiastical persons, whether male or female, from unchastity, under pain of forfeiting their whole properties and the privilege of Christian burial.[2] Monks and nuns are the parties brought unequivocally under the lash of this regulation; but it is rather loosely worded, and was most probably meant as a warning to the whole sacerdotal order. It had long been a popular

---

[1] The two archbishops, Odo and Wulfstan, and a large assemblage, both clerical and lay, were present: Easter was the time of year. The precise date is uncertain; but, as Edmund reigned from 941 to 946, this *witena-gemot* may be reasonably placed in 943, or thereabouts. The preamble calls it a *great synod;* but it cannot hence be necessarily inferred that the assembly was convened for ecclesiastical purposes only. Nor, indeed, does it appear certain that the very religious air worn by the preamble, in the printed editions of the councils, is contemporary. From these, Johnson thus renders the latter sentence of the preamble: " There were Odo and Wulfstan, archbishops, and many other *bishops, consulting for the good of their own souls, and of those who were subject to them.*" Now, in the Cotton MS., although Saxon is found answering to the words printed in *italics*, yet it seems an addition, the hand looking different, though ancient.—*Brit. Mus. Nero.* A. 1. f. 88.

[2] *LL. Eccl. Edm. R.* cap. 1. SPELM. i. 420. WILK. i. 214.

maxim among the stricter professors of religion, that however human laws might allow priests to marry, conscience demanded their celibacy. The monastic opinions now gaining ground so fast on the continent, and industriously patronised by one of the ablest heads in England, naturally brought this ascetic view into more than usual repute. Another of Edmund's constitutions enjoins the payment of tythes, *church-shot,* and *alms-fee*.[1] It is not easy to determine the exact nature of this last payment: hence it has been considered as identical with the *plough-alms* mentioned in Edward the Elder's treaty with Godrun.[2] Practically, the decision of such a question is of no great importance in modern times; not so the repeated legislative mention of assessments for ecclesiastical purposes, independently of tythes. From such notices, it is plain that the *church rates* of after ages are not the mere creatures of some ancient unwritten prescription, but the legitimate successors of more than one formal assessment, constitutionally imposed by the national legislature. It is remarkable, however, that Edmund has not provided civil penalties against defaulters: his legislature merely sanctions their excommunication. Another of his laws enjoins every bishop to repair God's house at his own see,[3] and to admonish the king of due pro-

---

[1] *LL. Eccl. Edm. R.* cap. 2. SPELM. i. 420. WILK. i. 214.

[2] *LL. Eccl. Edov. Sen. et Guth. ab Alur. et Guth. RR. primum conditæ,* cap 6. SPELM. i. 392. WILK. i. 203.

[3] There is an ellipse here, which occasions a difficulty. The Saxon stands, ᵹebete Ɠoƀeꞃ huꞃ on hiꞃ aᵹnum, literally, *better God's house on his own*. The last word may be plural. Hence Spelman has " suis ipsius *sumptibus*." Inett does not profess to trans-

vision for churches generally. This looks like another evidence that tythes were not regarded as the sole fund for the maintaining public worship. In other constitutions, Edmund legislates against bloodshedding, perjury, magical arts, and violation of sanctuary.

During his brief reign, the see of Canterbury became vacant, and Odo was translated to it from Sherborne. This prelate was of Danish blood and heathen parentage; but an early conversion, by which he mortally offended all his original connexions, secured his masculine understanding for the Christian ministry.[1] On receiving an offer of the metropolitical chair, he is reported to have demurred, because he was not a monk, alleging that he should want a recommendation which every successor of Augustine had hitherto possessed.[2] This allegation was probably never made, for there is reason to believe it untrue;[3] nor, therefore, need it pass for certain, that Odo surmounted his objection, either by taking the monastic habit at Fleury,[4] or by receiving it in England from the abbot, especially deputed thence for

---

late, but he thus paraphrases the canon: "The fifth requires the bishops to repair the churches in their own *demeans and lands*, and to inform the king of such others as want repairs." This appears a reasonable way of filling up the ellipse. Johnson's word, *see*, has however been used in the text, because the Saxon will not warrant Inett's word, *churches*, in the former clause. It merely says *God's house*, in the singular.

[1] OSBERN. Vita Odonis.—*Angl. Sacr.* ii. 78.   [2] *Ib.* 81.

[3] "Quod tamen a veritate alienum est: nam quosdam presbyteros fuisse supra retulimus."—*Antiqu. Britan.* 115.

[4] BROMPTON. *X. Script.* 863.

his accommodation:[1] but such relations discover plainly that the monkish era had now fairly begun. To the religious records of England Odo contributed ten extant canons and a synodical epistle, grave and pious compositions, very creditable to his memory. His canons claim immunity for the church from secular impositions, urge a sense of duty upon every class, from the throne downwards, enjoin fasting, alms-giving, and the observance of religious days, especially of Sunday, and insist upon the due payment of tythes.[2] These venerable monuments offer no superstitious admonition; nor, although solicitous of unity for the church, do they make any mention of a papal centre, but merely recommend Christians to become one body, by the common bond of faith, hope, and charity, under one head, Jesus Christ.[3] From one canon, it appears that the monkish profession was often little else than a pretence for vagrancy and idleness.[4] From the last, it is plain that the payment of tythes was not considered as a general release from liberality to the poor. Odo

---

[1] GERVAS. X. Script. 1644. OSBERN. Angl. Sacr. ii. 82.
[2] SPELM. i. 415. WILK. i. 212.
[3] Can. 8. SPELM. i. 417. WILK. i. 213.
[4] Can. 6. SPELM. i. 417. WILK. i. 213. Wigfrith, a visitor to Guthlac, the famous hermit of Croyland, told him that he had met with monkish impostors among the Scots. "Dicebat enim se inter Scottorum populos habitasse, et illic pseudo-anachoritas diversorum religionum simulatores vidisse."—(*Brit. Mus. MSS.* COTTON. *Nero.* E. 1. f. 191.) It might seem fair enough to charge all these impositions upon a rival party; but obviously, the monks of earlier, and the friars of later times, must have always had among them a considerable body of idle hypocrites. Odo's canon shews this to have been the case in his day.

says, that men are not only to live, but also to give alms, out of the nine parts remaining after piety has had her tenth. The synodical epistle appears to be imperfect, but it conveys admonition in a religious, humble, and earnest strain, every way worthy of a Christian prelate.[1]

Among the monks living under Dunstan at Glastonbury, was a well-born native of Winchester, named Ethelwold;[2] he had been ordained priest in company with his abbot,[3] and he cordially partook of all that eminent man's monastic enthusiasm. So anxious, indeed, was he to rival the most perfect of his order, that he was upon the point of leaving England for a residence among the foreign Benedictines, when the mother of Edred, now upon the throne, conjured her son to save his dominions from the loss of a personage so holy.[4] Edred was overcome by these persuasions, and, founding a monastery on a royal estate at Abingdon, he made Ethelwold its abbot. This was the second Benedictine house established in England. No exertion, however, of its new superior, was wanting to render it the parent of many others. He was aware that continental monasteries excelled in reading and singing; he therefore procured masters from Corby, to instruct his own society in these attractive arts.[5] He seems to

---

[1] SPELM. i. 418. WILK. i. 214.

[2] *Brit. Mus. MSS.* COTTON. *Nero.* E. 1. f. 416. Ethelwold's parents, we there learn, lived in the reign of Edward the Elder. Wulstan was the author of this life.

[3] *Ib.*   [4] MALMESB. *Script. post Bed.* 139.

[5] Hist. Cænob. Abendon.—*Angl. Sacr.* i. 165.

have doubted whether, even under Dunstan, there had been opportunities for a thorough acquaintance with monastic discipline: he sent, accordingly, one of his monks to Fleury for farther instruction.[1] Thus he laid a secure foundation of popularity for his favourite system, by the attractions of its public worship, and by the well-defined, rigid austerity of its discipline. Rightly, therefore, was he termed, in after ages, the *father of monks*.[2] Dunstan had, indeed, led the way, but his intellect was too comprehensive, and his ordinary habits were too secular, for maturing all those details which the system required for its complete success.

Monachism had, however, scarcely taken root, when Edred, its royal patron, prematurely died. His nephew, Edwy, a very handsome youth,[3] succeeded to the throne. This young prince, wearied by the coarse intemperance of his coronation day, withdrew from the festive hall into a private room. Disgusted at his absence, the carousing nobles despatched a remonstrance by Dunstan and a bishop, named Cynesius, related to him. On entering, the messengers found Edwy seated sportively between his wife and mother-in-law, while the crown lay negligently upon the ground. Expostulation being

---

[1] WULSTAN. *MSS.* COTTON. 417.

[2] " Pater monachorum, et sidus Anglorum."—(BROMPTON. X. *Script.* 877.) The former of these designations appears to have been borrowed from the *Saxon Chronicle*, which, mentioning Ethelwold's death under the year 984, styles him muneca fæðer, *father of monks*.

[3] " Præ nimiâ etenim pulchritudine *Pancali* sortitus est nomen."—ETHELWERD. *Script. post Bed.* 483.

found unavailing to procure the youthful king's return, a scene of violence ensued. Dunstan ended this by forcing Edwy from his seat, replacing the crown upon his head, and dragging him once more to join the offended revellers.[1] The whole transaction naturally gave mortal offence both to the king and his fair connexions. Dunstan, accordingly, was under the necessity of retiring to Glastonbury: thence he was driven soon after into exile, amidst the tears of his monks. Dunstan's panegyrical biography converts this natural incident into broad caricature, by contrasting the weeping community with the grinning face of Satan, whose peals of laughter, we are told, were distinctly heard, as the abbot's receding steps mournfully passed along the vestibule.[2] By Dunstan's disgrace, the royal vengeance was not satisfied: his abbey was dissolved, as was also that of Abingdon; and thus English monachism seemed only like some meteor, that brightly flashes, and then immediately disappears.

But Edwy had miscalculated his power. Dunstan's establishments were nurseries of fanaticism, and were studiously formed from admired continental

---

[1] *Cleop.* B. 13. 76. The queen's name is usually written *Elgiva*: the contemporary life of Dunstan has it *Æthelgifu*. Mr. Turner (*Hist. Angl. Sax.* ii. 252. note) may be consulted for authorities proving that this lady was Edwin's wife. She is branded as his mistress by some of the monastic writers, most probably because she was related to him within the prohibited degrees.

[2] " Audita est in atrio templi vox plaudentis diaboli, quasi vox juvenculæ acriter atque minute cachinnantis."—OSBERN. *Angl. Sacr.* ii. 105.

models, both powerful holds upon popular favour: the nobles, also, whose commission the exiled abbot had executed, probably regarded him as a victim in their cause, and hence justly entitled to their protection. An irresistible conspiracy, accordingly, soon secured his triumphant return from Flanders, where he had taken refuge. Nor was this humiliation all that Edwy had to undergo: his insurgent subjects raised Edgar, a younger brother, to the throne, assigning to him, as a kingdom, all England between the Humber and the Thames:[1] Elgiva, too, was divorced by Odo, as related to her unfortunate husband within the prohibited degrees.[2] With even this the archbishop was not contented: he branded her upon the face, and sent her away to Ireland. A short residence there healed her unsightly wounds, and she ventured upon a return into her native island. Having reached Gloucester, she was arrested, and under Odo's authority the tendons of her legs were barbarously severed.[3] Of this cruel mutilation she seems never to have recovered, being soon after overtaken by the hand of death. Elgiva's sufferings have effectually blasted with posterity the memory of Odo: but one age cannot safely measure the men of another by a standard of its own. The archbishop, who has long been regarded as rather a monster than

---

[1] *Cleop.* B. 13. 78.

[2] "A.D. 958. This year Archbishop Odo separated Edwy and Elfgiva, because they were too nearly related."—*Sax. Chr.* 150. Dr. INGRAM'S *Transl.*

[3] OSBERN. *Angl. Sacr.* II. 84.

a man, was known among contemporaries as *Odo the Good*.[1] His treatment of Elgiva, now ranked among the most inhuman outrages upon record, was attributed, probably, to the absolute necessity of restraining irregular passions, by occasional examples of just severity.

After a short interval, Edwy's untimely death, seemingly by violence, rendered his more fortunate brother master of all England. Upon the unhappy prince, thus cut off in the flower of his age, monkish writers have been immeasurably severe. Ethelwerd, however, a contemporary authority of high rank, assures us that he deserved his people's love.[1] He

---

[1] *Ode the Good.* (MALMESB. *Script. post Bed.* 115.) OSBERN (*Angl. Sacr.* ii. 86.) gives this designation in a Saxon form: "Odo se gode," (ϸe ᵹoꝺ.) The author of this compliment was Dunstan, who is said to have seen a dove in the cathedral of Canterbury, while he was celebrating mass, on Whitsunday, which, after a time, settled on Odo's tomb. This incident, which might easily have happened in a large building with many unglazed windows, was represented as a visible descent of the Holy Ghost, and an undeniable demonstration of Odo's sanctity. Dunstan, accordingly, never subsequently passed his tomb without a reverence, nor spoke of him but as *the good.* This designation, however, was readily adopted by others; and it had not worn out in popular discourse, especially at Canterbury, when Osbern wrote. Had Odo been viewed by his own age, as one unmanly outrage has made posterity view him, Dunstan's authority would not have been sufficient for thus embalming his memory.

This archbishop's name is variously written, *Odo, Oda,* and *Ode.* It seems to be the *Oddy* of modern English surnames.

[2] " Tenuit namque quadriennio *per regnum amandus.*" (*Script. post Bed.* 483.) Edwy's death occurred in 959 : that it was violent, may be inferred from probability and from the obscure language of ancient authorities. The contemporary life of Dunstan (*Cleop.* B. 13. f. 78) says : " Interea germanus ejusdem Eadgari,

was evidently quite unequal to the task of curbing a society so fierce and haughty, as that which owned allegiance to his crown: but this is no very serious imputation upon the memory of a sovereign cut off in youth, and hastily embroiled with such men as Odo and Dunstan.

The latter of these two obtained episcopal honours in the beginning of Edgar's reign. Worcester was his first bishopric, and shortly afterwards he added London to it,[1] both sees lying in the portion of England wrested from Edwy. During that young prince's life, a more splendid ecclesiastical prize became vacant by the death of Archbishop Odo; but Canterbury was under the authority of Edwy, and by his influence Elsin, bishop of Winchester, became the new metropolitan. This prelate, a decided enemy to their order, is charged by the monks with insulting Odo's grave, and with obtaining Canterbury by simony. He died, however, on his way to Rome, whither he was proceeding for the pall. His unexpected fate

quia justa Di sui judicia deviando dereliquit, novissimum flatum *miserâ morte* expiravit." An old manuscript chronicler, cited by Mr. Turner (*Hist. Angl. Sax.* ii. 257), says, however, expressly, that *he was slain in Gloucestershire.* Mr. Turner gives *Edwin* as the name of this young sovereign, and under a great weight of authority; but he is called *Eadwig* by the Saxon Chronicle, Ethelwerd, and the contemporary life of Dunstan.

[1] Dunstan was advanced to the see of Worcester in 957, and in the following year London was conferred upon him, to hold with it. The next year, being that of Edwy's death, saw his translation to Canterbury. Dunstan's monastic biographers represent that he was offered that see on the two former vacancies, but declined it. Edwy's authority would, however, be likely to prevent Dunstan from receiving any such compliment within the limits of his kingdom.

arose, it is said, from extreme cold encountered in crossing the Alps; but it is represented as a judicial visitation of offended Providence. Brithelm, bishop of Wells, was tantalised by being chosen in his room; but the necessary arrangements were incomplete on Edwy's immature decease: Canterbury, therefore, was not closed against Dunstan's ambition, and the primate elect was compelled to relinquish his claims.[1] Having thus attained the highest dignity within a subject's reach, Dunstan became virtually the most powerful man in England. Edgar was, indeed, a boy of sixteen when he ascended the throne, and he seems ever to have been under the influence of licentious, headstrong passions. Very rarely do such men fill important stations with any degree of credit to themselves, or of advantage to society: Edgar is, however, one of these uncommon instances. Monastic writers have naturally loaded his memory with panegyric; nor can inquirers, however unfavourable to monachism, deny that his rule was glorious and beneficial. He reigned in prosperity and peace, the admitted superior over a larger portion, perhaps, of the island than any one of his ancestors.[2] Under

---

[1] OSBERN. *Angl. Sacr.* II. 109. Brithelm is represented by Osbern as a good-natured man, who knew very well how to take care of himself, but who was unfit for active life. "Homo mansuetior quam industrior, et qui suæ magis quam alienæ vitæ nosset consulere." He seems to have been far from willing to relinquish Canterbury. "Jussus a rege, et omni populo, Cantuariâ discedit." —*Ib.*

[2] Þe recȝað to roðan þ ȝe tima pær ȝeræliȝ ⁊ pinrum on Ængelcÿnne þa þa Eadȝap cÿnincȝ þone Crirtendom ȝefÿnðrove· ⁊ fela munuclipa aræpve· ⁊ hir cyneþice pær puniȝende on ribbe· rpa þ man ne ȝehÿnde ȝif æniȝ rcyphepe pæþe buton aȝenþe leode þe þir land heoldon·

so much good fortune, he attested his exultation with pardonable vanity, by titles, borrowed seemingly from the imperial court of Constantinople.[1] To Dunstan, probably, Edgar was largely indebted for his enviable position.[2] The royal councils were directed chiefly by a man of extraordinary talent: the mind, indeed, of that illustrious adviser was rather warped upon monastic questions; but its ordinary produce was an enviable succession of views, clear, sound, comprehensive, and decided.

After a reign over all England of about two years, Edgar found his people oppressed by a calamity that no human wisdom could assuage. A dreadful pestilence raged, especially in London.[3] As usual in such

---

⁊ ealle þa cynınȝaſ þe on þyrum ıȝlanðe pæɲon· Cumeɲa ⁊ Scoττa· comon το Eadȝaɲe· hpılon aneſ dæȝeſ eahτa cynınȝaſ· ⁊ hı ealle ȝebuȝon το Eadȝaɲeſ pıſſunȝe. (*Brit. Mus. MSS.* COTTON. *Hom. in S. Swithun. Julius* E. 7. f. 101.) *We truly say that the time was happy and joyous in the English nation when King Eadgar furthered Christianity, and reared many monks' livings: and his reign continued in peace, so that no fleet was heard of, but of one's own people who hold this land: and all the kings who were in this island, Cumbrians and Scots, came to Eadgar, once in one day eight kings, and these all bowed to Eadgar's direction.* The eight kings meant, are Kenneth of Scotland, Malcolm of Cumbria, Macchus of Anglesey, three from Wales, and two others more difficult of identification.—See TURNER's *Hist. Angl. Sax.* ii. 265.

[1] " Ego, Edgarus, totius Albionis basileus, nec non maritimorum seu insulanorum regum circum habitantium." (MALMESB. *Script. post Bed.* 32.) " Ego, Edgarus, totius Albionis monarcha." —INGULPH. *ib.* 502.

[2] Afflaverat profecto cor regis divinitatis specie (*Dunst.* sc.), ut ejus consilium susciperet in omnibus incunctanter faciens quæcunque Pontifex jubenda putaret. Ille quoque quicquid famæ et saluti regis concinnum esse intelligeret, non omittere, differentem acrius urgere."—MALMESB. *Script. post Bed.* 115.

[3] In the year 961.—*Sax. Chr.* 153.

seasons, divine justice and human iniquity were anxiously contrasted in the public mind. Advantage was taken of these wholesome feelings to urge a plea in behalf of the Church: the needy and avaricious, disregarding conscience and the feeble sanctions of law, had commonly failed in the faithful discharge of tythes and other ecclesiastical dues. Their case was now represented as analogous to that of tenants failing in their payments to landowners. Men were exhorted to consider the little indulgence usually shewn to such defaulters, and to ask themselves, whether corresponding failures were likely to be excused by God; his vengeance rather might be justly feared by those who should fraudulently withhold that share from the provision for his service, which had been imposed upon them alike by law and conscience. Arguments of this kind appear to have prevailed in two legislative assemblies, the former of which was holden at Andover, then a royal domain. The rights of religion were now statutably protected by civil penalties; and thus was established a principle of imposing ecclesiastical rent-charges upon land, recoverable by the ordinary processes of law: no specific penalty, however, was provided, a discretionary power merely being given to the royal officers, which they were strictly enjoined to exercise for the punishment of defaulters.[1]

---

[1] See the document at the end. This venerable piece is bound up in the midst of an ancient MS. volume in the British Museum, chiefly occupied by the lives of saints. This position may be the chief reason why it seems to have been hitherto overlooked. It is entitled in a hand, perhaps, of James the First's time, *Carta Saxonica tem-*

In a subsequent meeting of the Saxon estates, this loose legislation was abandoned. Subtraction of tythes was now placed under cognisance of the civil and ecclesiastical authorities conjointly. The king's reeve, the bishop's, and the mass-priest entitled to recover, were to seize all the property tythable, but on which tythes had not been paid: they were to restore one-tenth of it to the defaulter, to render its tenth to the minister aggrieved, and to divide the remaining eight parts between the lord and the bishop.[1] This earliest of known statutes, guarding

---

pore Regis Edgari. The piece itself is probably coeval with the latter assembly recorded in it, and may not unreasonably be considered as a sort of proclamation, or authentic declaration, of certain legislative enactments despatched to some principal ecclesiastical establishment. It is followed by a similar exposition of enactments relating to affairs merely temporal. In the catalogue these documents are thus described: *Leges, sive constitutiones Eadgari Regis, quas occasione gravissimæ pestis, per totum regnum statuit observandas* (Saxonice): *folia bina ex libro quodam pœnitentiali avulsa.* The MS. volume is thought to have been chiefly written about the year 1000.

[1] "3. And let all the tythe of young animals be paid by Pentecost, and of the fruits of the earth by the Equinox: and let every church-scot be paid by Martin's mass, under pain of the full mulct, which the Doom-book mentions. And if any will not pay the tythe as we have commanded, let the king's reeve, and the bishop's reeve, and the mass-priest of the minster, go to him, and take by force the tenth part for the minster to which it belongs, and deliver to him the ninth part, and let the eight parts be divided into two; and let the lord take one half, the bishop the other, whether it be a king's man or a thane's man." (JOHNSON's *Transl.* SPELM. I. 444. WILK. I. 245.) There are no known means of affixing a certain date to these constitutions enacted under Edgar. Spelman would assign them to the year 967, or thereabouts, as being in the middle of Edgar's reign. There can be no reasonable doubt that they are posterior to the two legislative assemblies, whose acts are

tythe-owners in the possession of their property by a definite measure of coercion, appears chargeable with unjust severity: the times, however, were lawless and rude; hence the remedies provided for social evils were naturally tinged with unsparing harshness: ecclesiastical dues, also, really require a very full measure of protection. The dealer and artisan, the practitioner in law and medicine, are only controlled by competition in making terms with such as desire their commodities or aid; but the minister of God's word and sacraments enjoys no such advantage. All but fools and reprobates, indeed, freely concede importance to his profession. This acknowledgment, however, generally flows rather from cool, deliberate conviction, than from such feelings as maintain secular vocations. Minds fixed intently upon eternity, are alive to the value of religious ordinances: habitually the wants and cravings of mankind incline them to regard expenditure upon piety, as that which can be most agreeably, safely, and completely retrenched. Legislation, therefore, against such a shortsighted selfishness, is equally merciful and wise. It has planted a liberal profession, and a well-governed house of God, in every corner of England. Considerable seats of wealth and population might have commanded these advantages, and undoubtedly would,

---

recorded in the Cotton. MS., and which must have been holden after the pestilence, in 961. If they had been anterior to these assemblies, an arbitrary penalty, to be inflicted by the king's reeve alone, would not probably have been provided in the latter. The constitutions long printed are evidently an improvement upon such undefined enactments.

without national aid; but the country generally must have wanted them, unless a competent portion of all the people's industry had been legally reserved for their maintenance: nor, unless this portion had been jealously protected, could it have permanently stood its ground against that spirit of rapacity which human corruption ever keeps in vigour. Such protection, however, having been provided, every estate inherited or acquired was burdened with a variable rent-charge, reserved as the patrimony of religion. Hence opulent landlords were more easily induced to found and build churches upon their several properties. Nor usually did an endowment of glebe satisfy their pious liberality: in many cases, probably in all, they attested solemnly their individual approval of existing laws, by settling the tythes of their lands upon their new establishments. Thus English parochial churches, in themselves private foundations, can allege claims of two several kinds upon the properties around. Not only can they plead immemorial usage, and penal statutes of high antiquity, but also legal surrenders by very distant proprietors, confirmatory of such usage, and formally assenting to such statutes.

From another of Edgar's ecclesiastical laws, it is plain that the foundation of rural churches was in steady progress. The liberality of public bodies, however, seems to have lagged behind that of individuals. A founder was restrained from settling upon his church any more than a third of the tythes paid by its congregation: unless, indeed, it possessed a cemetery, every portion of the sacred tenth was denied. In such cases, it was probably considered rather as a private chapel: the proprietor, accordingly, was to maintain his priest out of the nine parts. Under no circumstance, however, does a thane appear to have been encouraged in providing religious instruction for his tenantry, by any transfer of the *church-shot*. The ancient minsters, immemorially entitled to it, might seem hitherto to have relaxed nothing from their claims upon this payment:[1] such tenacity must have acted injuriously upon the progress of parochial endowments; probably, to the great regret of pious and discerning minds. Although a great principle, however, calling for some particular sacrifice, might be generally acknowledged, yet its complete victory over individual prejudices and interests would naturally be slow: hence originates the prevailing uncertainty as to parochial foundations. These have arisen from no legislative compulsion, but from the liberality of individuals during many successive generations, encouraged by the gradual surrender of rights vested in anterior establishments.

---

[1] " 2. If there be any thane who hath, on land which he holds by written deed, a church with a burying-place belonging to it, let him pay the third part of his tythes into his own church. If he hath a church with no burying-place belonging to it, let him give his priest what he will out of the nine parts; and let every church-scot go into the ancient minster from all the ground of freemen." (JOHNSON's *Transl.* SPELM. i. 444. WILK. I. 245.) Perhaps it is doubtful whether any distinction is intended here between tythes and church-shot. *Shot* properly means a *payment*, hence the familiar English phrase, *pay the shot.* If such a general interpretation of the term *shot* be allowable in this place, it might seem not unreasonable to suppose that private founders were allowed to endow their churches with a third of *all* the ecclesiastical dues arising from their estates.

But although Edgar's ecclesiastical legislation, bearing upon the Church's patrimony, is that alone which has retained any practical importance, he is nowise indebted to it for his figure in religious history. He is the hero of monkish chroniclers, and his rule really exerted a lasting influence upon English society, because he was Dunstan's passive instrument in rooting the monastic system. During his brief reign, he seems to have established no fewer than forty-eight monasteries.[1] Had all these been new foundations, they must have wrought striking changes in the national habits and modes of thinking; many of them, however, reared their heads amidst a considerable mass of individual suffering, and greatly to the disapprobation of a numerous party. Clergymen were driven by the hand of power, either to become monks, or to relinquish the homes and livings in which they were legally seated around a minster.[2] If married, the former part of this alternative must have been felt as an intolerable hardship, to which submission was almost impossible. Nor could many of those who were single have regarded it otherwise than inexcusably tyrannical. Under pain of losing their bread, and of being branded as irreligious, they were called upon to renounce their natural liberty. Some of the abler heads among them, also, might

---

[1] EADMER, de Vita S. Osw. Archiep. Ebor. *Angl. Sacr.* ii. 201. Some of these were nunneries. Bromton is not equally precise, contenting himself with reckoning Edgar's monastic establishments at *more than forty.*—X. *Script.* 868.

[2] " Itaque clerici multarum ecclesiarum, datâ optione, aut ut amictum mutarent, aut locis valedicerent, cessêre melioribus, habitacula vacua facientes."—MALMESB. *Script. post Bed.* 115.

clearly discern that ostentatious observances, and substantial holiness, are by no means inseparable companions: but such considerations operate extensively upon the higher orders alone. Inferior life is little alive to the just rights and reasonable expectations of classes above itself: the ruder intellects also are ever liable to be duped by noisy pretension. It was, accordingly, among his more considerable subjects, that Edgar's alleged reformation encountered opposition; the great majority, probably, regarded him as piously and patriotically bent upon advancing sound religion, and reforming undeniable abuses.

Dunstan was little more than the adviser of this great ecclesiastical revolution. Ethelwold, bishop of Winchester, and Oswald, originally bishop of Worcester, eventually archbishop of York, were the principal agents in thus forcing a new character upon existing establishments, and in organising Benedictine societies, in situations where no religious house had previously stood. Ethelwold had been one of Dunstan's earliest inmates at Glastonbury, and had, from the first, gained his good opinion; otherwise he would never have recommended him as abbot on the foundation of Abingdon. Oswald was nephew to Archbishop Odo, and was placed by him in a canonry at Canterbury. There he imbibed strongly the rising taste for monachism, and passing over to Fleury, he became a Benedictine. By Dunstan he was introduced to Edgar, whose influence procured his election to the see of Worcester. Immediately he fixed his mind upon converting the cathedral there into a monastery of his own order; but the canons resolutely resisted, and being supported by powerful connexions, he was unable to overcome them. Under this disappointment he planted a rival house, duly supplied with monks, close to his rebellious chapter, in order that the populace might have full opportunity for drawing invidious comparisons between the two systems. This expedient succeeded: immense congregations waited upon the monks, while the canons ministered in a church more than half deserted. This mortification was embittered by serious loss. Worshippers brought offerings to the altar, and these were now taken to the Benedictine church. It was not long before these various causes began to operate: Wensinus, an elderly canon, much respected among his brethren, was the first to give way. Oswald immediately sent him to Ramsey for instruction in the Benedictine discipline. As usual, example proved infectious: other canons became monks, and Wensinus was quickly recalled to Worcester, as prior of the monastery which Oswald had now succeeded in substituting for his chapter.[1] Thus was consummated the first of these popular innovations; and, accordingly, the process of converting a chapter into a monastery became known as *Oswald's Law*.[2] Ethelwold seems, indeed, to have preceded

---

[1] EADMER, de Vita S. Osw.—*Angl. Sacr.* ii. 203.

[2] WHARTON in Eadm. *Angl. Sacr.* ii. 202. Florence of Worcester, there cited, assigns Oswald's innovation to 969. It appears, however, to have occupied two years from that time, before it was fully carried into effect. (*Ib.* i. 546.) Edgar's charter of *Oswald's Law*, as it is there styled, was granted in confirmation of Oswald's changes at Worcester, with the concurrence of the Saxon estates.

Oswald in such an attempt upon his own cathedral of Winchester. But he, probably, found more difficulty in accomplishing his design. Of the other bishops we hear nothing, and therefore they may fairly be considered as either indifferent, or hostile to the violence intended for every cathedral. But Dunstan, Ethelwold, and Oswald, formed a triumvirate, which, backed by the royal authority, might generally defy resistance. Hence Edgar's reign was marked by a succession of triumphs for the monastic party.

This victorious progress was undoubtedly secured by a strong current of popular affection. Besides parading themselves and their system as perfect models of self-denial, monks were most ingenious and indefatigable in supplying the vulgar appetite for marvels. Churches, never hitherto famed for any miraculous pretension, had no sooner passed into monastic hands, than their cemeteries were found mines of wonder-working relics.[1] Even monasteries, un-

It is printed by Spelman (i. 432), and by Wilkins (i. 239). It is remarkable, in general history, for a statement in the preamble, that Athelstan was the first of English kings to whom the whole island became subject. Even this assertion must, of course, be received with some limitation, but it evidently shews that the extent of Egbert's ascendancy is commonly overrated.

[1] Ethelwold, as might be expected, led the way in making these discoveries. " In illo tempore dictus vir venerabilis Ethelwoldus, Wintoniensis episcopus, monasteriorum constructor, a rege Edgaro impetravit, ut sanctorum corpora, quæ in destructis locis jacebant in negligentiâ, transferre sibi liceret in ea quæ construxerat monasteria." (BROMTON X. Script. 868.) From this it seems likely, that Ethelwold looked out for something to attract lovers of the marvellous, whenever he established a monastery, as an integral

recommended by a single promising interment, were careful to supply from a distance this mortifying and prejudicial deficiency.[1] Some departed saint, or at least, some part of one, was diligently sought and fairly gained. At other times, it was the shameful prize of either force or fraud. From whatever source this important acquisition came, the lucky house felt neither difficulty nor scruple in extracting from it both fame and fortune. Sickly pilgrims quickly crowded around their altar, and returned home enraptured by a cure. Nor is it doubtful that, among these invalids, many found a real benefit: change of air and scene, unwonted exercise, powerful excitement, are quite enough to give temporary relief under several human ailments. It would, however, be unfair to charge indiscriminately with dishonesty, this monastic provision for popular credulity. Among the monks were, probably, some few who valued relics merely as a productive source of revenue; but the

---

portion of its equipments It may seem amusing to be gravely told, that so long as the canons retained their ancient possessions in the church of Winchester, no miracles graced St. Swithin's tomb, but that the monks produced immediately a very different scene. " Quamdiu enim clerici inhabitabant ecclesiam Wentanam, nulla per sanctum Swythunum Deus miracula operatus est; sed *ipsis ejectis, statim miracula patrata sunt.*"—RUDBORNE *Angl. Sacr.* i. 223.

[1] " In the reign of Edgar, a shameful description of robbery had obtained among ecclesiastical bodies — the stealing of relics, upon a pretended divine revelation. In those days, it was no uncommon practice for powerful abbeys to despoil the weaker monasteries, or to rob defenceless villages of their sainted remains, in order to increase the celebrity of their own foundations."—GORHAM's *Hist. and Antiq. of Eynesbury and St. Neot's,* i. 48.

majority consisted of genuine fanatics. Now, such spirits have at all times, and under every circumstance, eagerly clung to miracle. Vainly for this tenacity do they live when knowledge is widely spread, or even when scoffers are abundant. Their vanity and credulity are very seldom proof against any disposition to give themselves, or their party, credit for supernatural endowments. Monastic bodies, therefore, in the tenth century, may reasonably claim indulgence from those who trace to them that particular species of religious imposture and delusion, which descended from their age uninterruptedly to the Reformation.[1]

It was not, however, within Dunstan's power to transfer a considerable mass of property from one order of men to another, without legislative intervention. Upon this necessity, the canons menaced with ejection anxiously relied. They naturally complained of gross injustice, and their cause was espoused by a majority among persons of condition. A convocation of the national estates afforded them, therefore, a reasonable hope of defeating royal policy and popular enthusiasm. Such an assembly was yielded to their importunities,[2] apparently in the year 968. Winchester was the place of its meeting, and it

---

[1] Fuller observes rather quaintly, but with great force and justice, " Whereas formerly corruptions came into the church at the wicket, now the broad gates were open for their entrance; monkery making way for ignorance and superstition to overspread the whole world.—*Ch. Hist.* Cent. x. 134.

[2] Fragmenta ex Aliâ Vitâ S. Dunst. autore Osberto Monacho Sæcul. 12.—*Acta SS. Ord. Benedict.* v. 706.

opened most ominously for the monastic party. Edgar, indeed, with the episcopal triumvirate, Dunstan, Ethelwold, and Oswald, brought heavy charges against married clergymen: these were met by assurances, that all reasonable causes of complaint should be removed. Nor did an overwhelming proportion of the assembled legislators discover any disposition to carry compliance farther. Edgar, accordingly, began to waver,[1] and was upon the point of siding with his nobles, when he and Dunstan are said to have heard, repeatedly and distinctly, from a crucifix in the wall, the following words: *God forbid it to be done: God forbid it to be done.*[2] In other parts of the hall, nothing more than some unintelligible noise appears to have been perceived: enough was heard, however, to raise curiosity and awe. The mysterious murmur was now explained, and the assembly felt a divine compulsion to drive the unhappy canons from their homes. This relation appears in the monastic writers generally; but Florence of Worcester, who mentions the council, has omitted it: hence modern Romish

---

[1] Even Dunstan also is represented as shaken. Osbern makes him say, immediately before the crucifix spoke, *Fateor vincere vos nolo. Ecclesiæ suæ causam Christo judici committo.* Wharton prefers Capgrave's version of his alleged speech. *Fateor, vinci nolo.*—De Vit. S. Dunst. Angl. Sacr. ii. 112.

[2] *Absit hoc ut fiat. Absit hoc ut fiat.* The crucifix appears, from Osbern, to have been eloquent no farther. The ancient MS. chronicle cited by Spelman, adds to these words the following: *Judicastis benè, mutaretis non benè.* It also adds, that all the assembly having fallen to the earth with alarm, the crucifix said, but again so that only Edgar and Dunstan could distinguish the words—*Surgite ne expavescatis, quia hodiè justitia et pax in monachis osculata sunt.*

authors are sufficiently justified in representing it as an apocryphal legend, posterior to the Conquest. Florence, however, places the council of Winchester after Edgar's death, and, indeed, leaves the whole transaction in considerable obscurity.[1] But, independently of ancient authority for placing this council in 968, it is plain that some new legislative powers were, about that time, required for giving efficacy to Edgar's intentions, actually brought into operation very shortly afterwards : nor without some ingenious contrivance were the canons likely to be deserted by their powerful friends.

On Edgar's premature decease,[2] their claims upon humanity and justice were promptly vindicated. The intrusive monks were generally expelled by persons in authority, and the clerical victims of an oppressive, calumnious fanaticism, again took possession of their homes and properties.[3] A large proportion of their

---

[1] Spelman (*Conc.* ii. 490) has collected the various printed authorities bearing upon the council of Winchester, and has added to them a citation from an ancient MS. chronicle. From this he is led to place the council in 968 ; and Wharton (*Angl. Sacr.* ii. 112) considers him to have judged rightly : evidently he has probability with him. It is a point, however, involved in much obscurity, the councils of Winchester and Calne having been commonly confounded together. There is a declamatory speech, extolling the monks and disparaging the canons, assigned to Edgar by Ethelred. (*X. Script.* 360.) The substance of this was, probably, spoken at the council of Winchester. The author of the *Antiquitates Britannicæ* (p. 127) would refer it to 969. It is reprinted there, and by Spelman, *Conc.* i. 476.

[2] Edgar died in 975, at the age of thirty-two.

[3] " Post obitum vero Edgari status regni turbabatur, nam plures magnates, ejectis monachis, de magnis monasteriis quos rex

protectors would fain have given them the security of a prince pledged in their favour. Under Edgar's son, by his second wife, they had a reasonable prospect of this advantage: but his own will, and the prior claims of Edward, his offspring by a former marriage, backed by the influence of Dunstan, were found irresistible.[1] In conceding this point, however, the more intelligent classes had no thought of surrendering also their clergy to proscription. The kingdom was agitated, accordingly, by angry debates, loud complaints, and harassing apprehensions.[2] For allaying these heats a legislative assembly was convened at Calne.[3] This was attended by Beornhelm, a Scottish prelate of commanding eloquence, as advocate for the menaced and insulted clergy.[4] The monastic party thus felt itself pressed, not only by a preponderating weight of property and intelligence, but also by talents for debate, probably superior to any within its own command. Hence Dunstan was almost over-

---

Edgarus et Dunstanus dudum instituerant, clericos cum uxoribus reduxerunt."—*Bibl. Lameth. MSS.* 12. JOHAN. TINMOUTH. *Hist. Aurea.* Pars. 3. f. 80.

[1] EADMER, de Vita S. Dunst.—*Angl. Sacr.* II. 220.

[2] " Multus indè tumultus in omni angulo Angliæ factus est."— INGULPH, *Script. post Bed.* 506.

[3] In 978. *Sax. Chr.* 163. Spelman doubts whether this council might not have been holden in the preceding year. In that year, a council was holden at Kirtlington. A third council was holden at Amesbury. This appears to have been for the purpose of completing the business broken off by the accident at Calne. But there are no decrees extant passed in any one of these three councils.

[4] Eadmer (*ut supra*) says, that the northern orator was hired upon very liberal terms: *magno conductum pretio.*

powered, when the floor suddenly gave way, and most of his auditors fell violently into a chamber underneath. Many were killed upon the spot, and others were extricated with such injuries as condemned them to suffering for life. The archbishop, and, according to some authorities, his friends also, wholly escaped, the beam under him remaining firm.[1] This extraordinary good fortune was interpreted as a divine manifestation in favour of monachism, and it secured its triumph. Among moderns, it has commonly fastened upon Dunstan an imputation of cruelty and fraud. It might have been accidental; but accidents very opportune, especially when occurring in an age of gross ignorance, are fairly open to suspicion.

Immaturity of years excused the king from attending this assembly;[2] and his violent death soon afterwards damped monastic hopes. He fell by the blow of an assassin, hired by his mother-in-law, who thus opened the throne for her own son's accession.[3] Edward's untimely fate was, therefore, owing merely

---

[1] The *Saxon Chronicle* says that Dunstan stood *alone*: Malmesbury says the same. On the other hand, Eadmer says, " Ubi vero Dunstanus *cum suis consistebat*, nulla ruina domus." John of Tinmouth also (*ut supra*), says, " Ubi vero *cum suis* scus accubitabat, ibi nulla ruine suffusio fiebat." Obviously the suspicion of contrivance is very much weakened, if Dunstan were the only party saved from falling: so say, however, the most ancient authorities. A particular examination of the case may be seen in Mr. Turner's *Hist. Angl. Sax.* ii. 277.

[2] " Absente propter ætatem rege."—MALMESB. *Script. post Bed.* 34.

[3] Edward was assassinated at Corfe Castle, the residence of his mother-in-law Elfrida, in 978.—*Sax. Chr.* 163.

to the vindictive and restless cupidity of an ambitious woman. His unfledged authority had, however, served as a rallying point for the monastic party; and accordingly he became known as *the martyr.* Nor were the monks tardy in discerning, that although dead he might advance their interest. His remains were invested with a saintly celebrity and devotees eagerly crowded around them.[1] This royal youth's assassination thus afforded a share of the seed eventually so prolific in superstition. Any extensive immediate benefit, however, does not seem to have gladdened the monastic party from his brief career. Domestic rivalry soon became, indeed, unequal to the full command of popular attention, for Scandinavia poured again her pirates over England. But the controversy between monks and canons could hardly fail of poisoning every considerable respite, and thus of undermining the Anglo-Saxon state. Hence, this unhappy strife may fairly be considered as a cause of that national decrepitude which allowed a temporary ascendancy to Denmark, and which eventually gave the Normans a secure establishment.

Under Ethelred, ignominiously known as *the Unready,* opened early a protracted series of harassing

---

[1] As this unfortunate lad, after losing his seat, was dragged a considerable distance in the stirrups, it is probable that his corpse was very much disfigured. This might occasion it to be burnt, which we find from Lupus, cited by Hickes, was the case. The ashes were buried at Wareham. The *Saxon Chronicle* speaks of those who " bow on their knees before his dead bones" (164.), but makes no mention of any miracles wrought. These, however, as might be expected, had arrived in full force before Malmesbury's time.—*Script. post Bed.* 34.

and disgraceful scenes.[1] In the year following his half-brother's assassination Dunstan crowned the young king, then only eleven years old, at Kingston.[2] The archbishop is said to have predicted that the sword having placed a diadem on his brow would never cease to shed misery over his reign.[3] He probably saw too plainly the prevalence of domestic dissension, and a fearful storm gathering in the north. Even such an intellect as his own might prove unequal to disarm the dangers provoked by a hasty and unjust attack upon established rights and institutions. But his age now forced attention steadily upon the the grave. Ethelred, also, was a mere child, and probably one in whom his discerning eye could rest upon little that was promising. There is no occasion therefore, to doubt Dunstan's prediction of an unhappy reign, or to believe, with his monkish biographers, that he spoke from inspiration. He lived to see his apprehensions considerably realised, but died before the king had attained complete maturity.[4]

---

[1] The pirates of Scandinavia recommenced their descents upon England in 980. (*Sax. Chr.* 165.) *Unready* means *ill-advised*, or *unprovided with a plan*. The Saxon word *ræd* is equivalent to *counsel*, evidently a Norman importation. *Ethelred* means *noble counsel*. The *Unready* seems to have been a derisory pun, very naturally suggested by the glaring contrast between the name and the administration of this most incompetent prince.

[2] In 979.—*Sax. Chr.* 164.

[3] INGULPH. *Script. post Bed.* 506.

[4] Dunstan died in 988. (*Sax. Chr.* 167.) Ethelred was then about twenty. Osbern makes the archbishop to have died at the age of seventy, or thereabouts. But this is inconsistent with the statement, made by himself and others, that Dunstan was born

In spite of all that monkish eulogists have done to render him ridiculous, his whole history proves him to have possessed uncommon talents. His prominence in monastic history may rather, perhaps, be regretted by many who feel a jealous interest in English records of departed genius. But although Dunstan originally moulded national fanaticism after Benedict, it should not be forgotten that others chiefly lent activity for the details of his ill-advised innovation. Nor does he seem chargeable with making that provision for popular credulity which the complete success of monachism demanded. Ethelwold and Oswald were the ejectors of canons; and the former of these prelates was the indefatigable rifler of tombs with saintly names. Around Dunstan's own cathedral of Canterbury the canons remained in possession of their homes.[1] This personal inactivity wears rather the appearance of selfish policy, but it affords, undoubtedly, a presumption that Dunstan's strength of mind raised him somewhat above the injustice and illusion which his favourite project

---

under Athelstan. In this case he could not have been more than sixty-four. The inaccuracy, however, is probably in the time assigned to his birth, not in the age ascribed to him.

[1] They were not disturbed until 1005, seventeen years, namely, after Dunstan's death. (*X. Script.* 1780.) Ælfric, then Archbishop of Canterbury, obtained authority from Ethelred and his legislature for this innovation: a copy of the instrument is preserved among the Cotton MSS. (*Claudius*, A. 3. f. 3.) and this is printed by SPELMAN (i. 504.) and by WILKINS (i. 282.) The intrusive monks, however, did not long maintain their ground, and it was reserved for Lanfranc, in 1074, to accomplish that expulsion of the dean and chapter which continued to the Reformation.—WHARTON, *Angl. Sacr.* i. 135.

naturally produced. A more unequivocal display of his intellectual vigour, and independence likewise, arose from his excommunication of a very powerful earl who had contracted an incestuous marriage. The offender, finding royal interference ineffectual, sent agents well supplied with money to Rome; the Pope was won over, and wrote a letter commanding and entreating Dunstan to grant the desired absolution. This was, however, positively refused until the sin had been forsaken, whoever might sue for such indulgence, and whatever danger might hang upon denying it.[1] A reply, so insubordinate, may surprise those who loosely consider the Church of England

---

[1] " Tunc ille seipso deterior immani est furore correptus, et nihil eorum quæ possidebat alicujus esse momenti reputans, ad hoc solum se totum studebat impendere, ut Dunstano excitaret scandalum, et Christianæ legis jugum, quo a suâ libidine coercebatur, sibi faceret alienum. Legatos itaque suos Romam destinat, et talibus assueta quorundam Romanorum corda et ora in suam causam largo munere, largiori sponsione, permutat. Quid inde? Præsul apostolicæ sedis Dunstano peccatori homini condescendere, verbis ac literis mandat, et eum Ecclesiæ gremio integrè conciliare monet, hortatur, imperat. Ad quæ Dunstanus ita respondet, *Equidem cum illum de quo agitur, sui delicti pœnitudinem gerere videro, præceptis domini Papæ libens parebo. Sed ut ipse in peccato suo jaceat, et immunis ab ecclesiasticâ disciplinâ nobis insultet, et exinde gaudeat; nolit Deus. Avertat etiam Deus a me, ut ego causâ alicujus mortalis hominis, vel pro redemptione capitis mei, postponam legem quam servandam statuit in suâ Ecclesiâ idem Dominus meus, Jesus Christus, Filius Dei.*" (SURIUS, *De Probatis SS. Historiis.* Colon. Agrip. 1572, tom. 3, p. 323.) Baronius, naturally scandalised by this relation, places the following gloss between the Pope's mandate and Dunstan's reply : " Sed si pœnitens peccatum relinqueret voluit mandatum intelligi; nec enim alter potuit intellexisse." (*Annal. Eccl. Luc.* 1744. Tom. 16. p. 203.) But this is merely a gratuitous inference.

identical in principles from Augustine to the Reformation. But Anglo-Saxon times knew nothing of papal jurisdiction. A close and deferential connexion with Rome was indeed assiduously cultivated. Authority for domestic purposes rested exclusively at home. Edgar, accordingly, though the passive instrument of Dunstan, and the corner-stone of English monachism, asserted expressly the royal supremacy, styling himself the *Vicar of Christ*.[1]

No literary remains bearing Dunstan's name are extant, but we have a body of penitential canons referable to his age, and compiled, probably, under his inspection. In one of these, a married person, ordained on the dismissal of his wife, and afterwards returning to cohabitation with her, is condemned to the same penance as a murderer.[2] The archbishop was buried in his cathedral at Canterbury; but Glastonbury pined under such a loss of honour and emolument. It was resolutely, therefore, maintained, that the earliest and most venerated of English Benedictine abbots had, like the founder of his order, been furtively removed, and that his mortal spoils really rested within his own loved isle of Avalon.[3]

---

[1] " Vitiorum cuneos Canonicorum e diversis nostri regiminis cœnobiis *Christi Vicarius* eliminavi."—*Monach. Hydens. LL. sub Edg. datæ. cap.* 8. SPELM. i. 438. WILK. i. 242.

[2] 40. " If a mass-priest, or monk, or deacon, had a lawful wife before he was ordained, and dismisses her and takes orders, and then receives her again by lying with her, let every one of them fast as for murder, and vehemently lament it."—JOHNSON's *Transl.* Canones sub Edg. R. cap. 31. SPELM. i. 465. WILK. i. 233.

[3] " Quidam ex vestris, noviter, ut putamus, inter vos conversi, prædicant antiquos patres vestros *fures fuisse et latrones, et quod*

Vainly did the monks of Canterbury shew his tomb, and defy their western rivals to prove its violation. A legend was produced, referring this to the darkest period of Danish anarchy : pilgrims, accordingly, were decoyed to Glastonbury during many ages, by the fame of Dunstan's relics. At length was announced an augmentation to their attraction, in a new shrine of unusual splendour. The cool, strong sense of Archbishop Warham revolted against such an abuse of popular credulity, and he desired his famed predecessor's coffin to be examined. In it were found a skeleton, and other fragments of mortality, proving incontestably that the hero of monastic story had been respected in his grave.[1] This discovery might mortify the monks of Glastonbury : their cupidity was proof against it. The abbot's reply to Warham expresses an apprehension lest, in damping the ardour which drew so many pilgrims to his house, he should incur Gamaliel's imputation of *fighting against God*.[2]

---

nequius est, etiam sacrilegos; idque illorum prædicandi laudi ascribunt, quod tales fuerunt, fortassis et eâdem voluntate debriati, non perpendentes quod diviná intonat paginâ. *Fures, sc. et latrones, regnum Dei non possessuros.* (EADMER, Epist. ad Glastonienses de Corp. S. Dunst. *Angl. Sacr.* II. 222.) The legend invented for detailing the alleged abstraction of Dunstan's remains from Canterbury, while that city lay ruined by the Danes, is very circumstantial, and may be seen in D'Achery and Mabillon's Collection. *Transl. S. Dunst. in Monast. Glaston. Acta SS. Ord. Benedict.* v. 713.

[1] Scrutinium factum circa feretrum beatissimi patris, Dunstani Archiep. ex mandato reverendissimi patris ac Domini, Willelmi Warham, Cant. Archiep. et Domini Thomæ Goldston, sacræ paginæ Prof. ejusd. eccl. Prioris digniss. A.D. 1508. Die 22. Ap.—*Angl. Sacr.* II. 227.

[2] Acts v. 39. Epist. Abbat. Glaston. *Ib.* 231.

In 1008, Ethelred held a legislative assembly at Eanham, probably the modern Ensham in Oxfordshire.[1] It was very numerously attended,[2] and it enacted laws for a general armament, both naval and military.[3] Among its ecclesiastical sanctions is a particular statement of dues, claimable by the church, but without any penal provision to enforce them. They stand thus: plough-alms to be paid within

---

[1] The date of this *witena-gemot* has been considered as not exactly ascertainable. Spelman refers it to *about* 1009, that year being at some distance both from 1006, when Elphege was translated to Canterbury, and 1013, when he was murdered by the Danes. Among the Cottonian MSS., however, in the British Museum (*Nero.* A. 1. f. 90), the proceedings at Eanham are thus headed: IN NOMINE DNI — AÑO NIC INCARN· M. VIII. Now, we learn from the *Saxon Chronicle* (p. 181), that Elphege went to Rome for his pall in 1007, and that Ethelred gave orders that all landowners should provide either ships, or armour, according to the magnitude of their several estates, in 1008. The king could make no such order without legislative authority: this was, most probably, obtained at Eanham.

[2] " Universi Anglorum optimates." (*Brit. Mus. MSS.* COTTON, *Claudius,* A. 3. f. 30.) This MS., which is in large octavo, excellently preserved, appears to be that which Sir Henry Spelman used in preparing his edition of the *Councils.* In the Cottonian MS., cited in the last note, which seems to have been more generally overlooked, the preamble to the proceedings stands thus: Ðiſ iſ ſeo ʒeꞃæðneſ þe Enʒla cynʒ· ⁊ æʒðeꞃ ʒehaꝺoðe· ʒelæpeðe piꞇan ʒecuꞃan ⁊ ʒeꞃæðꝺan. *This is the enactment which the king of the Angles, and both the ordained, and the lay senators, chose and enacted.* At the top of the page is written, in a hand of considerable age: " An act of parliament, as ytt were." Afterwards, we find in the same hand: " This is not in print."

[3] " A man possessed of 310 hides, to provide one galley, or skiff; and a man possessed of 8 hides only, to find a helmet and breastplate."—*Sax. Chr.* Dr. INGRAM's *Transl.* p. 181. *Brit. Mus. MSS.* COTTON, *Claudius,* A. 3. f. 32.

fifteen nights after Easter, tythe of young by Whitsuntide; of the earth's produce at All-Hallows, Romefee at St. Peter's mass, and light-shot thrice in a year. Soul-shot was to be paid on the opening of a grave; and in case of interment without the district in which the deceased had regularly gone to confession, the minster of that district was, nevertheless, to claim soul-shot. This ancient enactment is an obvious authority for the burial-fees, often claimed within their own parishes, from the relatives of parties interred without them. The Eanham legislators also forbade strictly, marketing and popular meetings, on Sunday; enjoined festivals in commemoration of the blessed Virgin and the Apostles; and instituted a solemn anniversary on the day of the late king's assassination.[1] This last enactment is a proof of successful

---

[1] Ʒelæꞃte man Ʒoðeꞃ ꞅeꞃihta ꞅeoꞃne· æꝼhpylce ꞅeaꞃe· Ꝺæt iꞅ· Sulh-ælmeꞅꞃan· xv niht on uꝼan Eaꞃtꞃan· ⁊ Ʒeoʒoðe teoðunʒe be Pentecoꞃten· ⁊ Eoꞃð pæꞃtma be Ealꞃa-halʒena mæꞃꞃan· ⁊ Rom-ꞅeoh be Petꞃeꞃ mæꞃꞃan· ⁊ Leoht-ʒeꞃcot þꞃipa on ʒeaꞃe· ⁊ Saul-ꞅceat iꞅ ꞅihtaꞃt ꝥ man ꞅymle ʒelæꞃte æt openum ʒꞃæꝼe· ⁊ ʒiꝼ man æniʒ lic oꝼ ꞅiht ꞃoꞅiꞅt-ꞃciꞃe elleꞃ-hꝥaꞃ lecʒe· ʒelæꞃte man Saul-ꞅceat ꞅꞃa þeh into þam mynꞅtꞃe þe hit to hyꞃde· ⁊ ealle Ʒodeꞃ ꞅeꞃihta pyꞃþiʒe man ʒeoꞃne· eal ꞅꞃa hit þeaꞅꝼ iꞅ· ⁊ Fꞃeolꞅa ⁊ ꝼæꞃtena healde man ꞃihtlice. ꝼꞃiman-dæʒeꞃ ꝼꞃeolꞅ healde man ʒeoꞃne ꞅꞃa þan to ʒebyꞃiʒe· ⁊ cypinʒa· ⁊ ꝼolc-ʒemota on þam halʒan dæʒe ʒeꞃꝼice man ʒeoꞃne· ⁊ ꝼore Maꞃian ꝼꞃeolꞅ-tida ealle peoꞃðie man ʒeoꞃne· æꝼeꞃt mid ꝼæꞃtene· ⁊ ꞅyððan mid ꝼꞃeolꞅe· ⁊ to æʒhpylceꞃ Aꝥoꞅtoleꞅ heah-tide ꝼæꞃte man ⁊ ꝼꞃeolꞃiʒe· buton to Philippuꞅ ⁊ Iacobuꞅ ꝼꞃeolꞃe ne beode pe nan ꝼæꞃten· ꝼoꞃ þam Eaꞅtoꞃlican ꝼꞃeolꞃe. Elleꞃ oðꞃe ꝼꞃeolꞅa ⁊ ꝼæꞃtena healde man ʒeoꞃne· ꞅꞃa ꞅꞃa þa heolðan þe þe betꞅt heolðan Ꝼnd ꝼoꞃe Eadpeꞃdeꞃ mæꞃꞃe-dæʒ pitan habban ʒeꞃoꞃen ꝥ man ꝼꞃeolꞅian ꞅceal oꝼeꞃ eal Engla land· on kl. Aꝥꞃiliꞅ· ⁊ ꝼæꞃtan ælce Fꞃiʒedæʒ butan hit ꝼꞃeolꞅ ꞅy. Oꞃdal ⁊ aðaꞃ ꞅynðan toꞃpeðen ꝼꞃeolꞅdaʒum ⁊ ꞅiht ymbeꞃ daʒum· ⁊ ꝼꞃnam Ꝼdventum Dñi oð octabaꞃ Epiphanie· ⁊ ꝼꞃnam Septuaʒeꞃimam oð xv oꝼeꞃ Eaꞃtꞃan. Beo ðam halʒan tidan eal ꞅꞃa hit ꞃiht iꞅ eallum Cꞃiꞅtenum mannum ꞅið ⁊ ꞅom ʒemæne· ⁊ ælc ꞅacu ʒetꞃæmed. (*Brit. Mus. MSS.* Cotton, *Nero*. A. 1. f. 91.) Let God's rights be paid earnestly every year: that is, plough-alms fifteen nights over Easter, and tythe of young by Pentecost, and

activity in the monastic party. No pains were spared, probably, to spread a belief, that, among national transgressions, now so severely visited, few had cried more loudly for vengeance than the murder of an innocent, well-disposed king. Such a topic might be easily so urged as to cast a shade of obloquy upon the persevering resistance of great men to a complete monastic triumph. Elphege, archbishop of Canterbury, eventually a victim to Danish violence,[1] ap-

---

fruits of the earth by All-Hallows' mass, and Rome-fee by Petre's mass, and light-shot thrice in a year, and soul-shot, it is rightest that a man ever pay at open grave ; and if a corpse be laid elsewhere out of its right shrift-shire, let soul-shot be paid nevertheless into the minster which had the pastorship of it : and let all God's rights be earnestly respected, even as it is needful, and let feasts and fasts be rightly holden. Let Sunday's feast be holden earnestly, even as it thereto belongeth ; and let marketings and folk-motes be earnestly avoided on that holy day : and let all St. Maria's festival tides be earnestly observed, erst with fast, and then with feast : and to each Apostle's high tide let there be a fast and feast ; but to Philippus and Jacobus' feast, we bid no fast, on account of the Easter feast. Else let other feasts and fasts be earnestly holden, even as those hold who hold them best. And St. Eadwerd's mass-day the senators have chosen to be made a feast over all the land of the Angles, on kal. Aprilis : and fast every Friday, unless it be a feast. Ordeal and oaths are forbidden on feast-days and right ember days; and from Adventum Domini until Octabas Epiphanie, and from Septuagesimam until xv. over Easter. In the holy tides, even as it right is, let peace and concord be common to all Christian men, and let every strife be laid aside.

Spelman's copy of the Eanham enactments (*Conc.* i. 517) mentions *church-shot* besides *light-shot*, takes no notice of St. Edward's day, and exhibits other variations. Johnson translates from this ; and he observes, from the reservation of tythes until All-Hallows, that corn tythes must have been paid in the grain.

[1] Elphege being taken prisoner on the capture of Canterbury by the Danes, had the offer of ransoming his life upon extravagant

peared at the head of his own order, in this meeting of the Saxon estates. In it, however, the services rendered by himself and the Archbishop of York were not merely deliberative : besides these, the two prelates communicated, to a crowd of people in attendance, such things as had been enacted, in the shape of an exhortation to obedience. Probably this was deemed a publication of these legislative acts, and was the usual practice.[1] This admonitory commucation also urges the duty of building churches, in all parts of the country.[2] For such a charge, it is most likely that the metropolitans had legislative sanction. It was one of those harassing and calamitous times, in which men earnestly think of propitiating. the favour of heaven. Obviously, however, that healthy tone of national morality, which has the promise of divine approbation, will arise from nothing so certainly, as from sufficient provision for a people's

---

terms. He refused, and being felled with bones, and other hard substances, he received his death-blow from a battle-axe. (*Sax. Chr.* 189. OSBERN, de Vit. S. Elph. *Angl. Sacr.* ii. 140.) Lanfranc denied him to be a true martyr, saying that he lost his life, " not for the confession of Christ's name, but because he would not redeem himself for money "—*Ib.* 134. note.

[1] " Post hæc igitur archipontifices predicti convocatâ plebis multitudine collecte, regis edicto supradicti, omniumque consensu catholicorum, omnibus communiter predicabant." (*Brit. Mus. MSS.* COTTON, *Claudius*, A. 3. f. 31.) The *preaching* begins with an exhortation to a right faith in the Trinity, proceeds to declaim against heathenism, and gradually unfolds a mass of sanctions ecclesiastical as well as civil. Among the latter appear penalties against neglect of the naval and military armaments enacted.

[2] " Ecclesias namque per loca singula edificate, in Dñi subsidio cunctipotentis, nec non et regis terreni."—*Ib.*

religious wants. In modern times, this archiepiscopal recommendation is chiefly worthy of attention, because it furnishes one, among the multitude of proofs, that our parochial churches are not national foundations, but the gradual fruits of individual liberality.

Men's anxiety to propitiate the wrath of heaven, by a strict attention to every Christian duty, was further attested in a legislative assembly holden at Haba, a place not identified.[1] It was there enacted, that a penny, either in money or in kind, should be rendered for every plough-land, and that the same sum should be paid by every member of a congregation.[2] This may be considered, probably, a statutable authority for Easter offerings. Another section earnestly enjoins an exact payment of *church-shot* and tythes. From this we learn, that the mode of tything was to surrender the produce of every tenth acre, as the plough went.[3] Other sections enforce, in general terms, a faithful discharge of all the

---

[1] Otherwise Bada, (WILK. I. 295.) It appears to have been so written in a MS. formerly belonging to the monastery of St. Augustine, at Canterbury. These enactments are undated; but Johnson refers them to 1014, when Ethelred had returned from Normandy, where he and his queen had taken refuge, and when he was promising the correction of his errors in administration.

[2] *Hirmannus.* "The priest's *hirman*, or *hyreman*, was what we call a parishioner." (JOHNSON). This writer conjectures, that the penny imposed upon plough-lands, in the former part of the clause, is not the old *plough-alms*, but an extraordinary benevolence, granted under the horror of Danish invasion. The Anglo-Saxon penny, it should be remembered, was equivalent to our threepence, to say nothing of alteration in the value of money.

[3] Cap. 4. SPELM. I. 531. WILK. i. 295.

Church's claims;[1] and one of them confirms established penalties for default :[2] a solemn fast of three days, also, is instituted before the feast of St. Michael,[3] and the people are urgently reminded of their

[1] These are thus enumerated in a MS. which must be about this age, as it is posterior to Dunstan, who is mentioned in f. 30. Æpeꞃꞇ ꞃulh-ælmeꞃꞃan· xv nihꞇ oꝼeꞃ Eaꞃꞇꞃan· ꝷeoꝷoꝺe ꞇeoꝺunꝷe be Penꞇecoꞃꞇen· Rom-ꝼeoh be Peꞇꞃeꞃ mæꞃꞃan· eoꞃꝺ-pæꞃꞇma be Ealꞃa-halꝷena mæꞃꞃan· cyꞃic-ꞃceaꞇ ꞇo Maꞃꞇinuꞃ mæꞃꞃan· ⁊ leohꞇ-ꞅeꞃceoꞇu þꞃiꞃa on ꝷeaꞃe· æꞃeꞃꞇ on Eaꞃꞇeꞃ-eꝼen· ⁊ oꝺꞃe ꞃiꝺe on Canꝺel-mæꞃꞃe-eꝼen· þꞃiꝺꝺan ꞃiꝺe on Ealꞃa-halꝷena-mæꞃꞃe-eꝼen· (Bibl. Bodl. MSS. *Junii* 121. f. 55.) *Erst, plough-alms xv. nights over Easter, tythe of young by Pentecost, Rome-fee by Peter's mass, fruits of the earth by All-Hallows' mass, church-shot at Martinus' mass, and light-shot thrice in a year; erst, on Easter-eve, and another time on Candlemas-eve, and the third time on All-Hallows' mass-eve.* Of these dues the clergy were solemnly to remind their congregations, at stated times. Rihꞇ iꞅ ꝥ ꞃneoꞃꞇaꞃ ꝼolc myneꝷian ꝥ hi Coꝺe ꝺon ꝼculon ꞇo ꝷeꞃihꞇum on ꞇeoꝺunꝷum· ⁊ on oꝺꞃum þinꝷum.

Rihꞇ iꞅ ꝥ man þiꞃꞃeꞅ myneꝷie ꞇo Eaꞃꞇꞃum· oꝺꞃe ꞃiꝺe ꞇo ꝷanꝷ-ꝺaꝷum· þꞃiꝺꝺan ꞃiꝺe ꞇo Miꝺꝺan-ꞃumeꞃa· þonne biꝺ mæꞃꞇ ꝼolceꞅ ꝷeꝷaꝺeꞃoꝺ. (*Ib.* ff. 54. 55.)

Right is that priests remind folk that they do what is right to God, in tythes and in other things

Right is that men be reminded of this at Easter, another time at the gang-days (Rogation days), a third time, at midsummer, when most folk is gathered.

[2] Cap. 7. SPELM. 1. 532. WILK. 1. 295.

[3] "While Apulia was infested by northern invaders, the Christians there obtained a signal victory, and were made to believe that this was done by the assistance of St. Michael, whose help they had invoked by three days' fasting and humiliation. There can be no doubt but that the fast here enjoined was in imitation of that of Italy. But it is observable, that there were in this age two Michaelmas days in the year; for a church was erected to this angel in Mount Garganus, where he was believed to have appeared, and to have obtained a victory for the Christians. The foundation of this church was laid on the 8th of May, and it was consecrated on the 29th of September, by which means both these days became stated festivals."—JOHNSON, *in loc.*

duties, both religious and moral. The reason expressly given for all this earnest exhortation, is the pressing necessity for God's blessing to secure victory and peace. Thus a whole nation was driven, by the force of overwhelming calamity, into that enviable disposition for serious thought, which individuals display when anguish weighs their spirits down, or death is before their eyes. At such a time, the spiritual profession appears in all its real value. Hitherto, perhaps, little occasion had been felt for any other than worldly callings; but new wants now crowd upon the mind, and men provide for the service of God, as if they deeply desired his honour and the welfare of their fellows. Ordinarily religion pleads in vain for that liberal care which the best interests of society really demand.

A ray from one illustrious name gleams brightly over the wretched and humiliating reign of Ethelred. While England bled at every pore, an admirable genius was indefatigably bent upon mitigating her distress, by furnishing abundantly the balm of sound instruction. It was Elfric who thus memorably laboured for his unhappy country. Nor has the age ennobled by such generous industry, alone had reason to rejoice in his appearance. His was the prolific pen to which we owe a very large proportion of extant Anglo-Saxon literature. Through him yet resounds a voice from our ancient Church, upon many questions in theology. Upon one, the witness borne is important above measure. It has retorted, with force irresistible, that odious imputation of a rash and indefensible disregard for antiquity by which

Romanists would fain cast obloquy upon the Reformation. Elfric brands indelibly with innovation, and in a vital point, the very principles which Cranmer found possessed of English pulpits. The venerable Anglo-Saxon thus convicts a party which claims exclusively his country's ancient faith, of an unconscious, but a perilous departure from it. He proves the teachers of a later period to have inculcated essential doctrines, even positively condemned by that honoured ancestry from whom the bulk of their endowments had descended.

His education was begun under a clergyman of slight attainments;[1] but completed at Winchester, in the celebrated school of Ethelwold.[2] For that popular and able prelate he ever entertained a filial reverence. Of personal communication with him he had probably enjoyed but little: his age forbidding it.[3]

---

[1] Hpilon ic pirte þ rum mærrepneort re þe min maʒirten pær on þam timan· hærðe þa boc Generir· ꝫ he cuþe beðæle Lyðen unðenrtanðan. *Once I knew that a mass-priest, who was my magister at the time, had the book of Genesis, and he could partly understand Latin.* (*Præfat. Ælf. in Genes.* HEPTATEUCH,&c. *Angl. Sax.* Oxon. 1698. p. 1.) This ecclesiastic, Elfric proceeds to say, used to talk of Jacob's four wives. Perhaps, in addition to his illiteracy, and his indiscreet conversation, he was not formed by temper for tuition; and thus Elfric might have imbibed, almost in infancy, a prejudice against ordinary clergymen.

[2] "Si alicui tamen displicuerit nostra interpretatio, dicat quomodo vult, nos contenti sumus, sicut didicimus in scholâ Athelwoldi, venerabilis præsulis, qui multos ad bonum imbuit."—ÆLF. Gramm. Præf. ad calcem *Somneri, Dict. Sax. Lat. Angl.* Oxon. 1659.

[3] " Dulce namque erat ei (Ethelw.) adolescentes et juvenes semper docere, et Latinos libros Anglicè eis solvere, et regulas

A deep sense of obligation could not, however, fail of overspreading his ingenuous mind towards one who had provided him access to learning. The general current of his thoughts led him also to venerate Ethelwold. Elfric zealously espoused monastic principles. He fully shared in prevailing prejudices against married clergymen.[1] It was his opinion, evidently, that, without obedience to the rule of Benedict, high ministerial qualities were nearly hopeless. As he seems to have been eminently sober-minded, his preference for the monastic party must have rested upon some substantial ground. Nothing, probably,

---

grammaticæ artis, ac metricæ rationis tradere, et jocundis alloquiis ad meliora hortari." (Vita S. Ethelw. Episc. WINTON. *Acta SS. Ord. Benedict*, v. 617.) Wolstan's name is affixed to this life; but he has done little else than copy Elfric, as appears from the variations that have been supplied by the editors, at the feet of the several pages. In the passage cited, Elfric evidently speaks from recollection; and it is a lad's recollection of a kind old man. Ethelwold died in 984. The monastery of Cerne was endowed by Æthelmer, or Ailmer, earl of Cornwall, in 987. Sigeric was archbishop of Canterbury from 989 to 994, and as Elfric sent his homilies from Cerne to the primate, styling himself *monk and mass-priest*, it is plain that he must have been ordained to the presbyterate by the year 989, or soon afterwards. He was probably, therefore, born about the year 965, and consequently he might be some nineteen years old when Ethelwold died. It is most likely that he went to Cerne immediately upon the establishment of that house, in the year 987.—*Monasticon*. i. 254.

[1] " Erant autem tunc in veteri monasterio" (Winton.) " ubi cathedra pontificalis habetur, canonici nefandis scelerum moribus implicati, elatione et insolentiâ atque luxuria præventi, adeo ut nonnulli eorum dedignarentur missas suo ordine celebrare, repudiantes uxores quas illicitè duxerant, et alias accipientes, gulæ et ebrietati jugiter dediti. Quod minimè ferens sanctus vir, Adelwoldus, datâ licentiâ a Rege Eadgaro, expulit citissimè detestandos

confirmed more strongly his conviction, than Benedictine services to literature. Whatever may be thought of the system generally established by Dunstan, Ethelwold, and Oswald, it is, indeed, indisputable, that these distinguished prelates instituted important seminaries for ecclesiastical education.[1]

His early years having been employed most advantageously at Winchester, Elfric was called away by Elfege, then bishop there. Ailmer, earl of Cornwall, had recently founded an abbey at Cerne, in Dorsetshire, and he requested Elfege to select a monk fit for establishing it upon a proper footing.

---

blasphematores Dei de monasterio; et adducens monachos de Abandoniâ, locavit illic, quibus ipse abbas et episcopus extitit." (Vit. S. Ethelw. *Acta. SS. Ord. Bened.* v. 614.) This harsh language, it is fair to believe, might have been substantiated by a few cases of gross misconduct. All large bodies of men will, unhappily, supply such, especially in a semi-barbarous age. But remove such cases out of sight, and Elfric's description will be found but little different from those libellous caricatures of clerical life, by which prejudice and malevolence have ever sought to blacken the character of ecclesiastics making no ascetic pretensions. It was a just retribution upon the monastic body, that its own eventual expulsion was promoted and defended upon like imputations of moral delinquency.

[1] "Ab initio enim Edgari Regis, ad annum circiter millesimum singuli ferè Angliæ episcopi et abbates ex monasteriis Abbendoniensi, Glastoniensi, et Wintoniensi delecti sunt (WHARTON, Dissert. de duobus Elfricis. *Angl. Sacr.* i. 126.) " Illo enim tempore, nulli ferè digni habebantur, qui monasteria et ecclesias seu regerent, seu instituerent, nisi qui e Dunstani, Ethelwoldi, aut Oswaldi scholis prodiissent." (*Ib.* 132.) The ascetic character earned in these admired seminaries was, no doubt, a powerful recommendation to the candidate for ecclesiastical promotion. But it must be supposed that this was commonly accompanied by more valuable qualities. In Elfric's case it was eminently so.

Elfric was chosen; but his new duties were insufficient for a mind so active, and he sought further occupation in an undertaking of great popular utility. Usage and authority demanded a sermon from the clergy on every Sunday.[1] Satisfactorily to answer such a call is far from easy to minds highly cultivated, and sufficiently provided with literary appliances. Among a priesthood, slightly educated, and with a very limited access to books, the weekly sermon must have often pained a hearer of any information, or of more than ordinary ability. Elfric kindly resolved upon providing a remedy for this evil. He selected and freely translated from those established authorities, Austin, Jerome, Bede, Gregory, Smaragdus, and occasionally Haymo, forty homilies on subjects chiefly scriptural. This course was deemed sufficient for a year. The volume being completed, he sent it to Sigeric, archbishop of Canterbury, especially calling his attention to the great care taken for avoiding heresy and error. By this prelate these discourses were highly approved, and their use authorised. The learned monk attested his gratification by transmitting forty more homilies to Sigeric. These are of a more legendary character; but again challenge a rigid inquiry into the soundness of their doctrine.[2] They were greeted with the

---

[1] Riht ir þ pneortar ælce Sunnan-bæʒe· folce boðian (*Sinodalia Decreta.* (*Bibl. Bodl. MSS. Junii* 121. f. 29.) *Right is that priests preach to the folk every Sunday.*

[2] " Ego, Ælfricus, alumnus Athelwoldi, benevoli et venerabilis præsulis, salutem exopto Domino Archiepiscopo Sigerico in Domino. —— Nec ubique transtulimus verbum ex verbo, sed sen-

same success as the former series. Another literary labour of great utility, was a Latin grammar, compiled from Priscian, and with Elfric's usual patriotism, in his native tongue.[1] Before this undertaking, probably, his diocesan, Wulfsine, bishop of Sherborne,[2] had requested him to prepare a summary

---

sum ex sensu, cavendo tamen diligentissimè deceptivos errores, ne inveniremur aliquâ hæresi seducti, seu fallaciâ fuscati. Hos namque auctores in hâc explanatione sumus secuti, videlicet Augustinum Hipponensum, Hieronimum, Bedam, Gregorium, Smaragdum, et aliquando Haymonem: horundemque auctoritas ab omnibus Catholicis libentissimè suscipitur. Quadraginta sententias in isto libro posuimus, credentes hoc sufficere posse per annum fidelibus, si integrè eis a ministris Domini recitentur in ecclesiâ. Precor modo obnixè Almitatem tuam, mitissime pater, Sigerice, ut digneris corrigere, per tuam industriam, si aliquos nævos malignæ hæresis, aut nebulosæ fallaciæ, in nostrâ interpretatione reperies; et ascribatur dehinc hic codicillus tuæ auctoritati, non utilitati nostræ despicabilis personæ." (HICKES, *Thes.* II. 153). " Quia nostrum studium nimium laudasti, gratanter illam interpretationem suscipiens, festinavimus hunc sequentem librum, sicuti omnipotentis Dei gratia nobis dictavit, interpretare. Igitur in anteriore opere ordinavimus XL. sermones; in isto vero non minor numerus sententiarum invenitur. Perlegat, quæso, Benignitas vestra hanc nostram interpretationem, quemadmodum et priorem, et dijudicet si fidelibus Catholicis habenda est, an abjicienda."— *Ib.* 157.

[1] " Ego Ælfricus, ut minus sapiens, has excerptiones de Prisciano minore, vel majore, vobis puerulis tenellis ad vestram linguam transferre studui." (*Ælf. Præf. Gramm.* SOMNER.) An ancient MS. of this Grammar in the Library of St. John's College, Oxford, appears to be entitled *Ælfrici Præsulis Grammatica*. (HICKES, *Thes.* II. 104.) Hence a recent author concludes that Elfric did not write the Grammar until he had attained a station of eminence. He considers him to have written it soon after his advancement to the abbotcy of Peterborough. *Ancient Hist. Engl. and Fr. exemplified.* Lond. 1830. p. 66.

[2] Great obscurity has attended the name of Wulfsine; but a

of admonition and information most needed by the clergy, and suitable for addressing to them. Obedience to this request produced a celebrated piece, yet extant, resembling the episcopal charges of later times. It illustrates, largely, existing religious usages, and is particularly valuable, because it establishes, incontrovertibly that ancient England and modern Rome are utterly at variance in an essential article of faith. A similar piece, happily extant also, afterwards proceeded from Elfric's pen, and it commands attention by a contradiction, equally strong, to the capital article of Romish belief. This interesting document apparently was prepared for Wolstan archbishop of York.[1] Other distinguished

---

charter, published by Wharton (*Angl. Sacr.* i. 170), renders it sufficiently plain that he was bishop of Sherborne about the close of the tenth century. This instrument, dated 998, under Ethelred, authorises Wulfsine to settle a community of monks around his cathedral of Sherborne. Elfric is known to have resided in Dorsetshire about that time, and Wulfsine's reformation at Sherborne was exactly such as might be expected from one who looked up to him for advice. In addition to these evidences of Wulfsine's identity, Wharton met with a MS. history of Westminster, by John Flete, in which that writer relates, on the authority of Sulcard, a monk living fifty years after the time, that Wulfsine was made bishop of Sherborne in 980, and so continued until about 998. (*Ib.* 132). Elfric's epistle to Wulfsine has been printed, more or less completely, by Lambarde, Spelman, and Wilkins, and it has been translated by Johnson. In it occurs one of the shorter testimonies against transubstantiation, printed by Foxe and L'Isle.

[1] There were two Wolstans, archbishops of York. The former died in 956, the latter in 1023, after something more than twenty years' possession of the see. (*Angl. Sacr.* i. 133. J. STUBBS, *X. Script.* 1700). To this latter, only, could Elfric have written.

persons naturally became desirous of benefitting by industry so able, pious, and unwearied. Elfric was, accordingly, led into his various translations from Scripture. He wrote, besides, a life of Ethelwold,[1] a glossary, a body of monastic discipline, and other pieces.[2] The learned energy of his earlier years has, indeed, rarely been surpassed; and although, like other Anglo-Saxons, he wrote but little quite original, yet, considering the time of his appearance, he has fully earned a foremost rank in the literature of England.

In his epistle, as extant in the Bodleian Library (*MSS Junii.* 121. f. 111), Elfric only speaks of himself as " a brother to masspriests." Hence might be thought to have written this epistle soon after the year 1002. But in the prologue to the two epistles published by Wilkins (*Leges, Angl. Sax.* Lond. 1721. p. 166), he designates himself " abbot." Of these two epistles, the second is the beginning of that in the Bodleian Library, mentioned above. If he really were abbot, when that piece was written, this must be referred, most probably, to some date after 1005.

[1] His *Life of Ethelwold* is said, in the preface, to have been written twenty years after that prelate's death. an event occurring in the middle of 984. It must have been written, therefore, either in the year 1004 or in the earlier part of 1005. It is dedicated to Kenulf, bishop of Winchester, who was advanced to that see in 1005, and who died in July, 1006. Elfric was now " abbot;" and he seems to have been made abbot of Peterborough in 1005.

[2] In the face of Elfric's voluminous authorship, and of several Anglo-Saxon pieces from other pens, it is amusing to read the following extract from Hardouin's *Chronologia Vet. Test.* (Amst. 1700, pp. 34, 35), in the Preface to Hickes's *Thesaurus* (p. xxiii): *At Saxonica quæ in quibusdam dubiæ* (ut Coptica) *fidei monumenta extat, nihil aliud quam Germanica illius ævi est, quo sunt hæc* (Coptica) *exarata characteribus ab artifice excogitatis, diversis certe ab his, quibus Offa rex suos olim nummos inscripsit, qui sunt omnino Latini, quales ii quibus id nomen hic exhibemus. Ejus autem linguæ est Saxonica Ælfrici nomine homilia de*

The history of this distinguished scholar is, however, involved in thick obscurity. To the scanty particulars already given from incidental passages in his own works, must be added, from the same source, that he was a priest and a monk, and that he became eventually both abbot and bishop.[1] Elfric was not merely, therefore, an industrious man of letters, valued by none but students, and even known to few besides. His transcendent qualities were duly acknowledged in professional elevation. Yet neither the abbey over

---

Eucharistia, Ratramni sensu stilo, atque ipso subinde sermone conscripta, hoc est, hæretico. At Ælfricus non Anglicum, Saxonicumve nomen est, sed Hebræum, DEUS REDEMPTOR. *Nam* אל *Deus est : quod nomen quoniam nihil interest, utrum* ÆL *an* AL *efferas, ideo et* ÆLFRICUS *et* ALFRICUS *in libris scribitur.* פרק *redimere est ex Vulgato interprete, Ps.* cxxxv. 24, *quem tum ob peritiam viri singularem, tum aliis de causis, talium nominum architecti sequuntur.* This curious passage, Hickes very truly observes, has as many errors as lines; for neither are Anglo-Saxon monuments few, nor of dubious faith, nor written in any characters invented for deception; nor are the characters on Offa's coins *altogether* Latin (if they were, it would not follow that MSS. must be written in the same), nor is Elfric a factitious word, coined by some Hebraist, intent upon imposition, but a Saxon proper name, borne by many individuals of that nation. This whole tissue of error and absurdity is, however, well worthy of notice, as a proof of the despairing embarrassment with which Romanists encounter Elfric, conscious that he overthrows the main peculiarity of their creed.

[1] " O, ye mass-priests, *my brethen !*" are the opening words in Elfric's epistle, prepared, as it is considered, for Archbishop Wolstan. Ælfric, munuc; *Ælfric, monk.* (*Prefat. in Genes.*) Ælfric, abbod; *Ælfric, abbot.* (*De Vet. Test.* edit. L'Isle.) " Elfricum demum episcopali dignitate auctum esse constat ex epistola ejus MS. in Collegio Corporis Christi Cantab. quæ inscribitur ; *Elfrici Episcopi ad jam nunc ordinatos.*"—*Ang. Sacr.* i. 33.

which he presided, nor the see that he occupied, can be named with absolute certainty. Contemporary bishops and abbots, most of them, probably, useful and able in their day, but without any particular claim upon posterity, are accurately commemorated in existing records. Inquiries into Elfric's preferments demand research; and will, at last, be requited by nothing more satisfactory than strong probabilities. The following appears to be an outline of his real history. His revered master, Ethelwold, had taken especial interest in re-establishing those future glories of England's fen district, the abbeys of Peterborough, Ely, and Thorney, ruined by the Danes;[1] converting them, of course, into regular Benedictine houses. Elfric, it is hardly doubtful, gained his title of abbot from the monastery first named.[2] He there seems

---

[1] BROMTON, X. Script. 868.

[2] Wharton supposes him to have been abbot of Winchester. He grounds this opinion upon his dedication to Kenulf, in which he calls himself " an abbot and a Winchester scholar, *Wintoniensem alumnum.*" Hence Wharton thinks that his education and abbacy must be referred to the same place; and he is confirmed in this belief by Stubbs, who designates Alfric, archbishop of York, *Wintoniensis præpositus.* (Acta PP. Ebor. X. Script. 1700.) This designation, however, is hardly sufficiently precise for a positive conclusion. The author of *Ancient History, English and French, exemplified in a Regular Dissection of the Saxon Chronicle,* says of Wharton, " No man knew better than he, if he had taken time, that the old monastery, or cathedral church of Winchester, of which he says Elfric was, beyond all doubt, abbot, never had an abbot, *nomine,* abbot; but, as well before Ethelwold's reform as afterwards, was governed by the bishop in place of an abbot." The principle of this is distinctly stated in Ethelred's charter to Wulfsine : " Et quia mos minime—ut in episcopali sede, abbas constituatur; fiat ipse episcopus eis abbas et pater." (*Angl. Sacr.* i. 170.) In the ex-

to have had a very narrow escape from a victorious party of invading Danes. Having succeeded in reaching the royal presence, Etheldred sent him, in charge of Emma the queen, over to Normandy, her native country.[1] After some stay upon the continent, Elfric returned home; and his unquestionable superiority recommended him to the discerning eye of Canute, then occupant of the throne.[2] Under that fortunate

---

tract also from the *Life of Ethelwold*, already used (p. 225), that prelate is said, most probably in Elfric's own words, to have been *abbas et episcopus* of the monks whom he transferred from Abingdon to Winchester. In November 1005, Sigeric, archbishop of Canterbury, died. Elphege, bishop of Winchester, succeeded him; and Kenulf, abbot of Peterborough, to whom Elfric dedicated his *Life of Ethelwold*, was advanced to the see of Winchester. The recent writer cited above, to whom inquirers into Elfric's history are much obliged, has very reasonably concluded (p. 64) that he was immediately preferred to the abbacy of Peterborough If he had not been abbot there, it seems strange that his corpse should have been carried thither for interment; and the probability is, that he was the immediate successor of his friend and patron, Kenulf.

[1] *Sax. Chr.* 191. He is there called *Ælfsige*, as the text stands; but the recent author, cited in the last note, conjectures that the name was designedly substituted for *se*, the Saxon definite article masculine. For the particulars of his escape, see INGULPH. (*Script. post Bed.* 507.) As the passage appears there, the transactions might seem to have occurred in 1018; but then they are mixed up with the name of Sweyne, under whom, in fact, they took place. Sweyne, however, died in 1014; Elfric's escape from Peterborough, and mission to Normandy with Queen Emma, happened in 1013. Ingulph, who relates the particulars of his escape, does not name him; but, probably, the text may not appear there exactly as Ingulph left it.

[2] Tu, Sacerdos egregie Ælfrica, nostri Regis C. obtutibus semper assistis, et secreta ejusdem consilia a te non sunt abscondita, sed per tuæ industriam sapientiæ discernendo rimantur." *Facun-*

and able Dane, we can trace him to the archbishopric of York; with which he probably held the bishopric of Worcester during several years.[1] He died at Southwell in 1051, and he was buried in the abbey of Peterborough.[2]

That such facts should be unascertainable by

---

dissimo Sacerd. Ælfr. ad calcem *Someri Dict.* p. 53) Wharton says, very truly, that *King C.* could be no other than *King Canute.* (*Angl. Sacr.* i. 134.) Elfric's promotion to the see of York under that prince is, indeed, strong evidence of his favour with him.

[1] One MS of the *Saxon Chronicle* has, under the year 1023, Heɲ ꝼoɲðꝼeɲðe þulꝼꝼꞃan aɲceb· ⁊ ꝼenʒ Ælꝼɲic to. *Here departed Wulfstan archb. and Ælfric took to.* (203) What did he *take to?* Undoubtedly to the see of York. But Wulstan held Worcester also, as had his immediate predecessors. Worcester cathedral was converted into a Benedictine monastery, which York was not; and, accordingly, the archbishops, being Benedictine monks, were allowed to hold *in commendam* a see which offered them a cathedral where they could reside in their proper character of abbot. It must appear probable that these precedents operated in Elfric's case; and that, if the clause cited from the *Saxon Chronicle* had been entire, we should find that he *took to* both sees. Existing catalogues of the Worcester bishops might, however, lead to a different conclusion. But there are difficulties in these which leave room for conjecturing that Elfric really held Worcester until the year 1034.—See *Anc. Hist. Engl. and Fr.* 89.

[2] STUBBS, *X Script* 1700. A MS. *Consuetudinary of the Monastery of Peterborough,* in the Lambeth library, has, accordingly, the following entry in the calendar : *Die IX. Calend. Februarii. Depositio Dompni Elfrici Archiepiscopi.* (WHARTON, *Angl Sacr.* i. 134.) The sacrilegious violence and fanaticism which disgraced the interval between Charles the First's troubles and his son's restoration, brought to light accidentally, in the cathedral of Peterborough, a chest or shrine, about three feet long, and containing human bones, inscribed *Elfricus.* This great man's remains, therefore, had been thought at one time worthy of translation, as it was called. (*Anc. Hist. Engl. and Fr.* 456.) Their original coffin must have been of larger dimensions.

direct testimony, is among the more striking of historical problems. It is true that, fifteen years after Elfric's death, Normandy gained firm possession of his native land, and reduced the language in which most of his works were patriotically written, to a vulgar dialect which superior families disdained. Authors, however, arose, diligent in examining the national records, and in forming them into materials for compositions of their own; especially such of them as were favourable to the monastic cause. Elfric had this recommendation. He was repeatedly employed in regulating monasteries.[1] Though gifted with a vigorous understanding, he had even imbibed a firm and zealous faith in the miraculous privileges of relics.[2] There were two writers in early Norman times particularly led by the nature of their pursuits, and the general bent of their minds, to preserve the incidents of such a person's life. Neither of these

---

[1] " In cod. Benedictino, quem asservat Col. S. Ben. seu CC. apud Cant. sub finem Evangelii secundum Matthæum, habentur sequentia, *Ego Ælfricus scripsi hunc librum in Monasterio Bathonio, et dedi Brihtwoldo Preposito.* (MARESCHALL, *Observ. in Vers. Angl. Sax.* 490.) Wharton conjectures, with great probability, that Elfric was sent to Bath by Elfege, bishop of Winchester, who had been the first abbot of that monastery; and that he might have been sent to other monasteries.—*Angl. Sacr.* i. 133.

[2] Elfric's homilies afford many proofs of this. His mind, accordingly, was eagerly bent upon the acquisition of relics, even while he lived with the queen in Normandy, an exile from his abbey. He found the abbey of Bonneval in great distress from the plunder which it had recently undergone, and hence willing to sell the body of St. Florentine. He bought this, all but the head, for five hundred pounds, and eventually lodged it at Peterborough.— *Sax. Chr.* 192.

writers might seem to have had any certain knowledge of his existence. One of them, namely Osbern, mentions incidentally an Elfric Bata, to whose impious activity he assigns a temporary cessation of the miracles expected by worshippers at Dunstan's tomb. The spirit of that sainted archbishop, we are told, was under the necessity of putting Bata to flight, before it could continue its accustomed deeds of mercy.[1] The other ancient author is William of Malmesbury, the great luminary of Anglo-Norman ecclesiastical antiquity; and he speaks of an Elfric, who was both an abbot and a prelate, and an able industrious translator. But he writes as if he had never examined his works. Their fame, he does not dissemble, had reached his ears; but, with exemplary caution, he expresses a doubt whether, from lapse of time, it might not have been greater than the pieces

---

[1] A cripple, Osbern says, having vainly sought relief at Dunstan's tomb, was returning homeward in despair. At a resting-place the saint appeared to him in his sleep, and said, " Non poteram his diebus requiem corporis mei visitare, nec præsentiam meam filiis ibidem manentibus exhibere. *Nam ecclesiam Dei Elfricus, cognomento Bata, exheredare tentavit.*" (De Mirac. S. Dunst. Auctore, OSBERNO MONACHO. *Acta. SS. Ord. Benedict.* v. 692.) Of course the saint announced himself now at liberty, and desired the cripple to return; who, obeying, found relief. The fact is, that there was an Elfric Bata, a disciple of the great Elfric, but a far inferior man; who made some additions to a colloquy of his illustrious master, for the use of boys. (HICKES, *Thes.* ii. 104, 105.) Osbern's object in detailing the legend as he has, could hardly be any other than to connect the name of Elfric with known inferiority, and to brand it in some undefined way with religious evil. It appears, however, from Elfric's addresses to Sigeric, that he was particularly careful to avoid the least imputation of heresy.

merited.[1] Yet the Elfric, upon whom, apparently, Malmesbury had fallen by mistake, though something anterior to the most illustrious bearer of that name, was only just before him. He was only removed by a very few generations from Malmesbury himself. It is, therefore, scarcely credible that a man should have grown up in bookish habits from childhood, as, probably, every literary man has; this, too, at a time when books were few; and yet should hardly have examined a voluminous national writer, of whose high character he was well aware,—one also whom even his own shewing would place at no considerable distance from himself. Such cases naturally lead to a suspicion of unfairness. It is not easy to acquit either Osbern or Malmesbury of a deliberate intention to suppress the memory of Elfric, and to bury his very name under a mass of hopeless uncertainty.

---

[1] " Eum peritum literarum, præsertimque elegantissimum interpretem, *nisi fallax tradit vetustas*. Elfricus sanè cum grandævus esset, in episcopum Cridiensem altatus, vix. IV annis superfuit. Reliquit aliquantos codices, non exigua ingenii monumenta, *Vitam Sancti Adelwoldi*, antequam eam Wolstanus operosius concinnaret, *Abbreviationem Passionis Sancti Edmundi*, libros multos ex Latino in patrium sermonem versos." (W. MALMESB. de vita Aldhelm. *Angl. Sacr.* ii. 33.) It is unquestionable that the author thus described was the great Elfric. But we know, from himself, that his *Life of Ethelwold* could not have been written before the year 1004. Now Wharton makes it appear that Elfric, bishop of Crediton, succeeded to that see about 977. By Malmesbury's own account, then, he must have died about 981. (*Angl. Sacr.* i. 129.) In the *Monasticon* (p 8), we read that " Elfric, bishop, abbot, and monk of Glastonbury," died in 988. This is equally irreconcilable with the known date of the *Life of Ethelwold*. Godwin (*De Præsul.*) makes Elfric, bishop of Crediton, to have died in 999. But even this will not do.

For this disingenuous policy, a reason may be readily conjectured. Osbern was the humble friend of Lanfranc, who found a passport to professional distinction in the controversy with Berenger. He fails not, accordingly, to introduce, among his histories of Anglo-Saxon times, legendary tales of miracles wrought in proof of transubstantiation.[1] Malmesbury, too, had taken decidedly the infection from that new theology which England received with her Norman conquerors. Hence his indignant zeal extorted from him an attack equally ludicrous and important upon the venerated character of Raban Maur.[2] Now Elfric's eucharistic doctrine and that of Raban are identical. Both of them wrote, after Paschasius Radbert had astonished studious men by his portentous novelty; and both, accordingly, have left such language upon record as only controversy commonly calls forth. Elfric's vocation, as homilist for the people, obliged him upon occasions to furnish lengthened, clear, and forcible expositions of the eucharist. In discharging this duty, he has freely used not only language from earlier authors unfavourable to transubstantiation, but also he has embodied, for the use of ordinary congregations, the substance of Ratramn's famous controversial piece. It is no wonder that

---

[1] A legend of sacramental wine, sensibly transubstantiated into blood by Odo, may be seen in Osbern's Life of that archbishop. (*Angl. Sacr.* ii. 82.) A like story, as to both the bread and wine, is related of Dunstan by this author. (SURIUS, iii. 330.) Such tales are not among the least striking evidences that Lanfranc's adherents were sadly embarrassed by the prevalence of a belief very different from their patron's.

[2] See *Bampt. Lect.* 413.

Lanfranc's admirers looked upon such an author with disgust and despair. Their master's fame rested upon endeavours to make his own eucharistic belief appear that of all Christendom in every age. Elfric proved not only that England, whose orthodoxy was unquestioned, had entertained no such doctrine, but even that she had expressly and intentionally contradicted it;[1] and Elfric died only fifteen years before the Conquest. Colour for charging him with innovation, there was none whatever. The century before him had produced Erigena, one of Radbert's earliest and most formidable opponents; yet the friend of Alfred. Erigena's doctrine, too, might be connected satisfactorily with Alcuin and Bede; only controversy had won for it an energy, breadth, and precision, for which earlier scholars had found no occasion. Thus Elfric merely finished, but with a

---

[1] To well-informed English Romanists, Elfric still occasions great embarrassment. Dr. Lingard, in the notes to his *Antiquities of the Anglo-Saxon Church*, (note M, p. 576, Fr. transl.) wishes to dispose of Elfric, by labouring to make it appear that his doctrine is not irreconcilable with Romanism, and that he was a writer " of inferior merit," who lived when Anglo-Saxon intelligence had seriously declined. Upon the former of these representations, the *Paschal Homily* especially may be left by Protestants to speak for itself. Against an imputation of " inferior merit," Elfric's numerous works are a triumphant defence. It is true that when he lived, the brightest age of Anglo-Saxon literature was over; but this national misfortune certainly was no great impediment to his own improvement. Nor did it affect his doctrine; he explained the eucharist in strict unison with all the most illustrious Anglo-Saxon divines. Undoubtedly he is more clear, full, and forcible. But then Radbert had written since Bede and Alcuin. Hence controversy had suggested and demanded language for which earlier theologians found no occasion.

vigour equalled, probably, by Erigena alone, that unyielding array of testimony against Lanfranc's new divinity which echoes from the whole theological school of ancient England. Against an author so recent, and in such full possession of the popular ear, discretion forbade a direct assault. But his unpalatable doctrine was conveyed in Saxon,—a language with which Anglo-Normans, of any distinction, were unacquainted. Hence, after a few years, no cultivated mind was ever likely to be awakened by hearing any of his homilies. Books were few; and such as Elfric left might shortly be rendered useless by refraining from translating them into Latin. The despised populace might imperceptibly be weaned from his opinions by retrenching such parts of the customary sermon as had grown unfashionable.[1] Authors might learn that great men, wishing him to be forgotten, were likely to be pleased by seeing his very name involved in obloquy and confusion. Such was the policy pursued; and being favoured by a prevailing disregard for Anglo-Saxon literature, even by general ignorance of the character in which it was preserved, Elfric's memory became all but wholly lost.

---

[1] For the manner in which the famous *Paschal Homily* has been treated in the C. C. C. C. MS. 162. see *Bampt. Lect.* 428. A like liberty was taken with the *Homily for St. Peter's Day*, also printed in that volume (p. 126). Among the Cottonian MSS. in the British Museum (VESPASIAN, D. 14, f. 122), is found the beginning of that homily; the part, namely, that details the privileges of St. Peter in the words of Scripture. But all the latter part, beginning with "Bede, the Expositor," is omitted. In this latter part, however, are several passages unfavourable to the papal pretensions.

When, accordingly, the monastic libraries were dispersed, and Englishmen eagerly inquired into the language and religion of their distant ancestry, they were at a loss to identify the principal author that they had recovered.

A presumption in favour of Elfric's alleged influence with Canute arises from many of that prince's acts. The Danish conqueror revived a taste for pilgrimages to Rome by undertaking one himself.[1] He was a liberal patron to the monastic order.[2] Under him was holden a legislative assembly at Winchester, which confirmed churches in their established inviolability, and re-enacted the penalties imposed under Edgar for withholding ecclesiastical dues.[3] Another of these laws displays that anxiety for clerical celibacy that distinguished Elfric. An unmarried clergyman was to enjoy the privileges of a thane.[4] In a different series of Canute's laws, is one proving the reparation of churches to have been a burthen imposed by the legislature upon property generally, and not exclusively upon the tythes. "All people," it is declared, "are bound of right to assist in repairing the church."[5]

---

[1] In 1031. (*Sax. Chr.* 206.) Malmesbury's date is the same, as he places it in the fifteenth year of his reign. Ingulph places it a year earlier; but Mr. Wheaton says that the Danish chronologists seem to have conclusively proved its occurrence in 1027.—*Hist. of the Northmen*, 327, Note.

[2] INGULPH. MALMESB. *Script. post Bed.* 507, 41.

[3] LL. Canut. R. cann. 8, 9, 10, 11, 12, 13. SPELM. I. 544. WILK. i. 302.

[4] *Ib.* can. 6. SPELM. I. 543. WILK. I. 301.

[5] To cynic-bote rceal eall folc fylrtan mio pihte· "Ad fanum reficiendum omnes quidem jure debebant." (LL. Canut. can. 63. LAMBARDE *de Priscis Anglorum Legibus.* (Cantab. 1644, p. 121)

In the same series appears a strict prohibition of all pagan worship and usages.[1]

The brief reigns of Canute's two sons, Harold Harefoot and Hardicanute, afford no materials for ecclesiastical history. Nor is it much otherwise with the succeeding reign of Edward the Confessor. England was naturally rejoiced in finding herself again under a prince of her ancient dynasty, and hence regarded Edward with fond partiality. His personal qualities, indeed, were worthy of the people's love. He was a mild and well-intentioned sovereign, who displayed upon the throne those dispositions that are most estimable in private life. Among monastic writers he has gained high celebrity. They could not fail of extolling that munificence which founded the noble Abbey of Westminster. Their eulogies were justly due to a monarch who made religion popular by the strictness of his own example. Their prejudices were highly gratified by the spectacle of a distinguished married man avoiding commerce with his wife. They were not likely to reason that even if this abstinence had ever been rigidly maintained, personal aversion or mere constitution might

---

Johnson has appended (*sub. an.* 1018,) the following note to his translation : " This law which is omitted by Sir H. S." (Spelman), " shews that the reparation of churches was devolved on the people sooner than is commonly thought." The preamble states that the body of statutes in which this occurs, was enacted in a *Witenagemot* holden at Winchester, at Christmas. It is said that Canute mið hiɼ piτena ɀeþeahτe ɀeneð: *decreed with his senators' advice.* (LAMB. 97.) He seems to have holden a legislative council at Winchester in 1021.

[1] LL. Canut. R. can. 5. SPELM. I. 553. WILK. I. 306.

be the real cause of it. Nor did it harmonise with cloistered habits to remark, that if no such impediment intervened Edward's conduct was any thing rather than wise and patriotic. He ought surely to have felt some anxiety for securing his country against the miseries of a disputed succession. In him, however, was merely discerned a sainted virgin king, fitted for occupying a conspicuous station among the heroes of monastic story, and for stamping credibility upon some of those legendary tales which delighted a superstitious age. But, although the Confessor stands conspicuously religious among English kings, he does not make much figure as an ecclesiastical legislator. There are, indeed, certain laws relating to the church which pass under his name. These, however, were compiled after William had conquered England; and they seem rather to be authorised statements of laws in force while Edward reigned, than enactments in his legislature. They confirm the church's immunities[1] and claims to tithes,[2] adding those upon profits in trading.[3] They likewise confirm the papal claim for Peter-pence. But they make no mention of the customary assessments for public worship. One of them is remarkable for kindly declaring that the Jews are under the king's protection.[4] Of that most memorable among nations great numbers had recently

---

[1] LL. S. Edw. R. et Conf. can. 2, 6, 7. SPELM. i. 619, 620. WILK. i. 310, 311.

[2] *Ib.* can. 8, 9.

[3] " De negotiationibus, et omnibus rebus quas dederit Dominus, decima pars ei reddenda est, qui novem partes simul cum decimâ largitur."—Can. 9. SPELM. i. 621. WILK. i. 311.

[4] Can. 22.

fled into western countries before the fanatic fury of Mahometanism; and it is pleasing to know that England did not deny them an asylum. Another of the Confessor's laws provides outlawry and confiscation as penalties of usury.[1]

Edward's Norman education had rendered him almost a foreigner,[2] and indiscreetly partial to the French. The numbers of them whom he patronised gave a powerful influence to their language and manners. To the Confessor's reign, accordingly, may be traced that prevailing affectation of continental usages which Englishmen have long ranked among their national weaknesses. The king probably spoke French more freely than his native tongue. His Norman courtiers, generally, must have been unable to master the Anglo-Saxon. Hence, that noble idiom was branded with vulgarity; and thus even before the Conquest English gentlemen used their humbler countrymen to regard the speaking of French as a mark of superior breeding.[3] One of Edward's Norman friends was Robert, a monk of Jumieges, to whom he had owed some obligations while in exile. Him he preferred to the see of London, and afterwards to that of Canterbury. Other sees were also filled by foreigners. At length national antipathies and envy being effectively aroused, a powerful combination drove these adventurers back to the continent.[4]

---

[1] Can. 23.

[2] " Penè in Gallicum transierat."—INGULPH, *Script. post Bed.* 509.

[3] " Gallicum idioma omnes magnates in suis curiis, *tanquam magnum gentilitium* loqui."—*Ib.*

[4] MALMESB. *Ib.* 116.

Canterbury was now bestowed upon Stigand, bishop of Winchester; a see which he continued to hold, thereby committing, as monastic writers represent, a very grave offence. They might seem to have forgotten that Dunstan's character is liable to a like imputation.[1] Stigand, however, was one of the many distinguished Anglo-Saxons whom William found it desirable to dispossess. Hence, writers who sought Norman patronage, are naturally anxious to paint him in unfavourable colours. They are, however, driven to admit his wisdom and efficiency.[2] His primacy deserves notice, because it was exercised under circumstances even then unusual, and eventually represented as fatal to the powers of a metropolitan. Stigand never presented himself at the papal court to sue for a pall. Upon occasions he seems to have used one his predecessor left behind:[3] or it may be that he wore one sent to him, during a contest for the papacy by a party who failed in maintaining his ground.[4] Certainty upon these points, if

---

[1] Dunstan held Worcester with London.

[2] "Archiepiscopatum septendecim annis tantis honoribus adjungeret: alias sanè nec imprudens, nec inefficax."—MALMESB. *Script. post Bed.* 116.

[3] MS. profession of Remigius, bishop of Lincoln, made to Lanfranc, cited by Inett (*Hist. of the Engl. Ch.* ch. i. 387.) Remigius had been consecrated by Stigand; and Lanfranc insisted upon a new profession, because he maintained that Stigand had been excommunicated by the pope for his contumacy. This, however, is nothing in favour of the papal cause, for it is clear that whatever Rome might have done against Stigand, England paid no attention to it.

[4] Inett (p. 384) examines this relation at considerable length, and shews it to be far from clear as to the particular pope, or pre-

attainable, would be of little or no importance. But it is otherwise with Stigand's indisputable reception as primate. In this, England manifested a feeling of ecclesiastical independence which may surprise those who have hastily asssumed her entire dependence upon Rome from Augustine to the Reformation.

Edward's unfortunate successor, Harold, had, previously to his brief possession of the crown, founded the noble monastery of Waltham. To this act of liberality, however, he does not seem to have been tempted by any partiality for the Benedictine order: he arranged his establishment for secular canons.[1] The monks, therefore, had not triumphed over all opposition. The ancient economy of an English religious house yet found powerful friends; and the two rival systems must have been often warmly contrasted with each other, down to the very edge of Norman times. Facilities were thus afforded, obviously, for William's enterprise. The monks and canons were not anxious merely for the prevalence of their opinions respectively; they were struggling also for the endowments which each other possessed: hence was extensively nurtured a disposition for political changes; a numerous party ever seeking adherents for them, in the hope of gaining some advantage hitherto unattainable.

---

tender, who is said to have complimented Stigand with a pall. The matter is, however, of but little importance on any account. The truth, most probably, appears in the profession of Remigius.

[1] The abbey of Waltham was founded in 1062; namely, four years before Harold's obtainment of the throne. (*Monast.* ii. 13.) In 1117 regular canons were substituted for the seculars under papal authority.—*Ib.*

Upon doctrines prevalent during the last period of Anglo-Saxon religious history, Elfric's remains afford much interesting information. They prove, forcibly and clearly, that the ancient Church of England never wavered in her invaluable testimony against transubstantiation.[1] They shew satisfactorily

---

[1] On þam halȝan husle ve þicȝeað Crıstes lichaman· se hlaf ıs soðlice hıs lichama ȝastlice· þeah þe se unȝelæneða-þær ȝe lysan ne cunne. (Serm. de Lege Dei. Bibl. Publ. Cant. MSS. ii. 4—6. p. 175.) *In the holy housel we receive Crist's body: the loaf is truly his body spiritually, though the unlearned know not how to believe it.* This passage is evidently the key to testimony from antiquity cited in favour of transubstantiation. The gross and irreligious identified completely the sacramental elements with ordinary food. Divines taught that consecration converted them *spiritually* into Christ's body and blood. Such conversion, however, applies to *spiritual* receiving alone. This ancient homily, therefore, teaches the same doctrine as the catechism of the reformed church of England. In this we learn that " the body and blood of Christ are verily and indeed taken and received *by the faithful* in the Lord's Supper."

With this view agrees the following passage from an ancient piece, *De Ecclesiasticis Gradibus.* (Bibl. Bodl. MSS. *Junii,* 121, f. 39.) Se mæsse-pseost ȝetacnað Crıst sylfne· ꝑ ꝥ altane ȝetacnað Crıstes sode ꝑ seo oflete ȝetacnað Crıstes lichaman· ꝑ pin ꝑ pæten on þam calice ȝefsutelað þa haliȝnesse þe of Crıstes siðan utfleopan· ꝥ pæs bloð ꝑ pæten. *The mass-priest betokeneth Crist himself, and the altar betokeneth Crist's rood* (cross), *and the oflet betokeneth Crist's body, and wine and water in the chalice manifesteth the holiness which from Crist's side outflowed, that was blood and water.* In this passage, the word *oflet* comes from the Latin *oblata,* which is *ab offerendo,* and denotes a small cake made for the sacrament, and as yet, according to Du Cange, unconsecrated. He cites Bromton for this opinion, who speaking of Hugh de St. Victor's death, in the time of King Stephen, says, that on his desire of the eucharist, " simplicem oblatam non consecratam attulerunt." (*X. Script.* 1035.) This is hardly sufficient, perhaps, to limit strictly the use of *oblata* even so late as Stephen's reign. At all events a believer in transubstantiation was likely to see the danger of saying that the sacramental bread in any state

that she did not hold such opinions upon St. Peter's alleged privileges, and upon papal jurisdiction, as Romanists have maintained in later years.[1] They are irreconcilable with that fascinating lure, provided by scholastic ingenuity, which would make mere attrition ample medicine for the soul. Elfric taught the people, from St. Jerome, that very doctrine which Tyndale subsequently recommended as a sound view of sacerdotal absolution.[2] A belief, however, in transubstantiation, and an implicit reliance upon absolution, are the corner-stones of modern Romanism. William the Conqueror, therefore, found established a religious system, different essentially from that which Henry the Eighth overthrew. Externally, the Church indeed had undergone no very striking change: the Anglo-Saxon ritual was nearly identical with that which prevailed until the Reformation. Ancient England was habituated to confession; it was her usage to offer prayers and eucharistic services for the dead: she was trained in a superstitious veneration for relics. In Elfric's time, and long before, she was encouraged in paying religious honours to images. Her great homilist entertained some obscure speculations upon purgatorial fires.[3] He

---

" *betokeneth* Christ's body." There might, however, be room for doubt upon such subjects, were not Elfric's Paschal Homily, and his two epistles, irresistible evidence that neither he nor the church of England in his day, held the eucharistic belief of modern Rome.

[1] See *Bampt. Lect.* Serm. iii. p. 135, and the preceding homily.

[2] *Ib.* p. 300.

[3] *Fundamentum aliud nemo potest ponere preter id quod positum est, quod est xpus ihs.* Ðæt is ne mæʒ nan mann lecʒan oðeþne ʒpnunð-peal on þæne halʒan ʒelaðunʒe buton þæne þæp ʒelæð is ꝥ is

lends occasional authority, as it seems, to the invo-

Hælend Crist. He is se ȝnund-peal þæne ȝartlican cyncan· ꞅpa ꞅpa þe
eop æp ꞅæbon· Se apoꞅtol cpæð· ꞅpa hpa ꞅpa ȝetimbꞃað oꝥeꞃ ꝥiꞃum ȝꞃund-
pealle ȝold· oððe ꞅeolꝥon. oððe deoꞃpyꞃðe ꞅtanap. oððe tꞃeopu·
ꞅꝥꞃeaꞃ· oððe ceaꝥ· aneꝥ ȝehpylceꞃ manneꞃ peoꞃc bið-ꞅputel· Codeꞃ
dæȝ hi ȝeꞅꝥutelað· ꝥoꞃðan þe he bið on ꝥyꞃe ætopod· ⁊ ꝥ ꝥyꞃ aꝥandað
hpylc hecꞃa ælceꞃ peoꞃc bið. Giꝥ hpæꞅ ȝetimbꞃunȝ þuꞃh-punað ⁊
pið-ꞅtent þam ꝥyꞃe· þonne undeꞃꝥeð ꞅe pyꞃhta hiꞅ edlean æt Code
hiꞅ peoꞃceꞅ. Giꝥ hpæꞅ peopc ꝥoꞃbyꞃnd· he hæꝥð þone heaꞃm· ⁊ bið
ꞅpa þeah ȝehealden þuꞃh ꝥ ꝥyꞃ. Ðaꞅ poꞃd pe ne maȝon buton micelꞃe
ꝥyꞃhtu tꞃahtnian· Ðuꞃh ꝥ ȝold þe undeꞃꞅtandað ȝeleaꝥan· ⁊ ȝod
inȝehyd þuꞃh ꝥ ꞅeolꝥoꞃ· ꞃihtlice ꞅpꞃæce ⁊ ȝetinȝniꞅꞅe on Codeꞃ
laꞃe· þuꞃh þa deoꞃpyꞃðan ꞅtaneꞅ haliȝe mihta· ⁊ ꞅe þe þyllic peoꞃc
ȝetimbꞃað on Codeꞃ ȝeladunȝe· ne mæȝ ꝥ ꝥyꞃ on domeꞅ dæȝe hiꞅ
ȝetimbꞃunȝe ꝥoꞃuuman· ꝥoꞃðan þe ꝥ ꝥyꞃ ne dꞃꝥað þam ȝodum· þeah
þe hit tintreȝꞃie þa unꞃihtꝥiꞃum. Cold ⁊ ꞅeolꝥoꞃ ⁊ deoꞃpyꞃðe ꞅtaneꞅ
beoð on ꝥyꞃe aꝥandode ac hi ne beoð ꞅpa þeah mid þæm ꝥyꞃe ꝥoꞃnumene
Spa eac þa þe habbað ȝode peoꞃc· ne þoliað naꞃe pinunȝa on þam
bꞃadum ꝥyꞃe þe oꝥeꞃ-ȝæð ealne middan-eaꞃd· ac hi ꝥaꞃað þuꞃh ꝥ
ꝥyꞃe to Criꞅte buton ælceꞃe daꞃe· ꞅpilce hi on ꞃunnan leoman ꝥaꞃan·
Se þe ȝetimbꞃað oꝥeꞃ þam ȝꞃund-pealle tꞃeopa· oððe ꞅtꞃeaꝥ· oððe
ceaꝥ· untꞃylice he mæȝ piꞅan ꝥ hiꞅ peoꞃc ꞅceal on þam micclum ꝥyꞃe
ꝥoꞃbyꞃnan. ⁊ he hæꝥð þone heaꞃm hiꞅ peoꞃceꞅ· ⁊ bið ꞅpa þeah
ȝehealden þuꞃh ꝥ ꝥyꞃ. Ðuꞃh þa tꞃeopu. ⁊ þam ꞅtꞃeaꝥe· ⁊ þam
ceaꝥe· ꞅynd ȝetacnode leohtlice ꞅynnu· þe beoð þuꞃh ꝥyꞃ aꝥeoꞃmode·
⁊ ꞅe pyꞃhta hæꝥð piꞅe þæꞅ peoꞃceꞅ. Bið ꞅpa ðeah aꝥeoꞃmod puꞃh ꝥ
ꝥyꞃ· ⁊ ꞅyððan he cymð þuꞃh mæꞃum eaꞃꝥoðniꞅꞅe to Codeꞃ ꞃice.
Soðlice ꞅe ðe þa heaꞃod leahtꞅaꞃ pyꞃcð. ⁊ on þam ȝe-endað· he mot
ꝥoꞃbyꞃnan on þam ecan ꝥyꞃe ⁊ ꞅpa þeah þa ꞅꝥæꞃan ꞅynnu ne beoð
næꝥꞃe aꝥeoꞃmode ꝥoꞃ naneꞃ ꝥyꞃeꞅ æliꞃȝe. (Bibl Bodl. MSS.
BODLEY, 342, f. 177. Hom. in Dedicatione Ecclesiæ.) *Fundamentum aliud, &c.* (1 Cor. III. 11.) *That is, no man can lay another ground-wall (foundation) in the holy congregation, but that which is laid, that is Jesus Crist. He is the ground-wall of the ghostly church, even as we to you ere said. The apostle quoth: Whoever buildeth over this ground-wall gold, or silver, or precious stones, or tree (wood), straw, or chaff, every man's work shall be manifest. God's day will manifest it, because it shall be revealed in fire, and that fire will prove what each man's work is. If any one's building lasteth-through and withstandeth the fire, then receiveth the workman his reward from God for his work. If any one's work burneth-up, he hath the harm, and is nevertheless holden through the fire. These words we cannot without great fear expound. By the gold we understand belief and a good*

cation of saints :[1] his homilies, however, do not display either of these principles, especially not the

conscience; by the silver, right, speech, and eloquence, in God's lore; by the precious stones, holy powers, and he who buildeth such works in God's congregation, the fire on dooms-day cannot consume his building, because the fire hurteth not the good though it torment the unrighteous. Gold, and silver, and precious stones, are proved in the fire, but nevertheless they are not with the fire consumed. So, also, he who hath good works suffereth not any torture in the broad fire which over-goeth all the earth, but they go through that fire to Crist without any hurt, as if they went in the sun's brightness. He who builds over the ground-wall, tree, or straw, or chaff, undoubtedly he may know that his work shall in the great fire burn up, and he will have the harm of his work, and will be, nevertheless, holden through the fire. By the tree, and the straw, and the chaff, are betokened light sins, which will be purged by fire, and the workman will have punishment for the work. He will be, nevertheless, purged by the fire, and then he cometh through great difficulty to God's kingdom. Truly he who committeth the capital vices, and in them endeth, he must burn up in the everlasting fire, and thus the heavy sins will never be purged in any fiery conflagration. The homilist subsequently says, Fela ꞃynꝺ eac pitnienꝺlic ꞅtopu þe manna ꞃapla ꞃoꞃ heoꞃa ᵹymeleaꞃte onþꞃopiaꝺ· be heoꞃa ᵹyltu mæꝺe· æꞃ þam ᵹemænilican ꝺome· ꞃpa þ hi ꞃume beoꝺ ꝼullice ᵹeclænꞃoꝺe· ⁊ ne þuꞃꞃon naht þꞃopian on þam ꞃoꞃe-ꞃæꝺan ꞃyꞃe. *Many are also the punishing places in which men's souls for their negligence suffer, according to the measure of their faults, ere the common judgment, so that some will be fully cleansed, and have no occasion to suffer any thing in the foresaid fire.* Thus, the principal purgatorial fire was not expected until the day of judgment, and even upon that remedy great sinners were not to calculate unless they amended before the end of life. But this view of purgatory is not that of modern Romanists, nor does the gloomy prospect offered to the more inveterate offenders agree with such representations of absolution as have long formed a powerful attraction within the papal church.

[1] Homiletic exhortations to invoke the Blessed Virgin, may be seen in note 21 to Serm. 4. (*Bampt. Lect.* 233.) Such an exhortation to invoke St. Laurence is found in p. 238. The homilies

latter, in a clear point of view. It is plain, rather, that both were making a stealthy progress, than that either had found a place among evidences of orthodoxy. Thus Elfric, in favouring some traditions which the Council of Trent erected into articles of faith, renders a service, at best equivocal. His homilies were manifestly written during a state of transition from one class of doctrines to another: but indications of such a state are far from advantageous to the Romish cause. They fatally undermine that claim to an uninterrupted stream of testimony, in which religious principles, incapable of Scriptural proof, seek support. Such evidence from Elfric's pen also subverts the most cherished opinion of English Romanists: it convicts them of a fond illusion, in identifying their own peculiar system with that of their earliest Christian ancestry. The Saxon homilies countenance, indeed, more or less, various opinions that the reformed Church of England has rejected; but their voice upon other distinctive points

---

most likely are Elfric's; at all events they were produced about his time, and are evidences, therefore, that the practice of invoking departed spirits was then gaining ground. But the Saxon homilies, as may be seen in notes 4 and 5 (p. 216) to that sermon, are far from favourable, upon the whole, to such invocation. It is perfectly obvious, from them and from liturgies of their time and of earlier dates, as the proofs to that sermon abundantly testify, that not even Anglo-Saxon usage, much less authority, was ever very favourable to any invocation but that of God. None other, indeed, seems to have entered the head of any man until a period but little removed from the Conquest. Johnson, accordingly, observes upon the fifth of the penitential canons, which he would attribute to Dunstan, and which he places under the year 963, " It is evident the fashion of confessing to angels and saints did not yet prevail."

is Protestant. Upon the whole, they demonstrate sufficiently, that England, in leaving Rome, regained substantially her ancient faith.

ADDITIONAL NOTE ON ELFRIC.

After this work was finished, it seemed doubtful whether some mention ought not to be made of a formal treatise which takes a view of Elfric's history, different from that in the foregoing pages. The piece is thus entitled: EDWARDI-ROWEI MORESI, *de Ælfrico Dorobernensi Archiepiscopo, Commentarius.* It was published by Thorkelin, in 1789, Mr. Mores being then dead, and its object is to identify the great Anglo-Saxon author with an archbishop of Canterbury of his name. It maintains that Elfric was educated at Abingdon, under Ethelwold; that he removed with him to Winchester; that he went to Cerne, as all accounts agree; that he was made Abbot of St. Albans in 988, Bishop of Wilton in the following year, Archbishop of Canterbury, in 994, and that he died in 1005. To his residence at Winchester are assigned his *Glossary, Monastic Colloquies, Biblical Versions,* and *Epistle to Wulfsine;* to Cerne, his first volume of homilies; to Wilton, the second volume of homilies, and, probably, also his grammar.

Upon these dates, so far as they concern Elfric or Alfric, in the see of Canterbury, there is no material question. Nor is it doubtful that Elfric, the homilist, produced his first volume of homilies, soon after his removal to Cerne, in 987, and his second volume about 991; for he speaks in it of the Danish troubles. But the identity of Elfric the homilist with his namesake the Archbishop of Canterbury is any thing rather than equally clear. In order to render it probable, Mr. Mores is driven to the necessity of naming Elfric Bata as the author of the *Life of Ethelwold* and the *Epistle to Wolstan.* Chronology forbids the assignment of these to Elfric, archbishop of Canterbury. The hypothesis, therefore, of Mr. Mores, labours under the disadvantage of finding two literary men for works which might have come from one, and apparently did so. It is, besides, only supported by a MS. memorandum, appended to the *Glossary* and *Colloquies,* in the Library of St. John's College, Oxford, which claims the credit of several additions to these pieces for Elfric Bata, a disciple of his namesake the abbot. For attributing to Bata the *Life of Ethelwold* and the *Epistle to Wolstan*, no reason is assigned; yet internal evidence renders it hardly questionable that this epistle came from the same pen that has obliged posterity by the *Epistle to Wulfsine*. Again, Elfric the homilist introduces his second volume as a *monk*. He was then, Mr. Mores contends, Bishop of Wilton. This difficulty, however, is met by Archbishop Peckham's usage, in the 13th century, of styling himself *friar*, when he was actually filling the see of Canterbury. But such an analogy is too remote for much attention. The light, indeed, in which Elfric's history has been placed by the ingenious author of *Anc. Hist. Engl. and Fr. exempl.*, appeared perfectly satisfactory. By thus identifying this illustrious Anglo-Saxon, a life of about eighty-six years will be assigned to him, and a series of works, all bearing his name, is referred to a single author.

It should be added, perhaps, that those who cite Elfric's invaluable testimony against Romish opinions, ought to remark the challenge of inquiry into the soundness of his doctrine with which he introduces both volumes of homilies. That these challenges were not idly given, we are sufficiently assured; for an archbishop of Canterbury approved the books. Dr. Lingard, who labours to discredit them in the notes (Note M) to his *Antiquities of the Anglo-Saxon Church*, certainly does not make his case any the stronger by espousing the prevailing opinion that Elfric himself became archbishop of Canterbury, immediately after these homilies were published and authorised According to this hypothesis, Elfric sent one volume of homilies to Siricius, about 987, another about 991, inviting a strict inquiry into the soundness of both, and was himself the successor of Siricius in 994. If such be the facts, they are pretty decisive against English belief in transubstantiation, at that time of the day. As for the intellectual inferiority of Elfric's age to that of a former period, which Dr. Lingard maintains, let it be remembered that this was the very age of Dunstan and Ethelwold. A Romish advocate would laud the great luminary of such an age to the skies—if he had not overthrown the main distinctive article of Romish belief.

CHAPTER V.

MISCELLANEOUS PARTICULARS.

GOD'S OFFER OF SALVATION TO CHRISTIANS REPRESENTED AS UNIVERSAL—PRACTICE ESTEEMED THE ONLY TEST OF RELIGIOUS SINCERITY—GOD'S LIKENeSS TO BE FOUND IN THE HUMAN SOUL—POPULAR EXPOSITIONS OF THE LORD'S PRAYER AND THE CREED ENJOINED—APOCRYPHAL LEGENDS—RESPECT FOR SUNDAY—FESTIVALS AND FASTS—ABSTINENCE FROM STRANGLED FOOD AND BLOOD—EPISCOPAL ELECTIONS—NO PROFESSION OF OBEDIENCE TO ROME REQUIRED FROM BISHOPS—NOR OF BELIEF IN TRANSUBSTANTIATION—BISHOPS AND ABBOTS MEMBERS OF THE NATIONAL LEGISLATURE—BISHOPS CONCURRENT JUDGES IN THE COUNTY COURTS—EPISCOPAL SEES—EPISCOPAL PRECEDENCE AND VISITATIONS—ORDINATION AND DUTIES OF PRIESTS—ANXIETY TO KEEP THEM UNMARRIED—SEVEN ORDERS OF ECCLESIASTICS—DIFFERENT KINDS OF MONKS—REGULATIONS RESPECTING THEM—ECCLESIASTICAL IMMUNITIES—GUILD-SHIPS OR SODALITIES—CORONATION COMPACT—BAPTISM—MARRIAGE—SECOND MARRIAGES—WAKES—DEDICATION OF CHURCHES—RELIGIOUS ARCHITECTURE—ORGANS—ORDEALS—TRUCE OF THE CHURCH—LUSTRAL WATER AND CHRISM USED AS CHARMS—THE PENITENTIAL SYSTEM—ANGLO-SAXON SAINTS—ANGLO-SAXON VERSIONS OF SCRIPTURE—CONCLUSION.

For the convenience of making a distinction, apparently, Englishmen have long spelt and pronounced differently the words *God* and *good*. Anglo-Saxon documents offer no such difference to the eye; nor, probably, in Anglo-Saxon speech did any such difference fall upon the ear. The great Creator might seem to have been known emphatically as *the Good*, a happy designation, at once expressive of his own most endearing attribute, and of his people's thankfulness. With equal felicity of expression, it must be mournfully acknowledged, was our Anglo-Norman ancestry contented to signify *humanity* and *wickedness* by the same word. *Man* meant indifferently either. In strict conformity with a name so appropriately found for the Great First Cause, were Anglo-Saxon views of his moral governance. All Christians were encouraged in believing themselves to have received an offer of salvation. The health of every soul was represented as the desire of God.[1]

---

[1] Drihten us mid rra micelne lufan lufað· he pilnað þ we ealle hale syn'd ¬ gesund· ¬ to þære soðan hreowe gecyrran· ¬ to þam soþan andgyte his godcundnesse· Drihten pile þ ure lif sy gestaþelod on clænnesse· ¬ on soðfæstnesse· nelt he þ se synfulla mann on his synnum þurh-punige· ¬ æfter his beaðe on ecum pitum spelte· Ac he pile þ pe in þisse lænan tide geeasnien þ pe on ecenesse ne fospurðan· Se arfesta Drihten ¬ se mildheorta ne bideð he æt us gold ne feolfor. ne nænig populd gestreon· ac he pilnað þ pe clænsien une sapla· ¬une lichaman þ pe magon heo him spa clæne agyfan spa he hi us æs clæne befærte. Œenn þa leofestan pe sceolon mid monig-fealdum godum une sapla clænsian· mid færtenum· ¬ mid ælmes-beadum· ¬ clænum gebedum forðon se monn se gelomlice to Drihtene clypað· þonne brecð he deofles mægn· ¬ his costnunge him fram aflemð.—(*Hom. De Letaniá Majore.* Bibl. Bodl. MSS. *Junii*, 22.) *The Lord with so great love us loveth, he desireth that we all be hale and sound, and turn to true repentance, and to true understanding of his divinity. The Lord desireth that our life be established in cleanness* (pur'ty); *and in truth he will not that the sinful man in his sins continue, and after his death in everlasting punishments die. But he desires that we, in this lean* (frail or transitory) *tide, earn that we for ever do not perish. The gracious Lord and the mild-hearted, asketh he not of us gold, nor silver, nor any worldly gain; but he desireth that we cleanse our soul and our body; that we may give it up to him as clean as he committed it ere clean to us. Men, the most beloved, we should with manifold goods our souls cleanse; with fastings, and with alms-deeds, and with clean prayers; for the man who constantly calleth to the Lord, then breaketh he the devil's main* (power), *and his temptation from him putteth to flight.*

Nor were gloomy forebodings awakened in any believing mind, unless an irreligious life denied the conscience peace.

When the Author of all goodness is thus attractively displayed, a serious mind inclines irresistibly to love him. Such an inclination might, however, merely generate a transient glow, productive neither of individual amelioration, nor of honour to the church. Wisely, therefore, for the ripening of heavenly seed, were the Anglo-Saxons taught distrust in any barren impulse, however warm and creditable. Men might please themselves in observing their hearts approach to a healthier, religious tone, and not unreasonably. Would they please God, also, Anglo-Saxon divinity bade them to remember that virtuous actions must prove their feelings energetic, no less than sound.[1] Thus were congregations guarded against illusions from a sanguine temperament and an enthusiastic brain; holy affections were tried by the sober-minded test of moral lives; men were warned against reckoning either upon their own love to God or upon the love from him indispensable for their wants, while the habits bore no witness to a change. Until this difficulty

---

[1] Uton þe nu forþon· men þa leofestan· neoman sibbe ⁊ lufe uf betpeonan· foþþon on þam bið eall Dpihtnef beboð mæft· Uton neoman clænneffe· ⁊ ʒefceaðpifneffe ealna ʒoðna peopea· foþþon buton þæm ne mæʒ nan man Ʋoðe lician.—(*Hom. De Letaniâ Majore*. Bibl. Bodl. MSS. *Junii*, 22.) *Come we now, then, men the most beloved, let us take peace and love among ourselves; for in them is the greatest of all God's commandments. Come, let us take cleanness and regard for good works; for without them no man can please God.*

was overcome, all claims to the love of God were branded as nothing better than false pretences.[1]

To the soundness of such divinity sensible men will ordinarily yield immediate assent. Nor do they overlook, when sunk in serious thought, the difficulty of thus attesting trustworthy principles. From this insight into their danger, and into their natural incompetence to overcome it, religious minds draw humility and aspirations after heavenly aid. Anglo-Saxon teachers inculcated, accordingly, the need of both. A proud heart was represented as fatal to the hope of divine assistance, and this latter as indispensable for establishing the soul in health.[2] It was to

---

[1] Eft cwæð se Hælend to his leorning-cnihtum· Se þe me lufað he hylt min bebod· ꝥ min Fæder hine lufað for þane gehyrsumnysse· ꝥ pyt cumað him to· ꝥ him mid puniað. Gehyrað mine gebroðra hwæt se Hælend cwæð. Se þe me lufað he hylt min bebod. Þære lufe fandung is þær peorces fremming. Iohannes se apostol eac beþyrum cwæð· Gif hwa cwyð ꝥ he lufige þone lufigendan God· ꝥ his bebodne hylt byð leas þonne. Soðlice we lufiath þone leofan Drihten gif we une unþeawas geemnyttað be his hæsum· ꝥ une pohnysse be his fordum gerihtað· ꝥ þurh unlustar his lufe ne forcpeðað.—(Hom. De Dilectione Dei et Proximi. Bibl. Bodl. MSS. Junii, 23.) *Then quoth the Healer to his learning-knights: He that loveth me, he holds my bidding, and my Father loveth him for the obedience, and we two come to him, and dwell with him. Hear, my brethren, what the Healer quoth: He that loveth me, he holds my bidding. The love's proof is the work's effect. Iohannes, the apostle, also of this quoth: If any one quoth that he loveth the loving God, and his bidding hold not, he is a liar then. Truly we love the beloved Lord, if we our ill-manners adjust by his commands, and our errors by his words correct, and through what displeases him, his love do not gainsay.*

[2] Dena getacniað þa eadmodan· buna þa modigan. On Drihtenes to-cyme purdon bena afyllede· ſ buna geeadmete· fra fra he fylſ cwæð· Ælc þæra þe hine onhefð bið eadmet· ꝥ se þe hine geeadmet bið geufepod. Spa fra pæten fcyt of þene dune ꝥ eft ſtent on dene' fra fra fonflið se Halga Gart modigra manna heortan· ꝥ nimeð pununge on

that invisible part to which the words of Moses were applied, when he speaks of man as originally created in the image of God.[1] When human aims, therefore, were directed by the divine perfections, men were only striving to regain what they had been taught to consider as integral portions of their proper nature. Adam's fall, however, they were informed had enslaved the will. This had been originally free in every sense of that word. It was now warped by a

---

þam eaðmoðan.—(*Hom. in Nativ. Sci Ioh. Bapt.* Bibl. Bodl. MSS. *Junii*, 24.) *Valleys betoken the humble, mountains the proud. At the Lord's advent were valleys filled up and mountains levelled, even as he himself quoth: Every one of those who exalt themselves shall be abased, and he that humbleth himself shall be exalted. Even as water shoots off the mountain, and then stands in the valley, even so fleeth the Holy Ghost proud men's hearts, and taketh a dwelling in the humble.*

Nu behoraþ uɲe ɼneoðom æɼne Ɡoðeɼ ɼulтume· ɼoɲþan þe ɼe ne boð nan ʒoð butan Ɡoðeɼ ɼulтume.—(*Hom. in Letaniá Majore.* Brit. Mus. MSS. Cotton, *Julius*, E. 7. f. 83.) *Now needeth our freedom ever God's aid, for we do no good without God's aid.*

Næɼð uɲe nannan leoht ænıʒɲe ʒoðnyɼɼe· buton oɼ Ɛɲıɼтeɼ ʒıɼe· ɼe þe ıɼ ɼoðɲe ɲıhтpıɼnyɼɼe ɼunne ʒehaтen.—(*Ib. Titus*, D. 27. f. 54.) *None of us hath any light of any goodness but of Christ's gift, who is called the sun of true righteousness.*

[1] Heɲ ʒe maʒon ʒehyɲan þa halʒan Ðɲynneɼɼe· ⁊ ɼoþe anneɼɼe· anɲe ʒoðcunðneɼɼe. Uтon pyɲcan mannan· þæɲ ıɼ ɼeo halʒe Ðɲynnyɲ. To uɲe anlıcneɼɼe· Dæɲ ıɼ ɼeo annyɼ· To anɲe anlıcneɼɼe· na тo þɲym anlıcneɼɼum. On þeɼ manneɼ ɼaple ıɼ Ɡoðeɼ anlıcneɼ· ɼoɲþan ıɼ ɼe man ɼelɲa þonne þa ɼaulleɼɼan nyтenu þe nan anðʒıт nabbaþ embe heoɲa aʒenne Scyppenð.—(*Hom.* 15. *De Exameron.* ꝑ ıɼ ᛒᛖ ᚷᚩᛞᛖᛋ ᛋᛁᛉ ᛞᚫᚷᚫ ᚹᛖᚩᚱᚳᚹᚩ. Bibl. Bodl. MSS. *Junii*, 24. p. 276.) *Here ye may hear the Holy Trinity and the true Unity in one Divinity. Come let us make man: there is the holy Trinity. To our likeness: there is the Unity. To one likeness, not to three likenesses. In man's soul is the likeness of God; therefore is man's soul better than the soul-less cattle, which have no understanding about their own Creator.*

constitutional bias towards iniquity; hence nothing short of divine interposition offered a hope of such courses as judgment and conscience would approve.[1]

A Latin liturgy naturally made the Anglo-Saxons partial to that language even in their offices of domestic piety. The Lord's Prayer, the creeds, and other devotional pieces were, indeed, rendered into the vernacular tongue. Nor was there any reason why individuals, worshipping God at home, should have used them under the disguise of a foreign idiom. But public solemnities take a powerful hold upon imagination, and human weakness is prone to invest with a mysterious potency such religious forms as are ordinarily unintelligible. Hence, clergymen were enjoined, as an especial duty, to supply popular expositions of the Lord's Prayer and Creed.[1] Men, it was intimated, ought to know what was the purport of their prayers, and what were the articles of their belief. How forcibly does such an intimation rebuke the usage of making religion speak an unknown tongue!

---

[1] Hpæt ıſ aȝen-cyne Hyæt ıſ ſnıȝꝺom to ȝeceoran ȝoꝺ oððe yꝼel. Ꝺone ſnıȝꝺom hæſꝺe mann on neorxenepanȝe· ac nu ıſ ſe ſnıꝺom ȝeðeortoꝺ· for ſe mann ne cann nan ȝoꝺ· bute Ꝼoꝺ punh hıſ ȝeoſe hım tæce. Ne þa ȝet ne mæıȝ he hıt ȝeſorðıȝen bute Ꝼoꝺ hım ſylſte þænto. (Brit. Mus. MSS. Cotton, *Vespasian*, D. 14, f. 157.) *What is free will? What is freedom to choose good or evil? The freedom had man in Paradise: but now is the freedom enslaved; for man can do no good, unless God, through his gift, him teach. Nor, then, can he go on with it, unless God aid him thereto.*

[2] Se laneop ſceal ſecȝan þam læpeꝺum mannum ꝥ anꝺȝıt to þam Paten nɲe· ⁊ þam Cɲeꝺan· ꝥ hı pıton hpæt hı bıꝺꝺað æt Ꝼoꝺe· ⁊ hu hı ſceolon on Ꝼoꝺ ȝelyſan. (*Hom. in Cap. Jejuni.* Brit. Mus. MSS. Cotton, *Julius*, E. 7, f. 65.) *The teacher shall say to the lay men, the meaning of the Pater n̄r, and the Creed, that they know what they pray of God, and how they should in God believe.*

As Anglo-Saxon divines lived long before the revival of sound criticism, they were naturally prone to admit hasty views of Scripture and apocryphal tales. They teach, accordingly, that Elias is reserved alive for a solemn appearance upon earth; when Antichrist has gained his destined ascendancy, immediately before the final consummation. Then, he is to bear an unavailing testimony against ungodliness and suffer martyrdom.[1] Christ's death, it was also believed, has effected a most important deliverance for the first pair, and the good of former times. All these had hitherto languished in the infernal regions; but Jesus descended to them, and on departing carried them away in his train, leaving impenitent spirits to brood in gloomy despair over augmented horrors reserved for the day of judgment.[2] Paradise was

---

[1] Eliaſ næfne ȝyt ƀeað ne þoloƀe· ac he iſ ȝyt on lichame libbenƀe on þam ſtope þe Ɖoð him hæfð iſæt· ⁊ he ſceal þæn abiƀæn runðfullice hiſ manṫyrðomeſ· oððet Dnihten aſenƀe hine æft hiƀen on miððæn-eanƀe æt ponulƀeſ enƀe· þ he ſceal þenne ſecȝæn ⁊ cuþæn moncynne Ɖoƀeſ laſe· ⁊ hiſ manṫynðom fon Cnirteſ lufæ þnopæn on Anteċnirteſ ðaȝum. (Bibl. Bodl. MSS. BODLEY, 343, f. 162.) *Elias never yet suffered death, but he is yet in the body living in the place where God hath set him; and he shall there happily abide his martyrdom, until the Lord send him away hereafter hither on earth, at the world's end, that he shall then say and testify to mankind God's lore, and undergo his martyrdom for Crist's love, in Antecrist's days.*

[2] Uſe Hælenð Cnirt tobnæc helle ȝatu ⁊ ȝeneſoðe Aðam ⁊ Euan ⁊ hiſ ȝeconenan of heona cynne· ⁊ fneolice of ƀeað aſaſ ⁊ hi famoð· ⁊ aſtah to heofonum Ða manfullan he let bæftan to þam ecum pitum· ⁊ iſ nu helle ȝat belocen nihipiſum mannum ⁊ æfne open unnihtnifum· (Bibl. Publ. Cant. MSS. 9 l. 4—6. *Hom. in Die Dom. Pasch.* p. 294.) *Our Healer, Crist, brake hell's gates, and delivered Adam and Eva, and his chosen of their kind, and freely from death arose, and they with him, and ascended to heaven. The wicked he left*

represented as a delightful abode miraculously suspended between heaven and earth.[1] A proof of the body's resurrection was rather strangely sought in the legend of the Seven Sleepers. Certain individuals, thus designated, being said to have awakened from a trance of nearly four centuries, it was inferred that the possibility of a general resurrection had been thereby completely established.[1] A more philoso-

---

behind, to everlasting punishments; and now is hell's gate locked against righteous men, and ever open to unrighteous. Another of these legendary statements is worthy of notice, because it is at variance with the chronology now commonly received. Ðæt ƿær Friȝedæȝ þ hie þa blæƀe þiȝƀon Aƀam ⁊ Eua· ⁊ hie eft fpulton on Friȝedæȝ· ⁊ þa eft æftep þon þ hie butu pæpon on helle Aƀam ⁊ Eua· fop þær ȝylief mycelneffe· fif þufenƀ pintpa ⁊ tpa hunƀ pintpa· æp þon heom Goƀ ȝemilƀpian polƀe· ⁊ heom þær ppæcef unbinƀan. (Brit. Mus. MSS. Cotton, *Tiberius*, A. 3. f. 41.) *It was Friday that they ate the fruit, Adam and Eva, and they afterwards died on Friday; and after that they both were in hell, Adam and Eva, for the guilt's greatness, five thousand winters, and two hundred winters, ere that God would have mercy on them, and release them from his vengeance.*

[1] Scs Iohannef ȝefeh ofep ȝapfeȝ fpylce hit an lanƀ pæpe. Ða ȝenam hine fe ænȝel ⁊ ȝebpohte hine to neoŗxenpanȝe. Neoŗxenpanȝe nif naƀep on heofene ne on eopƀe· Seo boc ræȝƀ þ Noef floƀ pær feoptiȝ feƀmen heh ofep þa heȝefta ƀunen þe on miƀƀan-eapƀe fynƀen· ⁊ neoŗxenepanȝ if feoptiȝ feƀme hepne þonne Noef floƀ pær· ⁊ hit hanȝeƀ betponen heofon ⁊ eopƀen punƀeŗlice· (Brit. Mus. MSS. Cotton, *Vespasian*, D. 14, f. 163.) *Scs Johannes saw over the ocean as if it were land. Then the angel took him, and brought him to Paradise. Paradise is neither in heaven nor in earth. The book saith, that Noe's flood was forty fathoms high over the highest mountains that are on earth, and Paradise is forty fathoms higher than Noe's flood was; and it hangeth between heaven and earth wonderfully.*

[2] Uf fecȝaƀ eac bec fpa fpa hit full roƀ if· þ ða feofon‾flæpepaf· þe flepon on þam timan fpam Decief ƀaȝum· ðær͜ƀeofellican cafepef· oƀ Theoƀofief timan þe on Dpihten ȝelyfƀe. þreo hunƀ ȝeapa fæc ⁊ tpa ⁊ hunƀ feofontiȝ ȝeapa· þ hi þa upp-apifon of þæpe eopþan acu-

phical age would probably have remarked the inconsistency of reasoning from a case in which the more active bodily functions were merely suspended, to one in which the body itself was wholly decomposed.

A similar credulity lent force to exhortations for the strict observance of Sunday. Against the desecration of that holy day numerous legislative acts made a wise and honourable provision.[1] Minds, however, impressed but slightly by religion, find a temptation, almost irresistible, to encroach upon it by business or amusement. Hence an Anglo-Saxon homily circulated a legend, representing legal and customary restrictions for guarding the sanctity of Sunday as express revelations from Heaven. Christians at Antioch were said to have become very remiss in hallowing the Lord's day. An angel was

---

coðe· forþan þe Crist polðe þam carene ʒerputelian þ pe ealle rceolon of ðeaðe apiran on þam enðenextan ðæʒe unum Drihtene toʒeaner· ꞇ unðenfon eðlean ealpa une ðæða· be þam þe pe æn ʒeronhton on þirrene ponulðe. (Brit. Mus. MSS. Cotton, Vitellius, C. 5. f. 95.) *Us tell us also books, even as it full true is, that the seven sleepers, who slept at a time, from Decie's days, the devilish emperor, to Theodosie's time, who believed in the Lord, three hundred and seventy two years' space, that they then up-arose from the earth alive, because Crist would manifest to the emperor that we all shall rise from death at the last day to meet our Lord, and receive the reward of all our deeds, according to that we ere wrought in this world.*

[1] Ina's legislation for Sunday has already been particularised. This was repeated at Berghampstead. The fourteenth canon of the council of Cloveshoo, forbids journeys to ecclesiastics, unless absolutely necessary, on Sundays. (Spelm. i. 249. Wilk. i. 96.) Athelstan imposed heavy penalties on Sunday-trading. (Spelm. i. 400. Wilk. i. 207.) At Eanham, hunting on Sundays was forbidden. (Spelm. i. 518. Wilk. i. 288.) This, with the other prohibitions, Canute repeated.—Spelm. i. 546. Wilk. i. 303.

therefore despatched to one Peter, then bishop there, for the purpose of detailing the claims of piety's own day to especial veneration, and of enjoining the manner of its observance.[1] This heavenly messenger is made to crowd into the sacred day a very large proportion of those incidents that most interest religious minds. Anglo-Saxon usage consecrated to devotion the whole space of time from three o'clock on Saturday afternoon to day-light on Monday morning.[2] Within this interval, it was represented, God created the soul of man. To the Lord's day were assigned also the passage of Israel through the Red Sea, the miraculous fall of manna, the birth of Christ, his change of water into wine, his baptism, and his wonderful repast to the five thousand.[3] His rise from

---

[1] Ða arenðe re ælmihtiga Ʌoð an æpenð-ʒeppit uran of heoronan be anum halʒan enʒle to anum birceope re hatte Petpur re þær bircop on Antiochia þæne bunh· þæn þæn Scs Petpur re aportol æpert ʒeræt hir bircop-retl on þam ʒeppite rtoð eall be þær ðæʒer haliʒnerre (*Bibl Lameth. MSS.* 489 f. 25. SERMO AD POPVLVM DOMINICIS DIEBVS.) *Then sent Almighty God an epistle from heaven above, by a holy angel, to a bishop named Petrus, who was bishop in the city of Antiochia, where Scs Petrus, the apostle erst, set his bishop's see, in the writing stood all about the day's holiness.*

[2] This custom of keeping eves appears to have been adopted from the Jewish practice. Among that nation it was ancient, as is evident from Judith, viii. 6. The homily thus enjoins it, assuming the person of God: Ic beoðe þ men healðan þone ðpihtenlican ðæʒ fram eallum þeopetlicum peopcum. þ ir fram Sæterner-ðæʒer none oð Ɔonan-ðæʒer lihtinʒe. *I bid that men keep the Lord's day from all servile works: that is, from Saturn's day noon* (ninth hour, reckoned from six in tne morning) *to Monday's dawn.* Legislative penalties reserved all this space of time for religion so early as the council of Berghampstead, in 697.—SPELM. 1. 195. WILK. 1. 60.

[3] Ɛac on þam ðæʒe he ʒerceop manna rapla· ⁊ þa þa Ɔoyrer· re

MISCELLANEOUS PARTICULARS.   259

the dead and the great day of Pentecost are naturally commemorated in this imposing catalogue. Another powerful claim for the consecration of Sunday is founded on the general judgment, which, it is asserted, will crown the various most remarkable distinctions of that holy day.[1]   God is accordingly represented as

---

heneroȝa· læbbe Ɫober folc of Eȝipta lanbe þa on þam bæȝe he hit læbbe ofen þa Reaban fæ· fpa ꝥ he floh mib aune ȝynbe on þa fæ· ꞇ heo to-eobe on tpa· ꞇ ꝥ folc fon betpux þam tpam pætenum on þam ȝnunbe ealle bniȝ-fceobe oð hi comon to þam lanbe up· ꞇ on þam bæȝe com ænefꞇ feo heofonlica mete ufan of heofonum þam ylcan folce to bilyfan· ꞇ Ɫob hi mib þam afebbe xl pintna on þam fefꞇene þe hi to fonon· ꞇ fe mete hatte manna ꞇ on þam bæȝe pær Cnifꞇ þær lifȝenban Ɫober funu· ȝebonen of S͞c͞a Manian innobe· fob man eal fpa he if fob Ɫob mibban eanbe to alyf-anne of beofles anpealbe· þe hif æn ȝepealb ahte fon Ðamef ȝylte· ꞇ ryðban he acenneb pær he apenbe on þam bæȝe pæten to pine· ꞇ on þam bæȝe he pær ȝefullob· ꞇ on þam bæȝe he ȝeneonbabe æt anum mæle — [obliterated] þufenb manna of fif benenum hlafum — [obliterated] fixum ryðban he hæfbe þone bilyfan mib heofoncunblicne bletfunȝa þam ylcan bæȝe ȝebletfob· ꞇ þa þa hi ealle fulle pænon þa bæn man up of þan þe hi læfbon tpelf leafaf fulle. (*Ib.* f 26.) *Also on that day he created man's soul, and when Moyses, the leader, led God's folk from Egypt's land, then on that day he led them over the Red Sea, after he smote with a wand on the sea, and it went in twain, and the people went between the two waters on the ground all dry-shod, until they came to the land up: and on that day, came erst the heavenly meat from heaven above for the same folk's food, and God fed them with it xl. winters in the wilderness that they travelled through, and the meat was called manna. and on that day was Crist, the living God's Son, born of S͞c͞a Maria's womb, true man as he is true God, the world to release from the devil's power, who ere possessed the power of it for Adam's guilt: and after he was born, he turned, on that day, water to wine; and on that day he was baptised: and on that day he refreshed at one meal —— thousand men from five barley loaves —— fishes, after he had the food with heavenly blessing on the same day blessed, then were borne up from that which they left twelve baskets full.*

[1] On þam bæȝe fynb mibban-eanb eall ȝeenbab· ꞇ on þam bæȝe cymað Ɫob to bemanne eallum mancynne ælcum be hif aȝenum ȝefynh-tum. (*Ib.*)   *On that day will the earth be all ended, and on*

insisting upon a rigid observance of it. His angelic messenger forbids all trafficking on Sundays, all exercise of an artisan's trade, all such household cares as are not necessarily of daily recurrence; and he even interdicts the barber from obeying a summons for assistance. Any transgressor of these restrictions, it was declared, God would treat as an outlaw, denying him his blessing, and reserving for him his wrath.[1]

Besides the Lord's day, conciliar authority enjoined the celebration of all such festivals in honour of saints as were established in the Roman martyrologies.[2] In process of time English saints made new calls upon the national devotion. It was, however, impressed upon the minds of men, that such services, although in honour of religion's brightest ornaments, were merely commemorative on their

---

that day cometh God to judge all mankind, every man according to his own works. Se Sunnan-dæg is se forma dæg ealra dagena· ꝺ he bið se ende nyhsta æt þyssene populde ende. (*Ib.* f. 27.) *Sunday is the first day of all days, and it will be the last at this world's end.*

[1] Spa hpa ſpa ænige cypinge on þam dæge begæð oððe oþne þing þ man claðaſ paxe· oððe ænig cpæftig-man him on hiſ cpæfte tylige· oððe man eferige oðepne man· oððe hpeað bace· oððe ænig ungelyfeð þing bega on þam dæge. he ſcel be on utlaga pið me· ꝺ ealle þa him to þam unpihte fylſtað ꝺ him geþafiað· ꝼoꝥþan þa men þe ſpylc þing begað ne begytað hi na mine blettſunge ne mine myltſe· ac heom becymð ꝼæplice min gnama ofeſ ꝼoꝥ þæſ dæges fopſepennyſſe. (*Ib.* f. 28.) *Whoever any dealing on that day exerciseth, or washeth clothes, or any artisan that works at his craft, or a man who trims the hair of another, or bakes bread, or plies any unallowed thing on that day, he shall be an outlaw with me, and all who aid him in the wrong, and approve him: for men who ply such things do not get my blessing or my mercy, but upon them cometh suddenly my wrath for the day's contempt.*

[1] *Conc. Clovesh.* can. 13. SPELM. I. 249. WILK. I. 96.

parts. To God himself the service was really addressed.[1] Upon the public generally these demands for pious exercises appear to have been far less numerous than they eventually became. It was, probably, monks and ecclesiastics only who were expected to vary their year by all the commemorative offices of the Roman calendar. Upon the week-day time of laymen the claim for festivals appears to have been merely for the holiday-seasons of Easter, Whitsuntide, and Christmas; for two days in honour of the Virgin; for one day in honour of St. Peter and St. Paul; and for single days in honour of the archangel Michael, of the Baptist, of the saints Martin and Andrew, and of the Epiphany; together with such martyrs or confessors as should be interred in that particular diocese which contained the party's residence.[2] English

---

[1] " Festivitates scorum apostolorum seu martyrum antiqui patres in venerationis misterio celebrari sanxerunt, vel ad excitandam imitationem, vel ut meritis eorum consociemur atque orationibus adjuvemur: *ita tamen ut nulli martyrum sed ipsi Deo martyrum sacrificemus;* quamvis in memoriâ martyrum constituamus altaria. Nemo enim Antistitum in locis sanctorum corporum assistens altari aliquando dixit, *offerimus tibi, Petre,* aut *Paule,* aut *Cypriane,* sed quid offertur, offertur Deo qui martyres coronavit."—Ex codice MS. C. C. C. C. apud, Hickes, *Thes.* ii. 148.

[2] *De Festivitatibus Anni.* " Festos dies in anno celebrare sancimus: hoc est diem dominicum pasche cum omni honore et sobrietate venerari: simili modo tamen ebdomadam illam observare decrevimus: Die ascensionis dñi pleniter celebrare in pentecosten similiter ut in pascha: In natale aplorum Petri et Pauli die unum: nativitatem sci Iohannis baptistæ: assumptionem sce Mariæ. Dedicationem sci Michaelis: natale sci Martini et sci Andree: in natale dñi dies iiii: Octavas dñi: Epiphania dñi: purificatio sce Mariæ, et illas festivitates martirum vel confessorum observare decrevimus quorum in unaquaque parrochiâ sca corpora requiescunt."

authorities also thought themselves bound by the ties of national gratitude to prescribe festivals in honour of Gregory and Augustine.[1]

Besides these calls to blend religion with festivity, the Anglo-Saxon church prescribed regular pious exercises of a different character. Every Friday, unless it happened to be a festival, was to be solemnised by fasting. It was the same with the eve of every festival, except that of St. Philip and St. James. This saint's day was always near the joyous time of Easter. Hence the church was unwilling then to insist upon any fast, but left such a mode of celebrating the eve optional with individuals.[2] The great fasts were four in number, one in every quarter of the year. These were distinguished as *legitimate fasts,* and were ordinarily observed with considerable rigour. Every person above twelve years of age was then required to abstain from food until nones, or three in the afternoon.[3] These four seasons of

---

(*Brit. Mus. MSS.* COTTON, *Tiberius,* A. 3. f. 165.) Wanley pronounces the MS. from which this extract has been made, anterior to the Conquest.—HICKES, *Thes.* ii. 192.

[1] *Conc. Clovesh.* can. 17. SPELM. i. 256. WILK. i. 97. The 18th of King Alfred's laws allows twelve days at Christmas, the day of Christ's victory over the devil, St. Gregory's day, St. Peter and St. Paul's day, All Saints' day, Passion week, the Easter week, and a full week before St. Mary's mass, in harvest. (SPELM. i. 370. WILK. i. 194.) The St. Mary's mass mentioned, is that for the feast of the assumption, Aug. 15 Johnson considers the day of Christ's victory over the devil to be either Ascension-day, or the first Sunday in Lent.

[2] *Conc. Eanh.* SPELM. i. 518 WILK. i. 288.

[3] " Primum legitimum ieiuniū erit in primâ ebdomadâ quadragesimâ. Scdm autem in ebdomadâ pentecosten. Sive ebdomada

religious abstinence were also called *ember weeks,* from the Saxon word signifying *a circuit* or *course.* Of this adaptation the meaning is obvious,—in the course of every year these fasts regularly recurred.[1]

Anglo-Saxon prejudices appear never to have been relaxed upon the subject of such aliments as the most venerable of councils, that of Jerusalem, had forbidden.[2] Although Jewish prejudices no longer needed conciliation, yet this was apparently quite overlooked. Ecclesiastical authorities implicitly fol-

---

post pentecosten. Tertium autē in ebdomadâ plenâ ante equinoctiū autumpnale. Quartū autē in ebdomadâ plenâ ante natale dni nri ihū xpī." (*Bibl. Bodl. MSS. Junii.* 99) This is from an ancient calendar at the beginning of the MS., written, as it appears, by a monk and priest, named Edric, who died 9 *Kal.,* Dec.; but the year is not mentioned. The calculations, however, are made to the year 1119.

Fæꞃtað eopeꞃ lencten ꝼæꞃten ꞃihtlice to noneꞃ ælc man þe beo oꝼeꞃ xii pintꞃe· ꞃ þa ꝼeopeꞃ ymbnenu on tꞃelꝼ monðu· þe ꝼoꞃ ꞃihtlice aꞃette ꞃynd· ꞃ þæꞃa haliꞃꞃa mæꞃꞃe-æꝼenaꞃ þe ꝼoꞃ Cꞃiꞃteꞃ luꝼon manꞃyꞃdom þꞃoꝼedon (Ex Hom. intitul. Heꞃ iꞃ halꞃenðlic Laꞃ *Here is wholesome Lore.* in eod. cod. f. 68.) *Fast your lenten fast rightly to nones, every man that is over xii winters, and the four embrens in the twelve months, which are rightly set for you, and the mass-evens of the saints who for Crist's love suffered martyrdom.*

[1] As *embering,* and *ember,* still occur in our Prayer-books, and occasionally elsewhere, various speculations upon the precise meaning of the term have been entertained among observers of language, unacquainted with Saxon. It comes from ymb, the Greek ἀμφὶ, *about,* and ꞃyne, *a run.* Some have hastily derived it from *embers,* meaning the ashes, anciently used on Ash-Wednesday; but Somner (*in voc.* Ymb-ꞃen), very well observes, that this usage was confined to one day in the whole four seasons Some questions and answers upon these four fasts, with various fanciful reasons for their observance, from the pen of Egbert, may be seen in WILKINS, *Conc.* i. 85.

[2] Acts xv. 29.

lowed Egbert's example in prohibiting the tasting of blood or of strangled animals.[1] A legal defilement was attributed even to the water into which such substances had fallen.[2] In the *Penitentials,* accordingly, are provided penances apportioned to all these breaches of the ceremonial law, whether accidental or

---

[1] Riht iſ ꝥ æniᵹ Criſten man bloð ne þycᵹe. (Sınodal. Decret. 53. Bibl. Bodl. MSS. *Junii.* 121. f. 29.) *Right is that any Cristen man take not blood.*

We cyþað cop ꝥ God ælmihtiᵹ cpæð hiſ aᵹenum muðe ꝥ nan man he mot abyrᵹean naneſ cyneſ bloðeſ· ne ꝼuᵹeleſ· ne nytenes· þe eop alyꝼeð iſ ꝥ ꝼlæſc to nyttienne, Ælc þæna þe abyrᵹð bloðeſ oꝼen Godeſ beboð ꝼceal ꝼoꝼpuꝼðan on ecenyſſe. (Ex Hom. ıntıtul. Heꝼ iſ halpenðlic Laꝼ. Bibl. Bodl. MSS. *Junii,* 99. f. 68.) *We tell you that God Almighty quoth by his own mouth, that no man may taste any kind of blood, neither fowl's, nor cattle's, whose flesh is allowed you to enjoy. Every one who tastes blood against God's command, shall perish for ever.*

It appears, from the 31st canon of Egbert's *Penitential* (WILK. i. 121), that women sometimes took the blood of their husbands as a medicine. This usage was, probably, founded on some old heathen superstition, and popular credulity was likely to gather strength from ecclesiastical prohibition.

In Egbert's 38th canon (*Ib.* 123) is given an express permission for the eating of horse-flesh, and of hares (the Saxon word for which, though almost identical with the modern English, is strangely rendered *halices* by Wilkins.) From such permissions, it seems hardly doubtful that some people scrupled about the eating of any thing that was Levitically unclean. The same canon, indeed, enjoins, that even water, into which a little pig had fallen, should be sprinkled with holy water and fumigated with incense before use. It allows, however, expressly the eating of unclean animals in cases of necessity.

[2] *Egb. Pen.* can. 39. 40. WILK. i. 123. 124. From the latter of these two canons, it appears that scruples were entertained about the eating of swine which had eaten carrion, or sucked up human blood. Egbert goes no further than to say, *We believe that they nevertheless are not to be cast away ;* but he adds, that they cannot be used *until they are clean.*

otherwise. It is this peculiarity which has made many regard certain canonical sanctions, occurring in Anglo-Saxon monuments, as irresistibly ludicrous. Readers have been unable to contain their laughter, on encountering grave denunciations against water that had come into contact with a dead mouse or weasel. Those who think, however, of Mosaic prohibitions and the council of Jerusalem, will recognise in such peculiarities interesting links connecting modern times with ancient. It was owing, probably, to Theodore of Tarsus[1] that these Asiatic restrictions were enjoined so rigidly by the Anglo-Saxon Church, and her deference for his authority remained unshaken to the last.

As this venerable community, like other ancient churches, was happily connected with apostolic times by an episcopal polity, sufficient care impressed laical apprehensions with a due perception of this essential feature in religious discipline. Opulence was, indeed, exhorted and allured abundantly to the foundation of churches, by the offer of patronage. But no trace appears of independent congregations, or of congregations federally connected. Every new church was considered as an additional member of that single religious body which, without episcopacy, must want its full integrity. Whenever a diocese, accordingly, lost that spiritual head, which is alike

---

[1] Theodore is cited in the 39th canon, as an authority for dispensing with some of these scruples. This may, perhaps, appear an additional reason for attributing chiefly to him the naturalisation of this Judaizing Christianity among the Anglo-Saxons. As usual, some of his admirers had gone further than he intended.

necessary for securing the apostolical succession of ministers, and for assimilating religious communities with primitive antiquity, all the more considerable inhabitants were convened. Both laity and clergy solemnly admitted a serious loss, for the speedy reparation of which they were equally concerned. Hence it was by their united suffrages that a successor was appointed to the vacant see.[1] His original nomination might seem to have rested with the crown, and the popular duty to have been that of approval or rejection. Having been chosen, the bishop elect was presented to the prelates of the province for examination. He was now interrogated as to the soundness of his belief, and required to give a solemn pledge for the due performance of his episcopal duties.[2] A profession of canonical obedience to his metropolitan was also exacted from him. Of obedience to the Roman see, or of a belief in transubstantiation, there appears no mention in our earliest pontificals.[3] Professions of such obedience and

---

[1] For the address of clergy and laity to the bishops of the province, see *Bampton Lectures*, 177.

[2] For some of the interrogatories, see *Bampton Lectures*, 94.

[3] Nasmith, in his printed Catalogue of Archbishop Parker's MSS. in the library of C. C. C. C., has the following remark on an ancient pontifical in that collection, No. 44 : " Promittit eps ordinandus se plebem ei commissum ex sacris Scripturis docturum, officium episcopale fideliter obsecuturum, ecclesiæ Dorobernensi se fore subjectum et obedientem, et articulis fidei assensum præbet. Nihil vero hic invenies de subjectione a sede Romanâ ab electis postea exactâ, nec de transubstantiatione."—P. 28.

For the interpolations respecting traditions and papal constitutions, see *Bampt. Lect.* 95 : for those respecting transubstantiation and remission of sins, see p. 420. It might have been remarked,

belief, are therefore, palpable innovations. Their occurrence in later pontificals only, deservedly stamps them as interpolations. Formularies, thus interpolated, contrasted with more ancient records, afford invaluable evidence against allegations of antiquity advanced by a Romish advocate.

The prelacy constituted a standing branch of the Saxon *witenagemot*, or parliament. Legislative assemblies merely lay were unknown to those who provided England with her envied constitution. It would be, indeed, a monstrous folly, as well as a gross injustice, to exclude from political deliberation that very class of considerable proprietors, in which alone information and morality are indispensable. On every meeting, accordingly, of the great national council, Anglo-Saxon archbishops, bishops, and abbots, were provided with appropriate places. Thus the civil polity of England was wisely established on a Christian basis. The clerical estate has formed an integral member of it from the first. An English prelate's right to occupy the legislative seat that has descended to him from the long line of his predecessors, is, therefore, founded on the most venerable of national prescriptions. It is no privilege derived from that Norman policy which converted episcopal endowments into baronies. It is far more ancient than the Conqueror's time; being

---

in the Sermon upon Attrition, that the insertion of an interrogation as to the remission of sins, in the later pontificals, is an incidental proof that the scholastic doctrine of sacramental absolution is of no high antiquity.

rooted amidst the very foundations of the monarchy.[1]

Under William, indeed, episcopal privileges were abridged. He found the bishop, and the earl, or alderman, sitting concurrently as judges in the county court; having for assessors the thanes or gentry within the shire. This tribunal entertained ordinary questions of litigation, and was open to appeals from the various hundred-courts. Its own decisions were liable to revision by the king alone. An Anglo-Saxon prelate was therefore continually before the public eye, invested with an important civil trust. After a reign of about seventeen years, the Conqueror abrogated this ancient usage, erecting separate places of judicature for ecclesiastical suits.[2] A principle of exclusion was thus established, which proud and selfish spirits would fain abuse, until they have reduced, at least one order of competitors for the more attractive advantages of society, to hopeless insignificance.

Soon after the conversion of Kent, an episcopal see was founded at Rochester, in subordination to that of Canterbury. To this, the archbishops are said to have nominated, until after the Conquest.[3]

---

[1] For information upon the clerical branch of the Anglo-Saxon legislature, see Archbishop Wake's *State of the Church*, p. 135, et. seq., and his *Authority of Christian Princes*, p. 161.

[2] HICKES, *Dissert. Epistolaris*. Thes. i. 4.

[3] GODWIN, *De Præsul.* 527. This archiepiscopal privilege, we are told, was relinquished in favour of the monks of Rochester, by Archbishop Theobald, in 1147. But Godwin's editor shews the statement to be inaccurate. The ancient usage appears to have been, that the monks of Rochester should choose their own bishop

When other kingdoms of the Heptarchy were converted, a single see was established in each. In Wessex this was the Oxfordshire Dorchester; in Essex, London; in East-Anglia, Dunwich; in Mercia, Lichfield; in Northumbria, Lindisfarne; and in Sussex, Selsey. Essex and Sussex remained permanently under one prelate. The diocese of Wessex was firstly dismembered by the foundation of a bishopric at Winchester;[1] subsequently still further, by such foundations at Sherborne,[2] Wilton,[3] Wells,[4] Crediton and Bodmin.[5] Mercia was gradually divided into the dioceses of Sidnacester, Leicester, Hereford,[6] Worcester,[7] and Lichfield. Of these, the two former coalesced, and were placed under a single bishop, who resided at Dorchester.[8]

---

in the chapter-house of Canterbury. Probably Theobald relieved them from this mark of subjection. It is obvious, that while the old practice continued, the archbishop would be likely to influence the election. The see of Rochester was founded in 604.

[1] The see of Dorchester was founded about 635; that of Winchester, about 663.—GODWIN, *De Præsul.* pp. 202. 203.

[2] The see of Sherborne was founded about 705; it was removed to Salisbury some years after 1046.—LE NEVE, *Fasti,* 255. 256.

[3] Founded in 905. Herman was chosen to it in 1046, and, subsequently obtaining Sherborne, he procured the union of the two sees. Before his death he fixed the see at Salisbury.—*Ib.* 256.

[4] Founded in 905.—*Ib.* 31.

[5] Both founded in 905; they coalesced about 1040, on the establishment of St. Peter's at Exeter, as a see for both Devonshire and Cornwall. The Cornish see had been removed from Bodmin to St. Germain's.—*Ib.* 79.

[6] Founded in 680.—*Ib.* 107.

[7] Founded in 680.—GODWIN, *De Præsul.* 447.

[8] Sidnacester was founded in 678; Leicester, in 737. This

Northumbria became two dioceses, of which a see for the southern, was fixed at York;[1] for the northern, eventually, at Durham.[2] East-Anglia owned subjection to two prelates, during a considerable interval — an additional see having been established at Elmham. In later Saxon times, however, this arrangement was overthrown; the bishop of Elmham having under him all East-Anglia. At the Conquest, accordingly, England's ecclesiastical superiors were two archbishops, and thirteen bishops. — Wilton and Sherborne having merged in Salisbury, the two sees of Devonshire and Cornwall in that of Exeter.

For such variations in diocesan arrangements as might meet existing circumstances, provision had been made in the council of Hertford. It was there enacted, that as the faithful became more numerous, so should episcopal sees.[3] No prelate was, however, to assume a discretionary power of providing for spiritual wants not placed regularly under his charge.

---

was soon transferred to Dorchester. That see was placed over also the diocese of Sidnacester, in the earlier part of the tenth century. —GODWIN, *De Præsul.* 281.

[1] Paulinus was nominally the first archbishop of York under the Anglo-Saxons; but he could not maintain his ground in Northumbria. After his flight, York remained without a prelate until the appointment of Chad in 664. From Chad, accordingly, the series of archbishops of York properly takes its beginning.

[2] The see of Lindisfarne, or Holy Island, was founded in 635; this place having been burned, the bishop removed, in 882, to Chester-le-Street. In 995 the episcopal see was transferred to Durham. (LE NEVE, *Fasti*, 345. 346.) During a long period a see was established at Hexham, which had under its inspection a large portion of the modern diocese of Durham.

[3] *Conc. Herudf.* can. 9. SPELM. I. 153. WILK. I. 43.

Every one was forbidden to interfere without his own diocese.[1] Precedence among bishops was regulated by the dates of their several consecrations.[2] Episcopal visitations were to be annually holden in suitable places throughout every diocese.[3] But this provision appears to have been made rather on account of the laity than of the clergy. The visiting bishop was to dispense among his people that sound religious instruction which must have been insufficiently supplied in a country but ill provided with rural churches. Especially was he to warn them against pagan rites, usages, and impostures. On the death of a bishop the tenth part of all his movable property was to be distributed in alms among the poor, and every Englishman, reduced to slavery in his days, was to be manumitted.[4] Of these charities, the reason assigned was, that he might obtain the fruit of retribution and indulgence of sins.[5] An additional provision for the welfare of his soul was imposed upon the laity, who were to be summoned to their several churches, and to sing there thirty psalms. Four times that number were expected from prelates and abbots generally. They were also to celebrate one

---

[1] *Conc. Herudf.* can. 2.   [2] *Ib.* can. 8.

[3] *Conc. Clovesh.* can. 3. SPELM. 1. 246. WILK. 1. 95. *Conc. Calc.* can. 3. SPELM. 1. 293. WILK. 1. 146.

[4] Johnson understands here every English slave belonging to himself. This limitation is most probable, but it does not appear in the text.

[5] " Ut per illud sui proprii laboris fructum retributionis mereatur, et indulgentiam peccatorum."—*Syn. ap Celych.* can. 10. SPELM. 1. 330. WILK 1 171.

hundred and twenty masses, and to manumit three slaves.[1]

Candidates for the sacred profession were required to spend a month, before ordination, with the bishop, who was allowed this time for examining and instructing them. As to their literary proficiency, expectations were, of course, extremely moderate. But pains were to be taken for ascertaining the soundness of their belief, and their opinions on the divine attributes. They were also to display their acquaintance with the forms of public worship, and with such mystical significations as approved authorities had imposed upon its various features. Nor were inquiries to be forgotten upon their knowledge of the canons, and upon their competency to calculate the times for celebrating festivals and fasts.[2]

---

[1] *Syn. ap Celych.* can. 10. SPELM. 1. 330. WILK. 1. 171.

[2] Se þe hafeþ pilnize cume anum monðe æp þam hað timan to þam b. ⁊ beo ryððan on fandunze þæp pe bifceop tæce· ⁊ zepapnize þ he hæbbe to þam fæde þa bizpifte on foðan ⁊ on foððpe þe he habban pcule· þ he mið þam þinzum nan þinz ne hefize· þæne he hif fandian pcule. Dif he þonne mið þær lapeopef tacne to b cume· þonne beo he hafe þenyp zif he foyð on eallum þam fylizean pille þe b him pifize. Donne if æpeft hif þæpe fandunze fpuma on hpilcan zeleafan he fy· ⁊ hu he pihtne zeleafan oðpum mannum zefputelian cunne· ⁊ hpæt he fputelice undefftande þæf þe þufh God zepeapð· oð þon zyt zepeonðan fceall. þonne hu he hif þenunze cunne· ⁊ hu he fulluht undefftande. ⁊ hu he mæffan zetacnvnze undefzyte· ⁊ eac oðfa cypic-þenunza· ⁊ hpæþep he canon cunne· be ænizum dæle· þonne hu he on zepim-cfæfte zeaf pyne to fceaðan cunne· Dif he þiffa þinza ealpa zepif bið· þonne bið he hafef þe bet pypðe. (Bibl. Bodl. MSS. *Junu.* 121. Be Gehafeðum Mannum. *Of ordained men,* f. 34.) *Let him who desires ordination come one month before the ordination time to the b., and be then upon examination under the bishop's teaching: and let him take care that he have for the time the provision in food and fodder which he should have, that he be not troubled about any of these things, while he shall be examined. If he come to the b. with*

The former kind of skill was requisite, both for comprehending the nature of clerical obligations, and for apportioning penances; the latter, for enabling clergymen to act as a sort of animated almanacks. At ordination, the porrection of sacred vessels was used, as it is now in the church of Rome. Simultaneously with this ceremony, when a priest was ordained, the bishop also said, " Take authority to offer sacrifice, and to celebrate mass, as well for the living as for the dead."[1] In the imposition of hands,

---

the instruction of a teacher, then he is the nearer ordination, provided he is henceforth willing to follow what the b̄. directs him. Then is first the beginning of his examination in what belief he may be, and what ability he has to explain a right belief to other men, and what he clearly understands of that which has been done by God, or yet shall be done: then how is his knowledge of divine service, and how he understands baptism, and how he comprehends the signification of the mass, and also of other church ministrations, and whether he knows the canons in any degree: then whether he knows enough of arithmetic to divide the year. If he be acquainted with all these things, then is he worthy of the ordination that he desires. An incidental presumption against the doctrine of transubstantiation appears fairly to arise from this extract. If a doctrine, so mysterious and incredible, had then been received by the English Church, it must appear strange that candidates for ordination should not have undergone a particular examination upon it. Instead of this, however, they were merely to be examined as to their acquaintance with the significations of the mass, and other divine offices. It was the usage to seek mystical, figurative meanings in all Scripture and religious formularies. To this egregious trifling, the examination, most probably, was to be directed. In the thirteenth century, however, when transubstantiation, both name and thing, had obtained a pretty secure establishment, very particular directions were given from authority for inculcating a belief in it.

[1] " Accipe potestatem offerre sacrificium Dō, missamque celebrare, tam pro vivis, quam et pro defunctis, in nomine Dn̄i."

T

however, the ancient church of England, like the modern, enjoined all priests present to unite with the bishop.[1]

After ordination, a priest was to consider himself as wedded to his church, and hence formally precluded from any prospect of changing it for another.[2] He was also to keep clear of interference within the districts of brother clergymen.[3] Nor was he to venture upon officiating in a strange diocese, until he had produced commendatory letters from his own bishop.[4] Among duties expected of him appears to have been the education of youth.[5] In the exercise

---

Fragment. libri Pontifical. pulcherrime et magnâ ex parte ante Conqu. Angl. scripti. (HICKES, ii. 220.) *Brit. Mus. MSS.* COTTON, *Tiberius*, C. 1. f. 158.

[1] " Presbiter cum ordinatur, epō eum benedicente, et manum super caput ejus imponente, etiam oms presbiteri qui præsentes sunt, manus suas juxta manum epi super caput illius ponant."— *Brit. Mus. MSS.* COTTON, *Claudius*, A. 3. f. 45.

[2] Cyrice iſ mid rihte racerdeſ æpe. (Be cyrican. *Of the Church.* Bibl. Bodl. MSS. *Junii.* 121. f. 58.) *The Church is with right a priest's wife.* Riht iſ þ ænig preoſt ſylf piller ne forlæte þa cyrican þe he to gebletſod pær· ac hæbbe þa him to riht æpe. (Sinodal. Decret. 8. Ibid. f. 26) *Right is that no priest of his own accord leave the church to which he was ordained, but keep to it as a right wife.*

[3] Riht iſ þ nan preoſt oðrum ne æt do ænig þæra þinga þe him to gebyrige· ne on hiſ mynrtre· ne on hiſ rcriſt-rcire· ne on hiſ gyldrcire· ne on ænigum þæra þinga þe him to gebyrige. (Ibid. 9.) *Right is that no priest do any of those things that belong to another, either in his minster, or in his shrift-shire* (district assigned to him for receiving confessions, *i e.* parish), *or in his guildship* (sodality, of which he might be a member), *or in any of the things that belong to him.*

[4] *Conc. Herudf.* can. 5. SPELM. i. 153. WILK. i. 43.

[5] *Capitul. incertæ editionis* 20. SPELM. i. 595. WILK. i. 270.

of his ordinary ministry, he was restrained from celebrating mass in private houses, unless in cases of sickness.[1] All the great luminaries of his profession most rigorously bound him to celibacy. Sacerdotal marriages were, indeed, commonly branded as execrable breaches of continence, and imaginary revelations threatened them with frightful retribution hereafter.[2] This rigour is, however, adverse to the

---

The body of canons among which this is found was compiled by Theodulf, bishop of Orleans. Johnson (*sub an.* 994) thinks them to have been translated into Saxon by Elfric, for the guidance of English clergymen.

[1] Riht is þ ænig preort on ænigum hure ne mæffige· butan on gehalgobe cyrican· butan hyt ry ron hpilcer manner oren-reocnerre· (Sinodal. Decret. Bibl. Bodl. MSS. *Junii*, 121. f. 29.) *Right is that no priest mass in any house but in a hallowed church, unless it be for some man's over-sickness.*

[2] Leoran men in libro virionum ir appiten hu þa mærre-preortar ¬ þa diaconar þe mirleoroban hen on populbe pen on pitnunge pel hneophce gerepene· rpa rpa re enczel gerputelobe on þæne geribþe. Hi rtobon gebunbenne þ hi abugan ne mihton to heanbum raglum æt heona hnicze on þa hellican ryne oð heona gynblar· ¬ þa eanman pirmen þe hi hy pið ronlagon· rtobon ætronan heom færte getigebe on þam hellican ryne· up or þone narban ealle bynnenbe æfne ætgæbene· ¬ re beorol hi berpang rpiðe gelome· on heona gecynblimum· rpa rpa re boc ur recgð· ¬ rpa rpa re enczel ræbe on þæne geryhðe. Dæn pænon gemengbe mærre-preortar ¬ biaconar on þæne crylmincge· ronðam þe hi Criste nolban clænlice þenian on hir clænum þeopbome. (Be Gehabedum Mannum. *Of Ordained Men.* Bibl. Bodl. MSS. *Junii*, 121. f. 34.) *Beloved men, in libro visionum it is written how the mass-priests and the deacons who mislived here in the world, were in purgatory full cruelly beholden, even as the angel explained at the sight. They stood bounden, so that they could not stoop, to hard stakes at their backs in the hellish fire up to their girdles, and the wretched women who had been improperly connected with them stood before them, fast tied in the hellish fire ever burning upwards, and the devil lashed them very often on their middles, even as the book saith to us, and even as the angel said at the sight. There were mingled mass-priests and deacons in the torture, because they would not cleanly serve Crist in his clean service.*

general stream of human feeling, and it proved, accordingly, inoperative upon a large proportion of the less distinguished ecclesiastics. They seem to have urged in their own vindication, that Moses, and others among the most eminent of God's servants, were married men.[1] The apocryphal views of a future state, which aimed at striking terror into themselves and their wives, acted upon them, probably, as little else than provocatives to laughter. In most particulars their credulity was naturally that of their age, but personal considerations sharpen human wits; and, most probably, many a married Anglo-Saxon priest could see the ludicrous absurdity of tales invented for interfering with his own domestic comfort.

The Anglo-Saxon church, like that of Rome, used a gradation of inferior ministers. Elfric pronounces ecclesiastical orders to be the following seven:— ostiary, reader, exorcist, acolyte, sub-deacon, deacon, and priest. The ostiary was to keep the church-doors, and to ring the bell. The reader was to read in church, and to preach God's word. Perhaps the accustomed homily was often heard from his lips. The exorcist was to adjure malignant spirits. The acolyte was to hold the candle, or taper, when the Gospel was read, or the eucharist hallowed. The sub-deacon was to carry the vessels to the deacon, and to wait upon him at the altar. The deacon was to wait upon the officiating priest, to place the offerings upon the altar, and to read the Gospel. He might baptise, and administer the eucharist. Priests, how-

---

[1] See *Bampton Lectures*, 118.

ever, appear occasionally to have dispensed with his attendance at the altar, probably, from motives of economy. Such are stigmatised by Elfric as rather nominal members of the sacerdotal order, than really worthy of its privileges. Between the priesthood and the episcopate, Elfric allows no other difference than that of office; bishops being especially charged with certain duties, which might interfere with the regular engagements of ordinary priests. These duties are stated to be ordination, confirmation, the consecration of churches, and the care of God's rights.[1] Some authorities were not contented with resting episcopal superiority upon such narrow grounds. Another Anglo-Saxon enumeration of the seven ecclesiastical orders omits that of acolytes, and makes that of bishops the highest in the series.[2] Thus, evidently, there were those who looked upon the episcopate not only as a distinguished office, but also as a separate order. Both bishops and priests were under an awful expectation of leading their several flocks to the heavenly judgment-seat.[3]

---

[1] *Ælf. ad Wulfsin.* SPELM. I. 575. WILK. I. 251.

[2] DE OFFICIIS SEPTE GRADVVM. (" *Ex S. Gregorio Papâ.*" WANLEY. HICKES, *Thes.* II. 220.) *Brit. Mus. MSS.* COTTON, *Tiberius,* C. 1. f. 85.

[3] After citing, with some laxity, Ezekiel's denunciation against the mercenary and unfaithful pastors of Israel (ch. xxxiv. 2, *et sequ.*), a Saxon homily proceeds: Eall þis is gecpcƀen be bircopum· ⁊ be mærre-pneoptum· þe Hober folc on ƀomer-ƀæʒ· to þam ƀome læƀan rculon· ælc þone ƀæl þe him hep on life betæht pær. (BE SACERDUM. Bibl. Bodl. MSS. *Junii,* 22. f. 200.) *All this is said of bishops and mass-priests, who, God's folk on Doom's day, to the judgment shall lead; every one that portion which was committed to him here in life.*

In Anglo-Saxon times, monks ordinarily were not members of the priesthood. Every monastery numbered among its inmates one or more of the sacerdotal order, to minister in sacred things; but the community was chiefly composed of ascetic laymen. The whole monastic body was divided into four several branches. The most respectable of these consisted of monks permanently domesticated in some conventual foundation, under the discipline of an abbot. Another was made up of anchorites, or hermits. These recluses were expected to have resided some time in a regular abbey, and not to have withdrawn from it until they had exhibited a strict conformity to the system there. After such probation it was deemed allowable to retire into a solitary cell, for the purpose of continuing, with augmented rigour, the austerities exacted by monastic obligations.[1] A third class of monks, passing under the oriental name of *Sarabaites*,[2] comprised such aspirants after unusual

---

[1] " Anachoritarum vitam non improbo eorum, videlicet, qui in coenobiis regularibus instructi disciplinis ordinabiliter ad eremum secedunt, quibus est solitudo paradisus, et civitas carcer: ut activam vitam de labore manuum viventes exerceant, aut dulcedine contemplativæ vitæ mentem reficiant, fontem vitæ ore cordis sitiant, et eorum quæ retro sunt obliti ad ea ultrà non respiciant."
—Ivo, Carnoten. *Epist.* 192. Paris, 1610, p. 342.

[2] Du Cange says that there are various opinions upon the etymology of this word. He makes it, however, to have come from Egypt. Other authors have referred the origin of *Sarabaite* to the Hebrew סרב, *refractory*. The correctness of this etymology appears to admit of no reasonable question. In the Cottonian MS., from which an extract is given below, Saxon equivalents are placed over several of the words. Over this stands ꞅylꝼ-ꝺemeɲꞃ laɲeopaꞃ, *self-judging teachers*. Ivo of Chartres, in the epistle

strictness as had adopted the tonsure, but would not embrace any received rule, or remain within a monastery. These devotees resided, as heretofore, in private houses, sometimes three or four together, probably under such regulations of their own as suited their particular ideas or convenience. Ascetic fervour under such laxity would be very liable to evaporate; and hence abodes adapted for it, but upon this independent principle, could hardly fail to shock admirers of over-strained religious rigour. The Sarabaites, accordingly, are described as a grievous reproach upon their profession. But monachism found its principal source of obloquy and mortification in the *Gyrovagi*, or *wandering monks*. These were noisy claimants of extraordinary holiness, but, in reality, idle vagabonds, who preferred hypocritical mendicity to labour.[1] Of such traders in religion

---

cited above (p. 340), asks of monks, which is better, to live regularly in monasteries, " an fieri Sarabaitas, ut in privatis locis proprio jure vivant, et victum sibi de substantiâ pauperum per manum raptorum, et de fœnore negociatorum accipiant?"

[1] These monks appear from Ivo, in the epistle before cited, to have worn ordinarily the *melote*. (" Pellis ovina, ex Græco μηλωτὴ, a μῆλον, *ovis*. *Melotes* pellis sordida, vel simplex, ex uno latere pendens, quâ monachi utuntur." Du Cange, *in voc.*) Elfric thus explains this term in his Glossary. *Melotes*, vel *Pera:* ʒæten, vel bɲoccen ɲooc: *a jacket* (rochet) *of goatskin*, or *broken*. Of the sanctimonious vagabonds who went about half-clad in these shaggy garments, Ivo proceeds to say (p. 342), " Verum cum quidam ex hâc professione in *melotis* suis vicos, castella, civitates girando perlustrent, humilitate vestium, vilitate ciborum, merita sua populis ostentant. Ambiunt fieri magistri qui nunquam fuerunt discipuli, deprimentes vitam omnium hominum, quia non sunt quod ipsi sunt. Hos nec eiemitas computandos intelligo, nec coenobitas, sed *girovagos*, aut Sarabaitas."

generally, the true character is highly sensual. These ostentatious pretenders to a self-denying piety seem, accordingly, to have been notorious for gross indulgence.[1]

Had England adhered rigidly to the discipline provided by Theodore, the credit of monachism would not have been impaired by such impositions. Among the canons enacted at Hertford under that able metropolitan, one provides that monks shall remain stationary in the several monasteries to which they originally belonged, unless they could obtain the abbot's leave of absence, or removal.[2] The nature of a monastery, strictly governed, was no doubt very

---

[1] " Monachorum quatuor genera esse manifestum est. Primum, *Coenobitarum*, hoc est, monasteriale militans sub regulâ vel abbate. Deinde, secundum genus est *Anachoritarum*, id est, heremitarum, qui non conversionis fervore novitio, sed monasterii probatione diuturnâ, didicerunt contra diabolum multorum solacio jam docti pugnare, et bene instructi fraternâ ex acie ad singularem pugnam heremi securi jam sine consolatione alterius, solâ manu vel brachio, contra vitia carnis vel cogitationum, Deo auxiliante, pugnare sufficiunt. Tertium vero monachorum teterrimum genus est *Sarabaitarum*, qui nullâ regulâ approbati experientiâ magistri, sicut aurum fornacis, sed in plumbi naturâ molliti, adhuc opibus servantes seculo, fidem mentiri Deo per tonsuram noscuntur Qui bini, aut terni, aut certè singuli, sine pastore, non dominicis, sed suis inclusi ovilibus, pro lege est desideriorum voluptas : cum quicquid putaverint, vel elegerint, hoc dicunt s̄cm, et quod noluerint, hoc putant non licere. Quartum vero genus est monachorum, quod nominatur *Gyrovagum*; qui tota vita sua per diversas provincias ternis aut quaternis diebus, per diversorum cellas hospitantur, semper vagi, et nunquam stabiles, et propriis voluptatibus, et gulæ illecebris servientes, et per omnia deteriores Sarabaitis. De quorum omnium miserimâ conversatione melius est silere quam loqui."—Regula S. Bened. *Brit. Mus. MSS.* COTTON, *Tiberius*, A. 3. f. 118.

[2] *Conc. Herudf.* can. 4. SPELM. I. 153. WILK. i. 43.

much that of a penitentiary prison. Even serious minds would be, therefore, very liable to become weary of such an abode, after the sharp edges of remorse had worn away, or the flame of fanaticism had abated. But the monk dignified his adoption of the cloister as later enthusiasts have their identification with certain religious parties. He termed it his *conversion,* and claimed a degree of sanctity which challenged admiration from the mass of men. Hence he could hardly complain of regulations indispensable for preserving the respectability of a body so numerous as his. Especially, was it reasonable to impose all this rigour upon monastics, because abuses of their character were crying public evils, and because they were largely indebted to the national liberality. Not only did many noble foundations provide for their sustenance and security, but also, in common with the clerical body, they enjoyed important immunities. Ecclesiastical property was, indeed, ordinarily liable to assessment for the repairs of bridges and highways; for the maintenance of fortifications; and for providing forces against hostile incursions.[1] This threefold liability was termed in Latin, *Trinoda necessitas,* and it was a burden imposed upon landed possessions generally. There were, however, instances

---

[1] The three members of the *Trinoda Necessitas* were called, in Saxon, Bɲicʒ-boꞇe, *Bridge-repair;* Buɲh-boꞇe, *Town,* or *Castle-repair,* and Fyɲꝺ, the *Army.* " Sometimes, instead of leaving the military contingent in uncertainty, the number of vassals and shields which the abbot was to send forth to the wars is specifically defined. In such a case, the land was held by military tenure."— PALGRAVE's *English Commonwealth,* I. 157.

in which the Church was allowed the remarkable privilege of exemption from this triple charge.[1] Nor were any of her estates denied a more than ordinary degree of protection.[2]

The whole frame-work of Anglo-Saxon society was, indeed, religious. Voluntary associations, or *Sodalities,* answering to modern clubs, were common in the nation. The principal objects of these were mutual protection, assistance under unusual pecuniary calls,[3] and conviviality. One mass, however, for deceased associates, another for those yet surviving, appears to have impressed a character of piety upon their meetings.[4] One of their objects also was to provide *soul-shot* on the death of every member; so that his disembodied spirit might enjoy the full benefit of such services as were proffered by the Church. Eventually, religious houses entered into these combinations.[5] In this case, the *Guild-ship,* as every

---

[1] PALGRAVE's *English Commonwealth,* i 159.

[2] *Conc. Becanc.* can 1. SPELM. i. 189. WILK. 1. 57. *Conc. Bergh.* can. 1. SPELM. 1. 194. WILK. 1. 60. The second canon, enacted at Berghampstead, imposes a fine of fifty shillings for violating the protection of the church. This was generally done by drawing offenders from sanctuary. But a law, guarding inviolability under a penalty so heavy, could hardly fail of throwing an unusual degree of security around all the church's rights and possessions.

[3] As undertaking a journey, having a house burnt down, or being amerced in a fine.—HICKES, *Thes.* 1. 21. 22.

[4] This appears among the articles of a *Sodality* formed at Exeter.—*Ib.* 22.

[5] Hickes has printed the articles of a *Sodality* formed of seven monasteries (*Thes.* 1. 19), and he mentions a confederacy of this kind yet more numerous. (*Ib.* 20.) Both cases are, however,

such confederacy was vernacularly called, proposed an interchange of masses for the benefit of each other. But it is not likely that mutual protection for possessions and privileges was overlooked. Convivial or personal views were necessarily precluded.

In general terms, the king was bound, at his coronation, to respect ecclesiastical rights. He solemnly pledged himself to preserve the Church in real peace. But this pledge could not be redeemed, unless properties and privileges, legally bestowed upon her, were guarded from spoliation or encroachment. The Anglo-Saxon throne thus rested upon the basis of Christianity, and the king's duties were considered to be religious, no less than civil. Indeed, the former took precedence of the latter. Of the three royal engagements, that which provided for religion stood first.[1] England has, therefore, inherited a constitution from the most venerable antiquity, which recognises attention to the spiritual wants of men as the first and most important of a sovereign's duties.

---

posterior to the Conquest. Mr. Turner has an interesting chapter upon the *Guild-ship.—Hist. Angl. Sax.* iii. 98.

[1] " In the name of Christ I promise three things to the Christian people, my subjects. First, that the church of God and all the Christian people shall always preserve true peace through our arbitration. Second, that I will forbid rapacity, and all iniquities to every condition. Third, that I will command equity and mercy in all judgments, that to me, and to you, the gracious and merciful God may extend his mercy." (SILVER's *Coronation Service of the Anglo-Saxon Kings.* Oxf. 1831. p. 20.) The original of this oath is found in the British Museum among the Cottonian MSS. (*Claudius,* A. 3, f. 7.) The service, which is in Latin, and has been printed by Dr. Silver, together with his translation of it, is entitled in a hand of no great antiquity, *Coronatio Athelredi Regis Anglo-*

The coronation compact reminded an Anglo-Saxon monarch that his principal title to allegiance rested on his acting as the Christian head of a Christian people.

This character was impressed upon the nation by many statutes, and by severe penalties. The laws of Ina provided that parents should bring their children for baptism, within thirty days after birth, under forfeiture of as many shillings. If the infant died unbaptised, all the parent's property was forfeited.[1] Subsequently, the great festivals of Easter and Whitsuntide were the ordinary times for administering baptism;[2] but it was, on no account, to be delayed,

---

Saxonum. Dr. Silver, accordingly, entitles it *The Ceremony of the Consecration of King Ethelred II. A.D.* 978. "The word *consecrated* king occurs first in the *Saxon Chronicle* in the reign of Offa, king of Mercia, the contemporary of Charlemagne, about a thousand years since, and it is very probable that the ceremony of Ethelred was then used."—SILVER, 148.

[1] LL. INÆ, can. 2. SPELM. i. 183   WILK. i 58.

[2] These festivals had long been signalised by the administration of baptism in the Roman church, and Charlemain rendered this usage general through the west. The fourth canon of the council of Mentz, holden under that famous emperor in 813, designates Easter and Whitsuntide as the legitimate times for baptising, and limits to them the administration of that sacrament, unless in cases of necessity. (LABB. et COSS. vii. 1242.) In England this regulation had been solemnly enacted at Calcuith, in 787. (*Conc. Calc.* can. 2. SPELM. i. 293. WILK. i. 146.) Probably, however, it failed of meeting with universal acquiescence in this island; for the tenth, among the *Laws of the Northumbrian Priests*, enjoins baptism within nine days after birth, and imposes penalties for default. (SPELM. i. 496. WILK. i. 218.) Towards the close of the twelfth century this appropriation of Easter and Whitsuntide fell silently into desuetude, neither pope nor council authorising the change, or seemingly observing it.—DALLÆUS, *De Cultibus Religionis Latinorum*, Genev. 1671, p. 21.

whenever there was an appearance of danger to the child. It was administered by total immersion; and priests were expressly forbidden merely to pour water upon the head.[1] The child undertook, by his sponsors, to renounce the devil, with his works and pomps. Of this engagement, these individuals were carefully to apprise him, as his faculties opened; and they were to teach him, besides, the Creed and the Lord's Prayer.[2] From the font it was also their duty to receive him, when baptism was completed.[3]

Anglo-Saxon ideas of female rights were just and liberal. Women were permitted to possess and dispose of property: nor was a person of any wealth enabled to marry, at all events among his equals, until he had made a legal settlement upon his intended wife.[4] It was, however, the usage of ancient England, as it also was of cognate nations,[5] to withhold the formal conveyance of this provision until the morning after marriage. Hence the dowry of an Anglo-Saxon lady was called her *morning's gift*.[6] Her friends had agreed upon a certain provision for her,

---

[1] *Syn. Celych.* can. 11. SPELM. i. 331. WILK. i. 171.

[2] *Conc. Calcuth* can. 2. SPELM. i. 293. WILK. i. 146.

[3] JOHNSON, *sub. an.* 785. Hence sponsors were called *susceptores*. Du Cange, *in voc.* suscipere.

[4] For many interesting particulars respecting Anglo-Saxon marriages see TURNER's *Hist. of the Angl. Sax.* iii. 68.

[5] HICKES, *Thes.* Præf. xlii. " Every Saxon woman had her *mundbora*, or guardian, without whose consent she could not be married; and the remains of this custom may be traced in the *marriage-service*, when the clergyman asks, *Who giveth this woman to be married to this man ?*"—SILVER's *Coronation Service of the Anglo-Saxon Kings,* 49.

[6] Morgen-gife, or gifu.

in the event of a proposed marriage; and until the contract was completed on her part, the husband was not expected to complete it on his. But although the preliminaries of marriage were necessarily civil, due care was taken for impressing it, upon the whole, with a very different character. The mass-priest was to pronounce a solemn blessing at nuptial ceremonies, unless one or both of the parties had been married before.[1] England has, therefore, ever treated marriage as " a holy estate,"—a contract essentially different from any other mutually made among Christians. Of this wise and Scriptural view the natural consequence was, that death alone was ordinarily considered a sufficient release from the nuptial tie.[2] Marriage was forbidden within four degrees of consanguinity: men were also prohibited from marrying their godmothers, or nuns, or divorced women, and from taking a second wife while the former one survived.[3] Second marriages, indeed, under any circumcumstances, were met by an ascetic principle of discouragement. A layman, who had lost his wife, was allowed to take another; nor was a widow denied a similar privilege. But such liberty was treated as a concession to the infirmity of the flesh, which could expect nothing beyond connivance. The Church did not venture to approve: the priest was, accordingly,

---

[1] *LL. Edm. R. Angl.* can. 8. SPELM. i. 426. WILK. i. 217.

[2] The council of Hertford allowed a man to dismiss his wife *fornicationis causâ.* But then it bound him, as he valued the name of Christian, to live single afterwards, unless he became reconciled to the offending woman.— *Conc. Herudf.* can. 10. SPELM. i. 153. WILK. i. 43.

[3] *Conc. Ænh.* can. 6. WILK i. 287.

to withhold his blessing. He was even prohibited from attending the nuptial feast; and the parties were to learn that they had committed an offence, for which a formal penance must atone.[1]

As a belief in some sort of posthumous purgation reserved for human souls was general among the Anglo-Saxons, few persons of much opulence departed from life without having made a provision for their *soul-shot*.[2] By this payment, clerical services were secured for the deceased's funeral, and prayers for the repose of his departed spirit. It was, most probably, with a view to render him the latter service, that mourning friends passed the night around his corpse. The *wakes* of ancient England led, however, to the same abuses as those of modern Ireland. The assembly was often rather one of gross revellers, than of pious mourners.[3] If the party had noto-

---

[1] *Ælf. ad Wulfsin.* SPELM. i. 574. WILK. i. 251. *Excerpt. Egb. Archiep. Ebor.* 89. SPELM. i. 267. ap. WILK. can. 91. i. 101. The Church of England here, as elsewhere, followed foreign churches. Mabillon says, in a note to his *Museum Italicum (Lut. Par.* 1687. tom. 1. p. 389): " Antiquissima est in ecclesiâ benedictio super nubentes, *super secundo nubentes rarior.*" Both Egbert and Elfric, indeed, adopt the seventh canon of the council of Neo-Cæsarea, holden in 314. (LABB. et Coss. 1. 1487.) But that canon has been understood as levelled against a plurality of wives, which construction it will bear. Elfric has expressly applied it to a second marriage, contracted by a widower or widow.

[1] *Dissertatio Epistolaris*, p. 53. HICKES, *Thes.* tom. 1. " Nothing can more strongly express the importance and necessity of this custom, than that several of their gilds seem to have been formed chiefly with a view to provide a fund for this purpose."— TURNER'S *Hist. of the Angl. Sax.* III. 146.

[3] Sume menn eac ꝺꝛincað æt ðeað manna lice oꝼeꞃ ealle þa niht ꞃpiðe unꞃihtlice· ⁊ ᵹꞃemiað God mið heoꞃa ᵹeᵹaꝼ ꞃꝓæce· þonne nan

riously spent a religious life, his body might be interred within the church.¹ Thus an usage, which has long been merely one among the distinctions of opulence, originated in veneration for acknowledged piety. The relics of martyrs, indeed, honourably enshrined in places of primitive worship, appear to have supplied the precedent on which have arisen the sepulchral glories of later churches.²

The Anglo-Saxon churches were separated regularly from profane uses, by the imposing solemnity of episcopal consecration. This ancient³ and becoming ceremony was performed with great magnificence, when the building to be dedicated was of superior importance.⁴

ʒebeoꞃꞃcipe ne ʒehynað æt lice· ac haliʒe ʒehebu þæn ʒebynað ꞃpiðon. (*Hom. in St. Swithun.* Brit. Mus. MSS. Cotton. *Julius,* E. 7. f. 99.) *Some men also drink at a dead man's wake, over all the night very unrightly, and provoke God with their idle talk · when no drinking-party is suitable for a wake, but holy prayers are rather suitable to it.*

¹ Riht iꞅ þ man innan cyꞃican ænine man ne byꞃiʒe· butan man pite þ he on liꞃe Lobe to þam pel ʒeoꞃembe þ man þuꞃh þ læte þ he ꞃy þæꞃ læʒeneꞃ pynðe. *Sinodal. Decret.* 29. Bibl. Bodl. MSS. *Junii,* 121. f 27.) *Right is that no man be buried within a church, unless it be known that in life he was well pleasing to God, that through that he be deemed worthy of his resting-place.*

² "Churches were commonly built over the sepulchres of the martyrs, or in the places where they suffered, or else the relics of the martyrs were translated into them."—Bingham's *Antiquities of the Christian Church,* i. 327.

³ It is known that churches were regularly consecrated in the fourth century, and it is probable that this usage is of much higher antiquity. (*Ib.* 324.) All schisms and irregularities were provided against by making episcopal consent necessary even to the building of a church. This was done by the council of Chalcedon, and by the emperor Justinian.—*Ib.* 325.

⁴ In the life of Ethelwold, attributed to Wolstan, are some curious Latin verses, describing the consecration of Winchester Cathedral in 980.—*Acta SS. Ord. Benedict.* v. 621.

Nor even in ordinary cases was its memory allowed to fall into oblivion, but annual solemnities taught a surrounding population to hail the happy day which had opened a house of God within an easy distance. Of this ancient religious holiday traces linger yet in our country villages. The petty feast or fair, now merely a yearly provocative to rustic revelry, commonly originated in the day when episcopal benediction hallowed that venerable pile which has trained so many generations for immortality. Anglo-Saxon churches, even of some note, were often built of wood:[1] hence *timbering* was the word in ordinary use for building.[2] When more durable materials were employed, the architects followed existing Roman models with as much fidelity as their own skill and that of their workmen would allow. This is proved sufficiently by specimens yet remaining. Their edifices naturally present some peculiarities, for which not even a hint is found in buildings of classical antiquity. But in general character, Anglo-Saxon and early Anglo-Norman buildings are little else than rude imitations of Roman architecture. A Norman clerestory window, centrally placed in the western

---

[1] Finan placed his episcopal seat at Lindisfarne in such a church. (BED. III. 25, p. 233.) The venerable historian, however, speaks of this as done *more Scotorum*. Hence it seems reasonable to infer that the more considerable Anglo-Saxon churches were ordinarily of stone. An ancient church of timber yet exists at Greensted, near Ongar, in Essex.

[2] Even where an erection was not of timber that word was in use. Thus the *Saxon Chronicle* (p. 202.) says that Canute had built *(timbered* in the original) at Assingdon, " a minster of stone and lime for the souls of the men who were there slain."

side of the north transept of St. Frideswide's church, at Oxford, even exhibits an Ionic volute. The opposite pilaster seems to have been intended for Corinthian.

Both vocal and instrumental music being used in public worship, the Anglo-Saxons were glad of organs for their larger churches. They were no strangers to that noblest of instruments early in the eighth century; and in the tenth, one of enormous size was erected at Winchester.[1] Seventy men, forming two companies which worked alternately, supplied it with wind. In the cathedral, probably, were many unglazed apertures; otherwise, machinery so colossal must have emitted sound almost beyond endurance.

Among the uses to which Anglo-Saxon churches were applied, was one inherited from Pagan times. The heathen warrior under accusation solemnly protested his innocence, offering to prove it by some hazardous appeal to his paternal gods. He would thus enter upon a field highly favourable for the display of stern, impudent daring, abject superstition, and serpentine cunning—the most striking distinctions of savage life. Hence this picturesque experiment was emphatically called *ordal*, or *ordeal*,

---

[1] A description of the organ discovered by Mr. Turner, in Aldhelm *De Laude Virginum*, proves that instrument to have been known in England before the poet's death in 709. Dr. Lingard subsequently cited a passage from the *Acta SS. Ord. Ben.* in which Wolstan's muse celebrates the prodigious organ provided for the cathedral of Winchester by Elphege.— *Hist. of the Angl. Sax.* III. 457, 458. *Antiqu. de l'Egl. Angl. Sax.* 575.

a northern word, signifying *the judgment* ;[1] as if it were a mode of trying guilt or innocence, satisfactory above all others. On the Anglo-Saxon conversion, this absurd, collusive, presumptuous, and superstitious test of integrity, was continued under Christian forms. An accused party, desirous of thus vindicating his character, was to give personal notice of such intention to the priest, three days before the time appointed. On these three days he was to live only on bread, salt, water, and herbs. He was regularly to attend mass, and make his offering on each day. On the day of his trial he was to receive the eucharist, and to declare his innocence upon oath. Fire was then to be carried into the church if the intended ordeal required it. This being done, the priest and the accused were to go into the church together, but no one was to be there besides. If hot iron were the test, a space was to be measured for carrying it exactly nine times the length of the accused party's foot. Notice was next given to the friends without, that the required heat had been reached, and two of them were to enter, one for the

---

[1] " Uрѣеl, igitur, Saxonicè, oрѣal, verbale est a veteri Franco, vel Teutonico Uрѣela, *judicare.*" (*Dissertatio Epistolaris*, 149. HICKES, *Thes.* tom. 1.) Dr. Hickes quotes the Cottonian harmony of the Gospels for this opinion, a venerable remain of antiquity then existing only MS. It was published at Munich in 1830, from a MS. formerly belonging to the cathedral of Bamberg. The word *urdeles,* as Hickes gives it, or *urdelies,* as it stands in print, occurs in *ll.* 13. 14. p. 43, of the published *Harmony*, or *Heliand,* as it is entitled. In the Saxon laws it is plain that *ordeal* means properly not the trial abstractedly, but the heated iron or other substance used.

accuser, the other for the accused, to ascertain this. Their report being satisfactory, twelve were to enter on either side, and to range themselves opposite each other along the church: no further heating was allowed. Holy water was then to be sprinkled upon the whole party; they were to kiss the Gospels and the cross, and a service was to be read. At the last collect, the iron, if this were the test, was to be removed from the fire, and laid upon a supporter at the end of the nine measured feet. From this, the accused was to remove it, his hand being previously sprinkled with holy water. He was only required to carry it along three of the nine feet, on reaching the last of which he was to throw it down, and hasten to the altar: there his hand was to be bound and sealed up. On the third day afterwards this bandage was to be opened, but not before. If the trial consisted in removing a heavy substance out of boiling water, when the two witnesses entered the church the same formalities were enjoined. Another ordeal was by casting the accused person into water, bound by a rope, and if he sank immediately he was declared innocent.[1]

Of these presumptuous absurdities, the red-hot iron ordeal appears to have been most in favour. It was, indeed, obviously the safest. The accused had scarcely to take the burning mass into his hand before he was allowed to throw it down. For this brief

---

[1] *LL. Æthelst.* can. 5   SPELM. I. 399.   *Ejusd. R. LL. quæ in Saxonico desiderantur*, can. 8. p. 404.   The service provided for ordeals was published by Brown in the *Fasciculus Rerum Expetend. et Fugiend.* from the *Textus Roffensis.*

interval most men probably gave the skin some preparation. It was not, besides, expected that the hand would remain unburnt. Innocence was established if the priest, after three days, pronounced the injured part to be healthy. Thus a good constitution, or even a priest inclined to be merciful, could hardly fail of acquitting the bulk of men tried in this way. In some instances, there can be no reasonable doubt, a bribe secured mercy from the priest. Most cases he would be likely to consider as calling for no very rigorous scrutiny. The Roman church very properly refused encouragement to such modes of tempting providence, and to her hierarchy Europe was eventually indebted for their discontinuance.[1]

---

[1] " It does not appear that the Church of Rome ever gave countenance to it; and it is a very singular instance of a gross corruption that it had not the pope or his creatures for its author. If it ever was directly authorised by any council in a foreign church it was only by some new converts in Germany in the ninth century. The council of Mentz, 847, c. 24, enjoins the ordeal of ploughshares to suspected servants. But to give the pope, I mean Stephen V., his due, he presently condemned it in an epistle to the Bishop of Mentz, in whose diocese it chiefly prevailed. Nay, Alexander II., the Conqueror's own ghostly father, absolutely forbade it. The first prohibition of ordeal mentioned by Sir H. S." (Spelman) " here in England, is in a letter from King Henry III. to his justices itinerant in the north, in the third year of his reign. Yet this learned knight observes, that eight years after this he granted the religious of Sempringham power to administer it. Great lawyers have said that it was suppressed by act of Parliament in the third year of his reign. But the record mentions only the king's letter, and the king's letter says it was done by the advice of his council, and gives this only reason, that *it was forbidden by the church of Rome.*" (JOHNSON, *sub an.* 1065. can. 2.) Ordeals, however,

As ordeals were esteemed a branch of civil jurisprudence, they were forbidden on days consecrated to religion. The same prohibition lay against judicial oaths.[1] Connected with such suspensions of ordinary business, was a regulation of the last importance in an age of violence and insecurity. The days that forbade an ordeal and a solemn oath, forbade also men's angry passions from venting themselves in warlike outrage. On these days the church mercifully proclaimed a general truce, and her holy voice was wisely seconded by the civil power. Thus, ferocious overbearing violence was continually arrested in its merciless career, and religion provided regular respites for the weak, which laws merely human could not safely promise. Happily the days were numerous on which the church insisted upon peace. In every year whole seasons were thus kindly consecrated. The truce of religion extended from the beginning of Advent until the eighth day after the Epiphany; from Septuagesima until the octaves of Easter; from Ascension day until the same time after Whitsunday; and through all the Ember weeks. Besides this the holy truce began at three o'clock on every Saturday afternoon, and lasted until Monday morning. The

---

cannot be accurately taken as extinguished under Henry III. For the trial by wager of battle is a mere ordeal, and the legal extinction of this is very recent. It was introduced under the Conqueror. A trace of the water ordeal lingered among the common people until the last century, in their disposition to try barbarous experiments upon unhappy creatures accused of witchcraft.

[1] *LL. Edov. Sen. et Guth RR.* c. 9. SPELM. I. 393. WILK. I. 203.

same happy privilege secured a joyful welcome for all the principal saints' days, and within particular districts for the festivals of those saints to whom their churches were severally dedicated. The eve came, and ferocity was hushed. Protection, also, was at all times extended to persons in their way to or from a church, or a synod, or a chapter.[1] Disregard of these provisions was properly cognisable before the bishop. If his authority were neglected or defied, it was to be rendered available in the civil courts.[2]

It was among the evils of religious usages introduced from Rome, that they tended to confirm the superstition of barbarian converts. A rude and ignorant populace could not fail of considering as powerful charms those substances which the church invested with a venerable character. Nor were the clerical members of such a community often likely to disturb the prejudices of their contemporaries. It appears accordingly, that water, oil, and other like ingredients, in Romish worship, were esteemed efficacious for eradicating bodily disease.[3] There is, indeed, always this

---

[1] *LL. Eccl. S. Edw. R. et Conf.* c. 3. SPELM. 1. 619. WILK. i. 311.

[2] *Ib.* c. 7.

[3] Mıð halezum pætene he ʒehælðe ꞅum pıꞅ· þæꞅ ealðoꞃmanneꞃ æpe· ꝼꞃam eaꞃmlıceꞃe coðe. ⁊ heo ꞃona ʒeꞅunð hım ꞃýlꝼum þenoðe· Eꝼt on þæꞃe ylcan tıðe he mıð ele ꞅmyꞃoðe an lıcʒenðe mæðen on lanʒꞅumum ꞃaꞃe· þuꞃh heꝼıʒ-tymum heaꞃoð-ece ⁊ hıꞃe ꞃona pæꞅ bæt. Sum eaꞃꝼæꞅt pen pæꞅ eac yꞅele ʒehæꝼð· ⁊ læʒ æt ꞅoꞃð-ꞃıðe hıꞅ ꝼꞃeonðum oꞃꞃene Da hæꝼðe heoꞃa ꞅum halıʒne hlaꝼ þone þe ꞅe eaðıʒa pen æn ʒebletꞃoðe· ⁊ he þæne þæꞃ ꞃıhte on pæꞅen beðypte· ⁊ hıꞅ aðlıʒum mæʒe on þone muðe beʒeat ⁊ he þæꞃ ꞃıhte þæꞃe aðle ʒeꞅtılðe. (*Hom. in Nat. S. Cuthb.* Bibl. Bodl. MSS. BODLEY, 340. f. 65.) *With holy water he healed a woman, the alderman's*

danger when material objects are connected with ordinary devotion. To the reflecting few these may be only interesting relics of a distant age: among the thoughtless many they will certainly find aliment for a grovelling superstition.

No feature was, however, more exceptionable in Anglo-Saxon theology than the penitential system. It might seem a very desirable check upon human corruption, especially among a gross and barbarous people, that every offence should rigorously exact a proportionable penalty. Nor, undoubtedly, could the solemn recognition of such a principle fail to render important public services. Yet these were far less than might have resulted from the system nakedly considered. Fasts of months or years, or even of a whole life, were denounced against iniquities according to their several magnitudes. But then all this rigour was open to commutation. The same authority that had provided a scale of personal austerity had also provided an equivalent scale far more agreeable. If a penitent were disquieted by the prospect of a day's fast, a penny would release him from the obligation.[1]

---

wife, from a miserable disease, and she, soon sound, waited upon himself. Afterwards at the same time, he with oil smeared a maiden lying in long affliction, through a grievous head-ache, and she was soon better of it. A certain pious man was also very ill, and lay at the point of death given over by his friends. One of these had some holy bread which the blessed man formerly consecrated, and he dipped it immediately in water, and moistened his kinsman's mouth with it, and he immediately assuaged the disease.

[1] *Man may one day's fast with one penny redeem.* (WANLEY apud HICKES, *Thes.* ii. 146.) Undoubtedly the Saxon penny answered to three of modern times, and the existing value of money rendered it a sum worth considering.

If he had incurred a more than common liability of this kind he might build a church, and ecclesiastical authorities would pronounce him free.[1] Thus wealthy sinners found no great reason to tax the penitentials with intolerable severity. Nor was poverty left under the necessity of drawing an opposite conclusion. The repetition of psalms was pronounced highly meritorious.[2] Hence he who shrank from a fast, yet wanted means to commute it for money, might still appease an accusing conscience by a proportionate number of psalms.[3] Among the reading and thinking few doubts appear to have been occasionally felt as to

---

[1] *Amends for deeds are provided in various ways. A great man may redeem with alms. Let him who has the power rear a church in God's honour, and, if he have an opportunity, let him give land thereto.*—WANLEY apud HICKES, *Thes.* ii. 198.

[2] "Delet peccata." (*Bibl. Lameth. MSS.* 427. f. 1.) The second leaf of this MS. contains the following prayer: "Suscipere dignare Dne ds omps hos psalmos consecratos quos ego indignus et peccator decantare cupio in honorem nominis tui dni nri Ihu Xpi, et beatæ Mariæ semper virginis, et omnium scorum, pro me misero infelici, et pro cunctis facinoribus meis, sive factis, sive dictis, sive cogitationibus concupiscentis iniquitatibus, sive omnibus negligentiis meis magnis ac minimis; ut isti psalmi proficiant mihi ad vitam æternam, et remissionem omnium peccatorum et spatium adjuvando, et vivam penitentiam faciendo: per." Wanley refers this MS. vol. generally to the time of Edgar, or even to an earlier date; but he pronounces the prayer above, and many other things in the book, to have been written at a period far more recent.—HICKES, *Thes.* ii. 268.

[3] *He who owes one week on bread and water, let him sing* 300 *psalms, kneeling, or* 320 *without kneeling, as it is said above. And he who must do penance a month's space on bread and water, let him sing a thousand psalms and* 200 *kneeling, and without kneeling* 1680. — Pœnitentiale D. Ecgbert. Arch. Ebor. i. 2. WILK. i. 115.

the soundness of this system; for it is recommended that repentance should not cease, although discipline may require nothing further, it being uncertain what value God may put upon such services.[1] But an observation of this kind was likely to pass unheeded amidst a vast mass of matter far more popular. Hence Anglo-Saxon penitential doctrines were calculated, upon the whole, to serve sound religion and morality very uncertainly and equivocally.

A party striving for ascendancy is naturally prone to magnify those who raise its credit. If religious, it proclaims the superior morality of its more serviceable members. Anglo-Saxon efforts for extirpating paganism and establishing monachism were thus facilitated. To many devotees, conspicuous for zeal or self-denial, was attributed a saintly character, and eventually their tombs were eagerly frequented as the seats of miraculous agency. Nor did their posthumous importance fade until the Reformation. Even then long prescription, and services really rendered in

---

[1] *If a layman slay another without guilt, let him fast* VII. *years on bread and water, and then* IIII. *as his confessor teaches him: and after the* VII. *years' amends, let him ever earnestly repent of his misdeeds, as far as he may, because it is unknown how acceptable his amends may be with God.* (WANLEY apud HICKES, *Thes.* II. 146.) Dr. Lingard, by saying that Theodore published a code of laws for the imposition of *sacramental* penance (*Antiqu. of the Angl. Sax. Ch.* Fr. Transl. p. 246), might lead his readers to suppose that the Anglo-Saxons had anticipated the schoolmen upon such subjects. The passage, however, here translated from Wanley's Saxon extract, sufficiently shews that there was no such anticipation. For further information upon Anglo-Saxon penitential doctrines, see *Bampt. Lect.* Serm. V. with the *Proofs and Illustrations.*

some cases to religion, pleaded successfully against a total exclusion of such names from the national calendar. Others of them have escaped oblivion from local associations.

Upon several among these ancient saints sufficient notice has already been bestowed incidentally. Chad, whom Theodore displaced from York and subsequently seated at Lichfield, may be further mentioned because the homily for his day proves wheel-carriages to have been then in use. Theodore found him in the habit of undertaking pedestrian journeys far above his strength to preach the Gospel. He not only mounted him on horseback, but insisted also on his using a *horse-wain* occasionally.[1]

Another exemplary personage whom Theodore drew from monastic privacy to episcopal cares, was Cuthbert, the saint of Durham. Few authentic particulars respecting him are, however, extant, beyond his great reluctance to become a bishop, and his rigid perseverance, after yielding to such compulsion, in the monkish dress and diet.[2]

---

[1] Hine ſe encebiſhop miþ hiſ aʒenne honþ on horſe ahoꝼ. ꝼoꞃðon he hine ꞅpiðe haliʒne peꞃ ʒemette. ⁊ he hine nebbe þ he ꞃpa hiþen on horſe-peʒen peꞃe· ꞃpa hit neoþ-þeaꞃſe peꞃe. (Bibl. Bodl. MSS. *Junii*, 24. Hom. 1.) *Him the archbishop with his own hand mounted on a horse, because he found him a very holy man: he compelled him also to travel about in a horse-wain, if the case required.* St. Chad's conveyance was, probably, a rude specimen of that kind, known latterly as the taxed cart. Chad had a brother of the same name, who was bishop of London.

[2] Æꝼteꞃ þyꞃꞃum poꞃðum peaꞃð ʒemot ʒehæꝼð· ⁊ Ecʒꝼꞃiþuꞃ þæn on ʒeꞃæt. ⁊ Ðeoðoꞃuꞃ þyꞃeꞃ iʒlanðeꞃ anceþiꞃcop· miþ maneʒum oðꞃum ʒeðunʒenum pitum. ⁊ hi ealle anmoþlice þone eaðiʒan Cuðþeꞃhnuꞃ to biꞃceope ʒecuꞃon Ða ꞃænðon heo ꞃona ʒeꞃniꞃu· miþ þam æꞃenðe to pam eaðiʒan peꞃe. ac hi ne mihton hine oꝼ hiꞅ mynꞅtꞃe ʒebꞃinʒan.

Ethelred, or Audrey, Ely's great attraction, was chiefly famed for an invincible refusal to gratify either of her husbands, and an ascetic piety hardly reconcilable with strict cleanliness.¹ Her death seems to have happened rather suddenly, from an operation undertaken by some empiric, as he thought,

Ða ƿeoþ ꞅe cyninᵹ ꞅỳlꞅ Ecᵹꞅꞃiꝺuꞅ to þam iᵹlanꝺe· ⁊ Tꞃumpine biꞅ-ceop· miꝺ oðꞃum eaꞃꝼæꞃtum peƿum ⁊ hi þone halᵹan ꞅꞃiðe halꞅuꝺon. heoꞃa cneopu biᵹꝺon· ⁊ miꝺ teaꞃum bæꝺon· oððæt hi hine pepenꝺe oꞅ þam peꞅtene atuᵹon to þam ꞅinoðe ꞅamoꝺ miꝺ him. (Bibl. Bodl. MSS. BODLEY, 340. *Hom. in Nat. S. Cuthb.* f. 64.) *After this an assembly was holden, and Ecgfridus sate therein, and Theodorus, archbishop of this island, with many other noble councillors, and they all unanimously chose the blessed Cuthberthus as bishop. Then they quickly sent a writ with a message to the blessed man; but they could not bring him from his minster. Then rowed the king himself Ecgfridus to the island* (Lindisfarne), *and bishop Trumwine, with other pious men, and they much besought the saint, bent their knees, and begged with tears, until they drew him weeping from the solitude to the synod together with them.* In the same folio we learn, that, after Cuthbert became bishop, Nolꝺe apenꝺan hiꞅ ᵹepunelican biᵹ-leoꞃan· ne niꞅ ᵹepæꝺa þe he on peꞅtene hæꝼꝺe. *He would not change his accustomed food, nor his weeds that he had in the solitude.*

"Notwithstanding the great character of Cuthbert's piety, 'tis plain he sided with King Ecgfrid and Theodore against Wilfrid: and, by consequence, took no notice of the sentence in Wilfrid's favour, decreed by the Roman synod. Had not the case stood thus, he would never have made use of King Ecgfrid's recommendation, nor have accepted the see of Holy Island, which was part of Wilfrid's jurisdiction, and taken out of the diocese of York, against his consent."—COLLIER, *Eccl. Hist.* i. 110.

¹ "After her entrance therein (the monastery of Ely), she ever wore woollen, and never linen about her; which, whether it made her more holy, or less cleanly, let others decide." (FULLER, *Church Hist.* 91.) The homily adds to the account of her dress, that she polꝺe ꞅelꝺ-hƿænne hiꞃe lic baðian butan to heah tiꝺum ⁊ þonne heo polꝺe æꞃeꞃt ealle þa baðian þe on þam mynꞅtꞃe pæꞃou. ⁊ polꝺe him þenian miꝺ hiꞃe ðinenum· ⁊ þonne hi ꞅỳlꞅe baðian. (Brit. Mus. MSS.

successfully; but his patient died on the third day afterwards.¹ Her virginity was regarded as indisputable, because her body was found undecomposed, sixteen years after death. Such a deviation from the ordinary course of nature was, indeed, regularly considered as a proof of unbroken continence.²

The memory of Frideswide yet lingers at Christchurch, pre-eminent even in Oxford, among seats and seminaries of learning and religion. She was daughter of Didan, a princely chieftain who ruled in that venerable city with some sort of delegated authority.³ Her title to saintly honours appears to

---

COTTON, *Julius*, E. 7. f. 93.) *would rarely bathe her body unless on high days, and then she would first have all them bathe who were in the minster, and would wait upon them with her maids, and then bathe herself.*

¹ Ða pær þæn ꞃum læce on þam ᵹeleaꝼꝼullum heape· Cẏneꝼnẏð ᵹehaten· ⁊ hı cpædon þa ꞃume þ ꞃe læce ꞃceolbe aꞃceotan þ ᵹeꞃpell. Ða bẏbe he ꞃona ꞃpa. ⁊ þæn ꞃah-ut pẏnnıꞃ. peanð hım þa ᵹeðuht ꞃpılce heo ᵹepuppan mihte. ac heo ᵹepat op populbe to Gobe on þam þnıðban bæᵹe ꞃẏððan ꞃe bolh pær ᵹeopenob. (*Ib.*) *There was a certain physician in the believing company, named Cynefryth, and some people told her that this physician would reduce the swelling, which he soon did, and relieved her from the pain. He thought that she might recover, but she passed out of the world with glory to God, on the third day after the ulcer was opened.* The ulcerated tumour which had so fatal a result, was under the chin, and Etheldred appears to have considered it as a sort of judgment for the pleasure that she had formerly taken in wearing necklaces.

² Hıt ıꞃ ꞃputol þ heo pær unᵹepemme'ꞃ mæbcn· þonne hıne lıchama ne mıhte ꞃonmolꞃnıan on eopðan. (*Ib.* f. 94.) *It is manifest that she was an undefiled maiden, when her body could not decompose in the ground.*

³ In one of the Bodleian MSS. (*Laud.* 114.) containing lives of saints, and St. Austin *De Doctrinâ Christianâ*, Frideswide's father is called a *subregulus*. f. 132.

have rested on a determination to live as a nun rather than as a distinguished married lady.[1]

Edmund, king of East-Anglia,[2] to whose admitted sanctity the Suffolk Bury owed eventually a splendid abbey, was unmercifully scourged against a tree by some Danish pirates; and, like another Sebastian, then transfixed with spears. The pagan bigotry of these fierce invaders formed a hateful contrast with the Christian resignation of their victim. Hence pious minds embalmed the memory of Edmund, and monastic revenue was certain to wait on his remains. His head being stricken off, was cast into a tangled thicket. There, ancient legends tell, it found protection from a hungry beast of prey. Perhaps a modern might suppose the animal to have been restrained by fear; for the same authorities that commemorate its abstinence, record another circumstance fully as remarkable. Different individuals of a party, scattered in a wood, were in the habit of calling out occasionally, "Where art thou, comrade?" To those in quest of Edmund's head the usual answer, "Here, here, here," was regulary returned from a single spot. To this all the stragglers

---

[1] "Migravit igitur beata Fritheswitcha virgo ad dñm quarto decimo Kalendas Novembris; anno ab incarnatione dñi septingentessimo vicessimo septimo." *Brit. Mus. MSS.* COTTON, *Nero.* E. 1. f. 363.

[2] Crowned at Bury, his royal residence, in 856, being then fifteen, and slain in 870. (ASSER, 14, 20.) He met his death at Hoxne, in Suffolk. The Danes were commanded by Hinguar, as the homily spells his name, but it is more usually spelt without the aspirate.

MISCELLANEOUS PARTICULARS.   303

naturally repaired, and were amazed on finding every reply to have come from no other than the object of their search, respectfully guarded within the claws of a wolf.[1]

Among the northern saints was Oswald, king of

---

[1] This is gravely introduced into the service for St. Edmund's day. " Dani vero relinquentes corpus, caput in silvâ recedentes asportaverunt, atque inter densa veprium fruticeta occultârunt. Quibus abeuntibus, Christiani corpus invenientes, caput quesierunt; atque Ubi es? aliis ad alios in silvâ clamantibus, caput respondit *Her, Her, Her,* quod est, Hic, Hic, Hic. (*Breviar Sarisb.* 20 Novem.) The wolf's connexion with this extraordinary head is detailed in another lesson. It will, probably, be generally thought, that a prayer-book presciibing such lessons was not reformed before its time. The homily is amusingly picturesque. Hi eodon þa recende ealle endemeſ· ꝼ rymle clypiȝende· ſpa ſpa hit ȝepunelic iſ þam þe on puꝺa ȝaꝺ oꝼt· Hpæn eanꞇ þu· ȝeꝼena· ꝼ him anꝺꝼynde ꝼ heaꝼoꝺ. Heꞃ Heꞃ· Heꞃ ꝼ ſpa ȝelome clypoꝺe· anꝺſpaꞃiȝende him eallum ſpa oꝼꞇ ſpa heona æniȝ clypoꝺe. oꝺ ꝼ hi ealle becomen ꝺuꞃh ꝺa clypunȝa him to. Ꝺa læȝ ꞃe ȝꞃæȝe pulꝼ þe beꝼiꞃꞇe ꝼ heaꝼoꝺ. ꝼ miꝺ hiſ ꞇpam ꝼoꞇum hæꝼde ꝼ heaꝼoꝺ beclyppeꝺ ȝꞃæꝺiȝ ꝼ hunȝꞃiȝ· ꝼ ꝼon Ꝉoꝺe ne ꝺoꞃſꞇe þæꞃ hæꝼꝺeꞃ abyꞃian· ꝼ heolꝺ hit piꝺ ꝺeoꞃ. Ꝺa puꞃꝺon hi oꝼpunꝺꞃoꝺe þær pulꝼeꞃ hyꞃꝺnæꝺenne ꝼ ꝼ haliȝe heaꝼoꝺ ham ꝼeꞃeꝺon miꝺ him. þanciȝenꝺe þam Ælmihtiȝan ealꞃa hiſ punꝺꞃa. Ꝛc ꞃe pulꝼ ꝼolȝoꝺe ꝼoꞃꝺ miꝺ þam heaꝼꝺe· oꝺ ꝼ hi to ꞇune comon· ſpilce he ꞇam pæꞃe. ꝼ ȝeꝼeꞃꝺe eꝼꞇ ꞃiꝺꝺan ꞇo puꝺa onȝean. (Brit. Mus. MSS. Cotton, *Julius,* E. 7. f. 203. Bibl. Bodl. MSS. Bodley, 343.) *They went then seeking all together, and constantly calling, as is the wont of those who oft go into woods, Where art thou, comrade? And to them answered the head, Here, Here, Here. Thus all were answered as often as any of them called, until they all came through the calling to it. There lay the grey wolf that guarded the head, and with his two feet had the head embraced, greedy and hungry, and for God durst not taste the head, and held it against wild beasts. Then were they astonished at the wolf's guardianship, and carried the holy head home with them, thanking the Almighty for all his wonders. But the wolf followed forth with the head, until they came to town, as if he were tame, and after that turned into the woods again.*

Northumbria. He had, indeed, fairly earned respectful remembrance in that part of England. It was largely indebted to him for conversion. But he rendered this important service by means of a native church. His invitation brought Aidan from Scotland; and that missionary's dialect being ill understood in Northumbria, Oswald acted as interpreter. His charitable disposition was displayed in the surrender of an Easter dinner, and of the silver dish containing it, to a crowd of hungry poor waiting for his alms. To this incident Oswald, identified completely as he was with the national party, seems to have been largely indebted for posthumous reverence. As he pointed to the dish, and so liberally directed its appropriation, Aidan said, *May that blessed hand defy corruption.* Soon afterwards, Oswald fell in battle, and his right hand, being found possessed of properties decidedly antiseptic,[1] became invaluable for strengthening a monastic treasury.

The fens of Lincolnshire gloried in an anchoret named Guthlac.[2] Originally, he was little better than

---

[1] *Brit. Mus. MSS.* COTTON, *Julius.* E. 7. ff. 152. 153. " Grant this miracle of Oswald's hand literally true in the latitude thereof; I desire any ingenuous papist to consider the time wherein it was acted. It was Easter-day, yea, such an Easter-day as was celebrated by the Quartodecimans, Aidan being present thereat, contrary to the time which the canons of Rome appointed. Now, did not a divine finger in Oswald his miraculous hand point out this day then to be truly observed ? Let the Papists produce such another miracle to grace, and credit their Easter, Roman style, and then they say something to the purpose."—FULLER, *Ch. Hist.* 82.

[2] This is, probably, the *Goodlake* of modern English surnames. Guthlac's parents were of some distinction, and lived in the time

a bold marauder; but higher principles gained upon him in early manhood, and overwhelmed him with remorse.[1] He sought Croyland[2] for his hermitage, as being a spot unusually repulsive. His choice eventually caused a spacious monastery to rear its majestic head over the watery waste. Improvements immediately began, which have gradually converted barren marshes into fruitful fields. Many similar services have been rendered by the Church. A long succession of owners, always resident, often intelligent, have taught repeatedly the dreary wilderness to supply no unimportant measure of a nation's wealth.

The Anglo-Saxons, it has commonly been supposed, were provided with a complete vernacular translation of Holy Scripture. No such volume has, however, been discovered. Hence the existence of such, at any time, is very questionable. The Bible, in fact, was evidently considered as a Latin book in ante-Norman England. Texts were generally cited in that language, and then rendered into the native idiom, according to the Romish usage of later times.

---

of Ethelred, king of Mercia. (*Brit. Mus. MSS.* COTTON, *Vespasian*, D. 21. f. 18.) Ethelred abdicated and retired into a monastery in 704.—*Sax. Chron.* 60.

[1] We learn, from the MS. cited in the last note, that he was *four-and-twenty winters old* when he forsook the habits of his earlier years. He then retired into the monastery of Repton, and remained there two years. Thus his age was twenty-six when he turned hermit, and he is considered the first of his nation who adopted that character. There is a life of Guthlac, in Latin, very ancient, corresponding with the Saxon (which is probably translated from it), among the Cottonian MSS. in the British Museum.—*Nero*, E 1. f. 183.

[2] Or Crowland.

Doubts even entered reflecting minds as to the expediency of opening Scripture unreservedly to vulgar eyes. But such hesitation, if sufficiently examined, will be found little serviceable to the cause of modern Rome. It arose not from the Church's alleged possession of an unwritten word, and from a consequent apprehension lest an analogy should be drawn between this and the similar Jewish claim so pointedly reprobated by our Saviour. Ante-Norman indecision upon an indiscriminate publication of the sacred record flowed from a perception of contemporary grossness. An abuse was feared of certain Scriptural relations to justify individual obliquities.[1] All their other feelings made learned Anglo-Saxons anxious to spread abroad a knowledge of the Bible.

To such anxiety several interesting versions bear honourable testimony. The eighth century is thought to have produced the four Gospels in a vernacular

---

[1] *Now it thinketh me, love, that that work* (the translation of Genesis) *is very dangerous for me or any men to undertake: because I dread lest some foolish man read this book, or hear it read, who should ween that he may live now under the new law, even as the old fathers lived then in that time, ere that the old law was established; or even as men lived under Moyses' law.* (Ælfric, monk, to Æthelwold, alderman *Prefatio Genesis, Anglice.* Ed. Thwaites, p. 1.) Elfric then proceeds to relate how an illiterate instructor of his own dwelt upon Jacob's matrimonial connexions with two sisters and their two maids. This passage has been partly used already in the note respecting Elfric's early education. His own account of the biblical versions made by him is to be found in a Saxon piece which he addressed to Sigwerd, of East-Heolon, and which was published by L'Isle in 1623.

dress.¹ A like antiquity may possibly be claimed for the Psalter.² Of the translator, in either case, nothing is certainly known. The Pentateuch, with most of Joshua and Judges, and some parts of Samuel, Kings, Chronicles, Esther, and Maccabees, was translated by Elfric. He presented his countrymen, also, with a brief homiletic sketch of Job. A poetic piece, now imperfect, founded upon the apocryphal book of Judith, and written, it is thought, in Dano-Saxon, is, probably, another extant evidence of his industry. In this last undertaking he had an eye to the Danish incursions; thinking that a harassed nation could dwell upon few pictures more advantageously than upon one of successful resistance to foreign aggression. The Anglo-Saxons likewise possessed in their native idiom the pseudo-gospel, passing under the name of Nicodemus.³ Pro-

---

[1] Bp. Marsh's *Michaelis*, ii. 637. The four Gospels in Anglo-Saxon were printed in London in 1571. There again in 1638, together with fragments both of the Old and New Testaments. The Gospels were afterwards printed at Dordrecht in 1665, and at Amsterdam in 1684. (*Ibid.*) " From the different styles of the Anglo-Saxon versions of the Gospels, they must have been translated oftener than once."—Turner's *Hist. Angl. Sax.* iii. 499.

[2] " De Authore autem hujus versionis haud quicquam statuimus. Primus Psalmorum in Linguam Saxonicam translator sub anno 709, laudatur Adelmus Episc. Shirburnensis; sed cum regem Alfredum Magnum, translationem etiam hujusmodi, paulo ante annum 900, adortum esse legimus, priorem illam ex Danica tempestate perusse verisimile est, et posteriorem sanè ex importuna Regis morte abortivam fuisse novimus."—Præf in *Psalt. Latino Saxonic. Vet.* a Joh. Spelmanno, edit. Lond. 1640.

[3] All these, except the selections from Samuel, Kings, Chronicles, Esther, and Maccabees, which are most probably lost, were

bably, this was considered a valuable supplement to the inspired records of our blessed Saviour's life. If any other Scriptural versions ever existed, authentic particulars of them are unknown. We have, indeed, besides, a paraphrastic view of the leading incidents detailed by Moses. Its author seems to have been that Cædmon, whose extraordinary talents Bede commemorates, and ascribes to inspiration. But his work is a sacred poem, not a biblical version.[1] There is, likewise, in the British Museum, an ancient Harmony

---

published by Thwaites, at Oxford, in 1698, under the following title: *Heptateuchus, Liber Job, et Evangelium Nicodemi, Anglo-Saxonice. Historiæ Judith Fragmentum: Dano-Saxonice.*

[1] Bede (iv 24. p. 327) relates, that Cædmon abruptly retired from a table, where the guests were singing in succession, when the harp came to him because he had no verse at command. In the course of the following night he dreamed that a stranger desired him to sing. He pleaded inability, but was told that he did not know his own powers. Being further pressed, he began to sing the *Creation*, and he subsequently retained the faculty of clothing in verse any sacred subject read or recited to him. A short specimen of his abilities is preserved by Bede. A considerable mass of poetry, on the subjects which occupied his muse, is extant in the Bodleian library, in a MS. referred to the tenth century. This was published by Junius in 1655, and it has been recently republished. Hickes doubted Cædmon's title to it, because he considered the language Dano-Saxon, and therefore of a later age. But, probably, neither this work, nor the fragment of Judith, is in Dano-Saxon. Their verbal peculiarities will be readily accounted for by the fact, that they are strictly poems. It is undoubtedly far from obvious why Elfric should have written Dano-Saxon. Yet we have his own authority for attributing to him a translation of Judith. (*De Vet. Test* 22) This can hardly be any other work than that of which a fragment still remains

Of both the *Judith* and the *Cædmon*, long and interesting accounts may be seen in Mr. Turner's *Hist. of the Angl. Sax.* (iii. 309). Of the latter, still fuller particulars are supplied in the

of the Gospels.¹ This again, is poetical, and obviously was never intended for the Anglo-Saxon people; not being in their tongue, but in a cognate dialect from the Gothic stock.

As the scanty remains of Anglo-Saxon biblical literature mount up to a high antiquity, they are not without importance in scriptural research. Use of them has, accordingly, been made in the delicate and difficult task of conjectural emendation.² But although these venerable monuments of English piety can hardly fail of preserving traces of Latin versions now lost, yet St. Jerome's translation was that, in fact, of ancient England.³ Existing Anglo-Saxon versions, besides, are not sufficiently complete and critical to throw extensive light upon biblical

---

Illustrations of Anglo-Saxon Poetry, for which we are indebted to the two Messrs Conybeare. (pp. 3. 183.)

A strong similarity has been observed in parts, between *Cædmon* and *Paradise Lost*. Hence Mr. Turner supposes that Milton might have had some hints from Junius (*Hist. Angl. Sax.* III. 316.) Speculations of this kind might be carried further. The *pseudo-gospel* of Nicodemus personifies Hell, and makes her (for the gender is feminine) hold a dialogue with Satan. Such reading brings to mind Milton's personifications of Sin and Death

¹ Published at Munich in 1830

² " Various readings from the Anglo-Saxon version of the Four Gospels were first quoted by Mill, who took them from the papers of Marshall "—Bp. MARSH's *Michaelis, ut supra*.

³ Ðer Hieronimus pep halig racepþ ⁊ ᵹeᴛoᵹen on Ebpeircum ᵹepeopðe· ⁊ on Gpecircum ⁊ on Leðenum pulppemeðlice· ⁊ he apenðe une Bibliothecan op Ebpeircum bocum ᴛo Leðen rppee. (Bibl. Bodl. MSS. *Junu*, 34. p. 93.) *This Hieronimus was a holy priest, and skilled in the Hebrew language, and in the Greek, and in the Latin, perfectly; and he turned our Bible from Hebrew books to the Latin speech*

inquiries. The translators evidently had no thought of any thing beyond popular utility. They reasoned, probably, that every reader of more than ordinary reflection and acquirements would consult the Latin text. Its language, indeed, had not yet become completely obsolete among persons of education. Hence many liberties were taken by Elfric, especially, both in paraphrasing and abridging.[1] No doubt a version was thus produced more level to popular apprehension. But its value to a critic is impaired. There can be little certainty as to the text used by a translator who, obviously, considered himself perfectly justified in departing from it to meet the illiteracy of those for whom he wrote.

In this respect, as in others, the Anglo-Saxon age betrays inherent imperfection. It is, however, eminently an interesting and important period: indeed, the cradle of a social system, admired and envied by all Europe. Its monuments, therefore, demand attention from such as would adequately understand this noble constitution. Especially is examination due to its ecclesiastical affairs. English episcopacy is thus traced beyond Augustine up to a native church, immemorially rooted in the country. This institution, then, has every advantage of prescription, even that of connexion with primitive antiquity. The national endowments of religion, also, meet an inquiring eye under an aspect highly venerable. They

---

[1] He commonly omits indelicate passages, and long successions of proper names. In some cases he introduces a gloss, and in others he gives Anglo-Saxon equivalents for proper names.

challenge any rigour of investigation; offering evidence of legal imposition that gives a modern air to the muniments of every private family. Landed acquisitions must have been made universally under existing liabilities to provide for public worship. It should be likewise generally known, that England largely owed conversion to British agency, and that her independence was never insulted by papal domination before the Conquest. Nor, again, ought the doctrinal evidence of Anglo-Saxon records to be overlooked. The Marian martyrs faced an agonising death rather than deny one leading article of faith maintained by their distant ancestry. Another fact, pregnant with instruction, in the religious annals of ancient England, is her indignant repudiation of image-worship. Her voice, too, in other points now controverted, but which she never saw particularly noticed, responds most ambiguously and insufficiently to the call of Rome for traditionary support. Even the last Henry's monastic policy may appeal for extenuation to Anglo-Saxon history. This displays the Benedictine struggle to undermine an older system, and monks employing an ungenerous detraction, eventually turned with fatal force against themselves. It convicts the cloister, too, of seeking popularity and opulence from the very first, by that debasing subserviency to superstition which dishonoured all its course. Long, then, as Anglo-Saxon times have passed away, their hoary monuments will abundantly requite a student's care. This, indeed, is fairly due to civil institutions in which every Englishman exults, to a religious polity which the great majority reveres. Inquiry may surprise a Romanist with opposition, encountered by some peculiarities of his church convicting them of innovation; with evidence of others, groping a stealthy and vacillating way through national ignorance and troubles. It will greet a Protestant with invaluable testimonies to the antiquity of his distinctive creed.

END OF THE HISTORY.

KING EDGAR'S PROCLAMATION.

¹ Her ir gerputelob on þirum geprite· hu Eabgar cyningc þær rmeagenbe hpæt to bote mihte· æt þam ræn-cpealme ðe hir leobrcipe rpiðe brehte ꝺ panobe gynb hir anpealb.

Dæt ir þonne ænerт ꝥ him þuhte ꝺ hir pitum· ꝥ þur gepab ungelimp mib rynnum· ꝺ mib orephyrnyrre Uober beboba geearnob pæne· ꝺ rpyðort mib þam ortige þær neab-garoler þe Crirtene men Uobe gelærtan rceolbon on heora teoðinge rceattum. He beþohte ꝺ armeabe ꝥ gobcunbe be populbgepunan· Uir geneat manna hpylc rongymelearað hir hlarorber garol ꝺ hit him to ðæm rihт anbagan ne gelært· pen ir gir re hlarorb milb-heort bið ꝥ he þa gymelearte to rorgyrenyrre læte· ꝺ to hir garole buton pitnunge ró Uir he þonne gelomlice þurh hir bybelar hir garoler myngað· ꝺ he þonne aheanbað· ꝺ hit þencð to æt-rtrengenne· pen ir ꝥ þær hlarorber grama to þan rpiðe peaxe ꝥ he him ne unne naðen ne æhta ne lirer Spa ir þen ꝥ ure Drihten bo þurh þa gebyrrtignyrre þe rolcer men piðhærton þære gelomlican myngunge þe ure láneorar bybon ymbe ꝥ neab-garol urer Drihtner ꝥ ryn ure teoðunga· ꝺ cyric-rceattar. Donne beobe ic· ꝺ re ancebircеор· ꝥ ge Uob ne grymman· ne naðen ne geearnian ne þone rænlican beað þirer anbrearban lirer ne huru þone torearban écene helle· mib ænegum ortige Uober geрihта ac ægðen ge earm ge eabig· þe ænige tylunge hæbbe· gelærte Uobe hir teoðunga mib ealne blirre· ꝺ mib eallum unnan rpa reo gepæbnyr tæce þe mine pitan æt Anberеран² gepæbbon ꝺ nu ert æt Pihtrorber-rtane mib pebbe gerærtnobon. Donne beobe ic minum gerеран be minum rneonbrcipe· ꝺ be eallum þam þe hi ágon ꝥ hy rtyran ælcum þara þe þir ne gelærte ꝺ minra ritena peb abrecan mib ænegum pacrcipe pille· rpa rpa him reo rorеræbе gepabner tæce· ꝺ on þære rteore ne ry nan rongirner. Uir he rpa earm bið ꝥ he aðen beð oððе þa gober panað hir raula to rorpyjibe oððе paccor mib mober gnaman hy behyrrð þonne ꝥ he him to agenum teleð· ðonne him micele

---

¹ *Brit. Mus. MSS.* Cotton, *Nero*, E. 1. f. 389.

² The legislative importance of Andover is thus commemorated by a poet, who celebrates the dedication of the church of the old monastery at Winchester, in 980; he was, probably, Elfric ·
" Post alii plures aderant, proceresque, ducesque,
Gentis et Anglorum maxima pars comitum,
Quos è concilio pariter collegerat illo
Quod fuit vico Regis in Andeveram."
Vita S. Ethelw. Episc. Winton. ACTA SS. ORD.
BENEDICT. Sæc. v. p. 621.

agenne is þ him æfne on ecnyrre gelært gif he hit mid unnan ⁊ mid fulne blisse don polde.

Donne pille ic þ þær Godes gerihta standan æghpær gelice on minum anpealde· ⁊ þa Godes þeopas þe þa rceattas underfoð þe þe Gode syllað· libban clænan life· þ hy þurh þa clænnysse us to Gode þingian mægen. And ic ⁊ mine þegnas pyldan une preostas to þan þe une saula hyrdas us tæcð· þ syndon une bisceopas· þe þe næfne misshypan ne scylon on nan þara þinga þe hy us for Gode tæcað· þ þe þurh þa hyrsomnysse þe þe heom for Gode hyrsomiað þ ece life geeannian þe hy us to pemað mid lane· ⁊ mid byrene goddra peorca.

KING EDGAR'S PROCLAMATION.

Here is manifested in this writ, how King Eadgar considered what might be amended, in the pestilence that greatly harassed and diminished his people widely through his kingdom.

This is then, first, what he and his *witan* thought, that this unfortunate state of things was earned by sins, and by disobedience to God's commandments; and chiefly by the subtraction of the bounden tribute which Christian men should yield to God in their tythe-payments. He bethought and considered the divine course by that of the world. If any agricultural tenant neglect his lord's tribute, and render it not to him at the right appointed time, one may judge if the lord will be so merciful as to forgive such a neglect, and to take his tribute without punishing him. If he then, frequently, through his messengers, admonish him of his tribute, and he then hardeneth himself, and thinketh to hold it out, one may think that the lord's anger will wax to such a pitch, that he will allow him neither property nor life. So, one may think, our Lord will do, through the boldness with which common men resist the frequent admonition which our teachers have given about our Lord's bounden tribute, which are our tythes and church-shots. Then bid I, and the archbishop, that ye provoke not God, nor earn a premature death in this life, nor, what is worse, the future everlasting hell, by any subtraction of God's rights: but let every one, whether poor or rich, who has any business, render to God his tythes as the act teaches, which my *witan* enacted at Andover, and now again at Wihtbordestane with a pledge confirmed. Moreover, I bid my reeves by my friendship, and by all that they possess, that they punish every one of those who pay not this, and break the pledge of my *witan* with any prevarication, even as the foresaid enactment teaches; and in the punishment let there be no forgiveness. Neither poverty nor anger will free from danger the soul of any man who diminishes this, or converts it to his own use; it is then that he consults for his own eternal interest when he renders it freely and with full satisfaction.

Then will I that God's rights stand every where alike in my dominions; and that God's servants, who receive the payments that we make to God, should live clean lives, that they should through their purity intercede for us to God. And I and my thanes enjoin our priests what is taught us by the pastors of our souls, that is, our bishops, whom we should never fail of hearing in any of the things that they teach us for God, that we, through the obedience that we yield to them for God, may earn the everlasting life which they persuade us to by teaching, and by the example of good works.

THE END.

www.ingramcontent.com/pod-product-compliance
Lightning Source LLC
Chambersburg PA
CBHW071228230426
43668CB00011B/1349